The Celtic Goddess

Great Queen or Demon Witch?

The Celtic Goddess

Great Queen or Demon Witch?

Claire French

Floris Books

First published in 2001 by Floris Books

British Library CIP Data available

ISBN 0-86315-358-5

Printed in Great Britain
by Bell & Bain, Glasgow

Contents

To my husband Jack for his patient support, and
to my children, Edith, Henry and John

PART I

Celts: Ancient, Medieval and Modern

Introduction

The Celtic Inheritance

Who were the Celts? As far as we can tell, they were one of the many Indo-European populations who came from around the Caspian Sea to settle in Europe between 1000 and 800 BC. They conquered the Illyrians in what is today Austria and the Ligurians in what is today France. Without ever forming a coherent, centralized state, they merged with the indigenous "first Europeans" and settled in numerous tribal units from Spain to Turkey and from the Rhine to Italy. Historians call these migrants the Early Celts.

Long before the Romans they organized an economic network all over Europe, trading with their Greek and Etruscan neighbours in salt, weapons, hardware *(iron* is a Celtic word), chariots, horses and slaves. It is not exaggerated to say that they laid the foundations of European civilization north of the Alps, where place names, sanctuaries and sumptuous princes' graves remind us of their former presence.

Around 500 BC they crossed the Channel and settled in the British Isles, where their language and literature escaped merging with that of the Romans in the south and that of the Germans in the north as in the rest of Europe. But before this happened, the Celts had already split into two different language groups: the older Gaelic or Q-Celts and the later Brythonic or P-Celts. Gaelic is the language of Ireland, Scotland and the Isle of Man. Brythonic, the language once spoken over the whole of Britain, is now spoken only in Wales, with a related branch in Brittany in the north west of France and awaiting resurrection in Cornwall.

Apart from their language and technical knowhow the Celts brought to the conquered natives a new religion — Druidism and the cult of the sky gods: Esus the Lord, Taranis the Thunderer and Toutatis the God of the Tribe. As befits a nation of warriors and technocrats, theirs was a patriarchal religion that favoured the male gender in law, government and service to the gods. But this was to change. We know that the Neolithic first Europeans had themselves reached a high degree of sophistication in the field of stone building, geomancy, astronomy and natural science. This can be seen from the style of their sanctuaries of which Stonehenge remains the supreme example. They worshipped the Earth as a divine Woman who manifested as a beautiful Maiden in spring, a loving Mother in summer, and as Wise Old Woman/Death Goddess during the dead season or winter. The amalgamation of this belief system with that of the Celts was to occupy the following centuries. The readiness with which later Celtic kings adopted Christianity can perhaps be seen as a consequence of this age-old fusion.

Writing in the first century AD, Julius Caesar informs us that Celtic society was divided into three classes: Druids (including the bards), warriors, tradespeople and farmers. What puzzled those early classical observers was the fact that Celtic women were (almost) equal in law to their husbands, that they could practise any profession they desired, fight in battles, divorce their husbands and even rule independently as queens. It seems that this relatively high status of women had come about as a consequence of the Celtic style of conquest: their invasions were accomplished by all-male raiding parties who massacred the men and married the women by force. These freeborn women, used to their high status as clan mothers in the Neolithic, were not inclined to give it up. As givers, nurturers and preservers of Life they had been equal partners with their menfolk and they intended to remain so with their new husbands. The conquerors had to come to a *modus vivendi* with them and it took centuries before patriarchal rules (later reinforced by Roman and Germanic laws), finally prevailed again in Celtic lands.

Apart from a few sentences here and there in classical writings, we know very little about those dark centuries, because the Celts were not in the habit of recording their history. Their priests, the Druids, although highly erudite, shunned writing. Like St Paul they believed that "the letter killeth" and that it was preferable to keep their secrets in their heads rather than to share them with the populace.

One important class of Druids were the bards, whose task it was to sing the praises of their kings and aristocratic patrons and to legitimize leading families by stories of divine intervention. These sagas of gods and fighting men would be long forgotten, had it not been for the arrival of Christianity. The new religion lifted the embargo on writing and gave the early Christian clergy in Ireland and Wales scope to collect the oral literature of their people and thus save it from oblivion. So it came to pass that long afterwards, during the time of the nineteenth century Romantic revival, there began a frantic search for manuscripts containing remnants of the oldest European literature north of the Alps. It was fired by Irish and Welsh patriots, and financed, at least in part, by such exalted persons as Napoleon III.

Understandably, England had little interest in the search, but a lady of British high society, Charlotte Guest, heard of such a buried treasure in Wales. She got two Welsh clergymen to translate the stories contained in the medieval manuscripts, the *White Book of Rhydderch* (1300–1325) and the *Red Book of Hergest* (1375–1425) and published them under her own name between 1838–49. She gave them the misleading title *Mabinogion,* because she understood it to be the plural of *mabinogi,* in the mistaken belief of the time that they were tales which young bards had to master.[1]

Modern editions of the *Mabinogion* usually present the collection in three parts:

The Four Branches, which are four loosely connected tales titled *Pwyll, Prince of Dyfed; Branwen Daughter of Llyr; Manawydan Son of Llyr; Math Son of Mathonwy.* The connecting thread is the fate of Pryderi, the son of Rhiannon (originally Mabon son of Modron) from his conception to his death in combat.

Four Independent Native Tales: *The Dream of Macsen Wledig; Lludd and Llefelys; Culhwch and Olwen; The Dream of Rhonabwy.*
The Three Romances: *The Lady of the Fountain; Peredur Son of Efrawg; Gereint Son of Erbin.*

Many scholars are reluctant to discuss the *Mabinogion* because of the problem of its origins and compilation, for it is an enigma who penned the medieval manuscripts. They are missing in the so-called bardic collections of Wales and their style reveals that they were not the work of trained bards, but of popular storytellers, whom the professional bards heartily disdained for their illiteracy and lack of education. But if the storytellers themselves could not write, who, then, penned these medieval documents?

For the *Four Branches* at least, certain stylistic characteristics would indicate the hand of a woman. Compared with the powerful passions displayed in the Irish sagas, the *Mabinogion* stories are tame and almost "civilized," so that French authors at first attributed them to Norman minstrels. However, research has since shown that the material is much older and authentically Celtic, the work of Brythons who fled westwards before the invading Angles and Jutes, until they came to settle in the mountain fastnesses of Wales. Another part of the Celtic population of Britain joined a well-organized migration and resettlement to Armorica, in the northwest of France, the region now called Brittany (Little Britain). As their ancient Celtic-Brythonic language goes back to the same roots as Welsh, Welsh and Breton storytellers exchanged their repertoire and brought it to the medieval courts of Europe, whence it became known as the Matter of Britain.

Outside Welsh patriots and continental medievalists this collection is little known and mostly ignored by mythologists and collectors of folk-tales alike. The reasons for the general neglect of the *Mabinogion* collection may be found in the scarcity of Celtic scholars conversant with medieval Welsh, in the difficulties of the texts, and last but not least, in an attitude of superiority towards a society which was falsely seen as marginalized and backward.

Although they are coherent stories, the *Mabinogion* tales also seem to present great difficulties for the professional scholar, because of the inexplicable contradictions they often present. The reason is to be sought in the obscurities of Celtic social structure and Celtic spirituality — so very different from the Apollonian clarity of the classical world. Only very few authors have dared to shine a torch into these so-called obscurities. One of them is Jean Markale, professor of Celtic Studies at the Sorbonne. In his *Women of the Celts,* he writes:

> Celtic society is full of archaisms largely gathered and integrated from the original inhabitants of Western Europe. It was halfway between the patriarchal type of society which was agricultural and based on the ownership of land by the father of the family, and matriarchal societies, in which the mother, or women in general remained the basic link in the family, and a symbol of fertility.[2]

We do not know when the change from matriarchy to patriarchy took place in the Celtic realms. Nor do we know how long the struggle between goddess worship and the worship of sky gods and/or Christianity lasted. It must have been a process that continued for centuries and affected different parts of Europe in different ways. But it seems that the turning point (if we can call it such) may have come later in the British Isles than in the rest of Europe. It may also have left deeper traces there in the form of literature, folkloric customs and archaeology. With every wave of immigrants that hit the British shores from East or West the balance may have been tipped in favour of the one or the other belief system. Today it is impossible to reconstruct the exact course of events, but a certain sequence can be discerned. The prehistoric megalith builders may have had an egalitarian organization, but other groups of immigrants from the fifth century onwards, particularly immigrants from Gaul and the German plains, have been shown to be much more socially stratified and hence more patriarchal in their outlook. So were the Germanic tribes who invaded Britain in the fifth and sixth centuries AD. So we can say that Celtic culture held sway over the British Isles from 500 BC to about AD 500 — a time span of one thousand years, including five hundred years of Roman occupation in Britain. The Anglo-Norman invasion in Wales is not very much earlier than the manuscripts that preserved the *Mabinogion* stories.

Since the beginning of the twentieth century, auxiliary disciplines such as archaeology, anthropology and ethnology have helped us to answer many open questions in this field and many prejudices have been overcome. Yet still the *Mabinogion* stories are almost unknown outside Wales in spite of the fact that a scholar of the calibre of Martin Buber thought them important enough to translate them for his collection of world literature.

About thirty years ago the American author Evangeline Walton published the *Four Branches of the Mabinogi* in the form of four historical novels (see *Further Reading).* In these narratives she was able to convey the culture shock which the indigenous matriarchal Brythons must have felt when meeting with the patriarchal attitudes of the Celtic invaders. Thus she was able to solve many riddles and tie up loose ends which make the stories in the original text so hard to grasp for modern readers.

Gleaned from the medieval manuscripts the *Mabinogion* stories give us a vivid impression of the collision of the Indo-European Celtic gods with the triple goddess of Old Europe in her different manifestations. As we shall see, the fallout of the shock is to be found in Celtic Law of the medieval period, reflecting a considerable loss of former status of women.

Stylistic considerations

Students of Celtic literature frequently complain about the difficulties presented by the style of the *Mabinogi,* even in English translation. They are due, on the one hand to the stylistic brevity of presentation, which expects the audience to contribute its own knowledge and understanding; but more importantly to a stylistic device of the Middle Ages known as "interlace technique." This style recalls in many ways the endless interlacing of ribbons and plant elements in medieval stone masonry and woodcarvings, as well as in illuminated manuscripts such as the famous Celtic gospel books. The interlacing can refer to topics such as life and death, war and peace, love and hate, and many others. Most importantly it attempts to symbolize the intricate patterns of destiny which none can avoid.

The Four Branches are the stories of four different sexual unions. Two of them are fertile and/or redeeming, two are unhappy and doomed. The reasons for success or failure are seen in attitudes towards the Goddess and her life-giving powers, more specifically in the virtues of love, affection, respect, compassion and friendship of both partners. *Manawydan Son of Llyr* is the prime example of positive behaviour, *Math Son of Mathonwy* shows the negative side in spite of Math's wisdom and "righteousness."

Further, interlace technique serves the same purpose as Wagnerian leitmotivs: whenever two events are intrinsically connected, yet separated by time and space, the storyteller creates a parallel, thus reminding his audience of a connection. A typical example would be Gwawl being caught in Pwyll's magic bag, which Manawydan recalls and repeats with the mouse tied into his mitten at the very moment when he is about to end Gwawl's revenge forever; Rhiannon's initial reproach to Pwyll for abusing his horse, and then suffering the same abuses during her unjust "penance"; Arawn's otherworldly gift of pigs, which will eventually cause Pryderi's death, connects with the magic sow of Menawr Bennard which eats Llew's flesh, thereby preparing him for his resurrection.

By the memorizing device of the triads, bards and storytellers were trained to remember these symbols and motifs in groups of three. Triads often refer to mythical, ethical or supernatural themes and/or provide a symbol for them. Expecting their audience to understand their allusions, the storytellers enjoyed playing endless riddling games with their listeners. In fact, like the hidden ornaments in the *Book of Kells,* the art of the storyteller was judged by the amount of "hidden motifs" he could conceal in any given story. Today this kind of playfulness is thought to be misplaced in a narrative, except where we rather like to amuse ourselves with the clues scattered throughout a detective novel. But we should not criticize the medieval storyteller for using these devices. They were expected of him, and regarded as an important measure of his art. From this perspective the *Four Branches of the Mabinogi* are a great narrative achievement. Yet we Westerners have been so accustomed to the clear transparency of Classical writers that we find it difficult to recognize our own pagan roots. By reawakening our interest, our eyes will be opened and we will be rewarded with new and unexpected insights.

CHAPTER 1

The Collision of Two World Views

We are relatively well informed about the cultural achievements of the Celts and about their life style. Yet we know little about their religion and their spiritual beliefs. Julius Caesar in his *Gallic Wars* tells us, firstly, that the Celts "are exceedingly devout," and secondly that they worship the same gods as the Romans, "only under different names." The first statement is correct, but not the second. For instance the Celts had no god of war, like the Roman Mars. Instead, in military matters, the Celts invariably invoked a goddess. On the other hand they had no goddess of Love, like Venus or Aphrodite, a fact which was interpreted as a distinct lack of erotic culture on their part. Not so, writes French Celticist Marie-Louise Sjoestedt:

> Strangely, this lack [of a love goddess] ... is seen as proof of Celtic purity ... This is a mistake, as most Celtic goddesses show a pronounced erotic character. But to look [in their religion] for a goddess who is solely competent in matters of sexual love would be to misinterpret the Celtic character and attribute to it alien features.[1]

It follows that Roman and Celtic mythology differ. In particular we have to consider that Celtic goddesses were basically evolved from different manifestations of the triple *Magna Mater* of the Neolithic: Virgin, Mother and Wise Old Woman/Death Goddess. Mythologists emphasise that this goddess is usually territorial and this is not surprising when we consider that the Celtic goddess was above all identified with the Earth, the tribal territory, its fertile soil and life-giving waters.

We find it hard to grasp that our ancestors saw their homeland literally as "the Goddess," that their respective tribal territories could appear personified as an otherworldly woman who was fully identified with the tribal land and therefore the Mother and absolute Sovereign of all its inhabitants. She was "Lady Sovereignty" in a much more concrete sense than that in which Catholic countries place themselves under the protection and patronage of Mary.

Therefore all political power was originally invested in the tribal goddess and her agent, the queen — and not with the king, who only filled a largely protective and priestly function. The story of the Boudiccan uprising proves that the Romans failed to understand this fundamental principal of Celtic power distribution: namely the king's basic subservience to the tribal goddess and her representative, the queen as her priestess.

The king's enthronement was ritualized as a symbolic marriage of the king with the land.[2] Only the influence of the Roman Church and the introduction of the Frankish Salic Law gave the Celtic kings the position of absolute sovereignty we have come to expect and we can speculate that their originally weak position greatly facilitated their conversion to Christianity.[3]

The Celtic world view which accorded supremacy to the feminine principle in war and peace was also at the root of medieval chivalry, as we shall see. It was this abject devotion to the numinous Earth as a female deity which informed the Celtic character and rendered it open to criticism by the more pragmatic Anglo-Saxons.

In his book *Celtic Religion* Jan de Vries observed that the Celts had been among the first of the Indo-Europeans to subdue the neolithic farmers of Old Europe, a conquest which took place from perhaps the eighth to the fifth pre-Christian century. Hence it happened to them as so often befalls culturally superior invaders: they were "contaminated" (*angesteckt*) by the religion of the conquered tribes. Stonehenge and other megalithic achievements notwithstanding, de Vries naturally assumes the spiritual beliefs of neolithic and megalithic Europe to be inferior to those of the head-hunting Celts who conquered it. He accepts by implication that the subdued tribes had been "matriarchally structured," a malaise concomitant with "racial inferiority" and in his opinion this was a misfortune for their "racially superior" conquerors.[4]

By contrast, the Irish historian Eoin MacNeill explains the facts more realistically when he writes:

> It should be noted that an invading force in these far-off times would consist of men without wives, to whom the wives of those conquered fell as part of the booty. These women, reared in ... liberty, would hardly agree to accepting a lower status than what they were accustomed to. One can subdue a man by threats of death and servitude, but one must come to terms with a woman with whom one wishes to have a close relationship. No man can live forever on rape, especially with a freeminded and spirited woman.[5]

So much for the situation of the women in countries overrun by the Celts. Added to this we must remember that the conquerors comprised a military élite, whose life consisted only of war and the hunt. In order to live in the conquered lands they needed the indigenous farmers, their labour as well their agricultural experience. And this experience was closely connected with the cult of the Earth goddess, her sacred year and its festivals.

The French Celticist J.J. Hatt of Strasbourg University attempts to reconstruct Celtic religion in its relation to the indigenous pre-Celtic population of Gaul. In this he follows the scheme of the three divine functions developed by Georges Dumézil:

1. Sovereignty;
2. War;
3. Production, affluence, life after death.[6]

He concludes that a regional study of Celtic religion in Roman Gaul reveals two basic categories of deities and their cult:

—A heaven with three gods (Esus, Taranis, Toutatis), principally in those regions in which the Celts have lived since the beginning of the later Bronze Age or earlier: Alsace-Lorraine, South Champagne and Ile de France.

—A god and a goddess, who exercise several functions together. This cult is prevalent in Provence, in the Central Pyrenees, in the realm of the Treveri in the Moselle valley, in the region of the Sequani in Burgundy and to the west of it. In these latter regions it is the god who has several functions, because he is simultaneously the god of heaven and of the mountains, the god of water and of all human activities, the god of the community, of possessions and of the dead.

The former religious structure pertains evidently to those regions where Celts were predominant. The latter, by contrast, is found wherever the pre-Celtic element prevailed. The various changes and amalgamations of divine functions must have originated through mutual influences between the Celtic and formerly non-Celtic cultures.[7] Hatt never mentions the functions of the goddess in the second group. His silence is typical for mythographers who as a rule are not prepared to allow the goddess any function beyond the purely ornamental or an orgiastic "fertility cult." Yet Hatt is aware that this was not always the case, that the pre-Celtic population must have had different beliefs and rituals, which "were blended with Celtic cult habits." And he adds cautiously: "Perhaps this fusion started a long time ago, especially during the creative period of Celtic culture and religion at the beginning of the fifth century BC."[8]

He is obviously not interested in the pre-Celtic period. Yet our present-day archaeological knowledge reaches several millennia further back than the fifth century BC, and monuments such as Stonehenge, Avebury or Silbury Hill reveal the scientific and ritualistic sophistication of the pre-Celtic era. Hatt writes about the mutual interdependence of the two cultures, yet omits to mention the importance and functions of the female deity and her possible role among the people of the Celtic realms.

Panel 1: Taranis, the god of thunder.

The message of the Gundestrup Cauldron

However Hatt presents quite a different picture when he attempts to interpret the mythological images of the Gundestrup Cauldron. This silver cauldron, so called after the place where it was found in a Danish moor, is the most famous known cult object of the Celts. It is usually dated from the first century AD and consists of a number of images on silver panels fixed to a round base that carries the image of a sacrificed bull.

Here is Hatt's description and explanation of the most important panels:

Panel 1: Taranis, the god of thunder, holds in his right hand a wheel, the Celtic symbol of lightning and attribute of his power ... The wheel will fall on the Earth and collide with the powers of the Underworld, symbolized by the ram-headed serpent ...

Panel 2: Esus-Cernunnos, the god with the stag antlers, who is represented here in his typical cross-legged position ... He is beardless and carries a mighty pair of antlers on his head. He

Panel 2: Esus-Cernunnos, the god with the stag antlers.

wears the torque (the typical neck ring worn by every Celt), and holds a second torque in his right hand, which belongs to his spouse, the goddess, who is temporarily separated from him, probably because her presence is required on Earth during summertime, or because Taranis holds her captive. In his left hand he holds the ram-headed serpent. At his right we notice a stag, at his left a wolf and above them a small bull. The Celts used to sacrifice stags and bulls at annual festivals for the benefit of the dead.

The other half of the panel shows the soul's journey to the Celtic paradise: the soul is represented by a small man riding on a dolphin and under Esus' protection reaches the Islands of the Blessed, thus escaping the fangs of the dangerous beasts which symbolize "evil death," i.e. total annihilation according to ancient beliefs. (A similar scene is described in the Mabinogion story *Culhwch and Olwen:* the hero rides on the back of a salmon, the sacred fish of the Celts, to liberate Mabon, the Son of the Goddess. See Chapter 8).

Panel 3: This panel shows the Mother Goddess between Taranis, her first husband, and Esus, her second spouse. This can be concluded from the fact that the face on her right is very similar to Taranis on Panel 1, the face on her left resembles Esus-Cernunnos on Panel 2, but without the antlers. The Mother Goddess and Esus wear headbands, possibly symbols of betrothal or marriage.

Panel 4: The Mother Goddess, spouse of Taranis is here portrayed as Queen of Heaven. She is flanked by two elephants symbolizing her power to protect the warriors on the battlefield. Celtic mercenaries who had served in Near Eastern and African armies were acquainted with the military role of elephants. The rosettes on the right and left of her represent the starry sky. Beneath the goddess prowls a fierce beast, flanked by two

Panel 3: The Mother Goddess between Taranis and Esus.

Panel 4: The Mother Goddess as Queen of Heaven.

gryphons which symbolize the help the goddess receives from Belenos-Apollo against the vengeful wrath of Taranis.

Panel 5: The Mother Goddess on her way to the Underworld. Her second husband, Esus-Cernunnos, expects to meet her there. To her right her terrestrial champion Smertrius throttles and kills the savage beast Taranis has sent to avenge himself. To her left Smertrius is jubilant about his victory over the beast.

It is safe to assume that in matriarchal mythology the goddess had all power in Heaven, on Earth and under the Earth. Cernunnos may have been her original creative partner, the spirit of plant life and lord of the animals. Hercules-Smertrius (a Gaulish hero) appears to be her chosen human lover, the Year King, whose fate it is to die a sacrificial death at the end of each year, as Robert Grave explains.[9]

Hatt's interpretation of the images of the Gundestrup Cauldron is important for our argument, because it is proof of the fusion of old (matriarchal) and new (patriarchal) mythic themes and meaning. The assumed marriage of the pre-Celtic

Earth Mother with the Indo-European trinity of gods prepares us for the themes which we will meet in the medieval collection of *Mabinogion* stories.

There are however a few assumptions in Hatt's scheme which are open to debate, for instance where he identifies the Celtic Esus with the pre-Celtic Cernunnos. Such an identification may have taken place, but we know Cernunnos to be a much older deity. An image of a deity like Cernunnos complete with antlers, torque and ram-headed serpent, appears on a petroglyph at Zurla in Valcamonica, Lombardy and dates from the fourth century BC. A similar deity was discovered in the ruins of Mohenjodaro in the Indus Valley, dating back to the third pre-Christian millennium.

Panel 5: The Mother Goddess on her way to the Underworld.

Cernunnos would therefore have been a deity similar to the Hellenic Pan, and known as the Lord of the Forest and the Animals. His image has been preserved in folklore as "the Green Man," "the Leaf Man," "the Jack in the Green," and in Arthurian literature as the Lord of Animals, the Black Giant and the Green Knight (see Chapters 10 and 12). As mentioned, he may have been the first partner of the Goddess in pre-Celtic times.

The Year of the Goddess

The agricultural calendar of Europe had been fixed by Nature since the agricultural revolution which took place in the Middle East in the ninth millennium BC, and in Europe in the fifth millennium BC, and neither the Druids nor the Church of Rome had cause to change it. A certain amount of compromise between the gods and the goddess seemed inevitable, yet it was minimal. It is true that in Christian times the Year of the Goddess became the Year of the Lord, but the dates of the main festivals of Neolithic times remained the same.

On the Gundestrup Cauldron the age-old seasonal myth of the goddess's wandering between the Underworld (winter) and the Earth (summer) in order to secure the continuation of Life on Earth has become trivialized into a marriage conflict. Here we have an important change in mythological thinking: whereas in the matriarchal era the goddess Inanna descended to the Underworld of her own free will to retrieve the Laws of Life from her dark sister, in patriarchal Europe Demeter's *alter ego*, Persephone, is abducted and raped by Hades, and Rigani flees from her (enforced?) marriage to Taranis to rejoin her former husband Cernunnos.

Similarly the *Third Branch* tells the story of the abduction and captivity of Rhiannon and her son Pryderi at the behest of her rejected suitor. Her captivity causes the "desolation of Dyfed," the barrenness of the land during winter, which disappears as soon as the goddess and her son return.

Another panel of the Gundestrup Cauldron shows the high point of such a seasonal festival, the feast of the living for the dead which takes places at the end of the agrarian year, on the

Panel showing the feast of the living for the dead

first day of November.[10] This is the beginning of winter, the dark season of the year when all life seems to slow down and the Goddess is absent. A host of warriors is about to be purified and consecrated for the battle ahead. The ceremony includes military music, pageantry and sacrifices. A tree which has been torn out by the roots is carried in procession, consecrated and then thrown into a deep earth shaft. This rite invokes the union of the world of the living with the Otherworld, where the ancestors go after death and where the goddess resides during the winter months.

Her year begins on February 1, when the snow is melting, the first grass appears and the ewes drop their lambs. This is *Imbolc,* the time when the goddess leaves the Underworld and returns to her children on Earth, so that life and growth may begin again. The young people prepare her way with much noise and mummery to chase away evil spirits. The women go to meet her in procession, lighting her way with burning candles and singing hymns of welcome. The Church celebrates this day as the Feast of St Brigid and also as Candlemas, in memory of Our Lady's Purification.[11]

The next great festival begins on the night of April 30/May 1. This is *Beltain,* the feast of the sun fires. According to pagan beliefs, on this night the gates to the Otherworld are opened and the Goddess chooses the Year King, her champion and earthly lover from among the young heroes of the country. Traditionally, all were invited to take part in this festival and the celebrations lasted for a whole week or even a month.[12]

The third festival in the Year of the Goddess falls on August 1, the pan-European harvest festival. According to Irish mythology this was *Lughnasadh* (pronounced Lunasa or Lammas), the day on which the Sun hero Lugh came to free Eriu's land from the thraldom of the giant Balor of the Evil Eye. In Anglo-Saxon realms the corn harvest was seen as the sacrificial death of "John Barleycorn," the harvested cereal that would feed the people in the year to come.

The last festival of the goddess was *Samhain.* It began on the night of October 31/November 1. This night, once more the doors to the Otherworld stood open as the goddess returned to her subterranean realm and the Dead Season, the dark months of the year, began.

Now too is the season of the hunt and the Celtic aristocracy engaged in its favourite pastime with passion. Hence the pre-Celtic Cernunnos, God of the Hunt, has survived to this day in folklore as Herne the Hunter in the New Forest, or as Arawn in the *Mabinogion* who leads the hunt of the Goddess with her pack of red-eared white dogs (see Chapter 4).[13]

The hunting season was the time when the chosen champion of the goddess, the Year King, met with sacrificial death. The ritual murder was usually staged as a hunting accident, as in the case of the Irish hero Diarmuid. Mythology reveals many parallels: Tumuzi in Sumer, Osiris in Egypt, Attis in Syria, Hercules in Greece, Siegfried in Germany.

In the first Christian centuries, when the ritual murder was abolished, legends and hagiography tell of the appearance of a miraculous stag with a crucifix between its antlers, which leads the hunter into paradise or at least succeeds in converting him to Christianity. This is the case of Theodoric king of the Ostrogoths, of St Eustache and St Hubert. Typically, the *Four Branches of the Mabinogi* begin and end with a magic stag hunt, the first with a positive, the last with a negative outcome.

In order to counteract the pagan festival, in the year 731 Pope Gregory III declared November 1st as All Saints Day. A century later, in 837 the Emperor Louis I, son and successor of Charlemagne, in order to overcome paganism in his realm, ordained the observation of All Souls Day throughout the Frankish empire, which in those days comprised present day France and most of Germany. In England and Scotland it became *Hallowe'en,* that is All Hallows (All Saints) Even, the Vigil of All Saints Day.

These measures show how difficult it was for the authorities to exorcise the ancient pagan beliefs. In the end they succeeded only by permitting the worship of Mary, who was pronounced to have been both "virgin" and "mother" like the Goddess. This adaptation of pagan rites and beliefs to the Christian doctrine continued over many centuries and caused a considerable loss of status for women.

The gods of the Celts

We owe our knowledge of the Celtic gods partly to classical writers, partly to archaeological finds (altars and coins) and partly to the remnants of Irish and Welsh sagas, such as the *Lebor Gabala* (Book of Conquests) and the *Mabinogion.* Understandably, the reports of the classical writers, who saw the Celts primarily as barbarians and mortal enemies, vary considerably from Irish and Welsh saga material. One consequence of this difference is the fact that the gods of the Insular Celts appear so much more human and less demonized than their continental counterparts. The earliest Continental Celts who sacked Rome in the third century BC had a terrifying effect on the Romans, who never forgot the *furor gallicus* and strived for centuries to avoid a similar experience. Later they came to terms with the barbarians, recognized them as confederates, enlisted them in their armies and traded with them peacefully. Hence the testimony of later Roman writers such as Tacitus is perhaps more trustworthy.

As we have seen, the three principal gods of the Continental Celts were Esus, Taranis and Toutatis (Teutates). Esus was a god of the Forest, who was identified with the pre-Celtic Cernunnos. Like the Greek Pan he was most popular with the farmers, graziers and woodsmen, and as the Lord of Animals he survived into the Arthurian epics.

Taranis, a sky god, wields the terrible weapon of lightning, just like the Greek Zeus. His name is his attribute: *taran* is the Celtic word for thunder. However he is hardly ever mentioned in the legends of the Insular Celts. Among the Gauls his name was Sucellos, "the Good Striker," and he is represented carrying a hammer on a long pole.

The third member of the trinity is Toutatis or Teutates, a name which simply means "the god of the tribe." "I swear by the god by whom my tribe swears," was the time-honoured Celtic oath, suggesting that each tribe had its own god whose name was kept secret. Hence all Celtic tribes had their own Toutatis whom they honoured by giving him a special honorary title: *Toutiorix,* Tribal King; *Albiorix,* King of the World; *Catorix,* Battle-king, and many others. French archaeologists have discovered three hundred and seventy-four names of tribal gods, of which three hundred were found only once.[14]

Contrary to Latin sources the two names most frequently found were those of the Sun God: Grannos and Belenos. Understandably, the Romans identified Belenos with Apollo and built him a splendid temple at Aquileja. However, Belenos was not the only Celtic god identified with Apollo. More frequently we find as the "Celtic Apollo" a youthful god by the name of Maponos (in Gaul) and Mabon (in Britain). His full name is *Mab ap Modron,* "the Son of the Mother," and he was the fatherless son of the Goddess, a god of spring, a huntsman like Cernunnos, a healer and musician like Apollo. As often happens in the myth of divine babes, he was abducted by demonic powers in the night of his birth, as related in the *First Branch of the Mabinogi.* The *Third Branch* tells of his second abduction during a hunting expedition, where both he and his mother are held in captivity until Mannanan mac Llyr succeeds in breaking the spell which holds them both imprisoned (see Chapters 4 and 6). Further, the oldest Arthurian story, *Culhwch and Olwen,* describes his liberation by Arthur and his men (see Chapter 8).

The Greek historian Diodorus of Sicily mentions a report by his colleague Hecateus, dating from the sixth century BC. It seems to trace the identification of Mabon with Apollo to the most ancient of times. Hecateus writes:

> Opposite the coast of Gaul there is an island to the north, not smaller than Sicily, which is inhabited by the Hyperboreans, so called after the North Wind. This island has a good climate and fertile soil, so that crops can be harvested twice a year.
>
> According to tradition the goddess Latona was born there and therefore the inhabitants of the island worship [her son] Apollo above all other gods. One can say that they are the priests of Apollo, as they praise him daily with hymns and honour him greatly.
>
> In this island there is also a magnificent sacred grove of Apollo and a splendid temple built in the round, which is decorated with many votive offerings. There is also a city dedicated to Apollo. Most of the inhabitants are harpers who constantly play in Apollo's temple and praise his deeds in songs.
>
> The Hyperboreans speak a strange idiom and have a special relationship with the Greeks, in particular with the Athenians and the inhabitants of Delos.[15]

There are many parallels between Greek and Celtic mythology, and the sufferings of the Greek goddesses Latona and Demeter for their children are similar to those of the Celtic Epona/Rhiannon. The Welsh scholar W.J. Gruffydd sees in the abduction of Mabon and the search for him the *Urmyth* of the Insular Celts (see Chapter 4), yet wonders why Mabon's father is not in evidence. If we assume that this myth pre-dates the Celtic invasion of Britain, the lack of the Father and the persecution of the fatherless son of the goddess is easy to understand as a consequence of a change in religion, very much like the myth of Demeter and Persephone at Eleusis.

In Ireland and Gaul, the principal god of the Celts was not Maponos the Son of the Mother, but Lugh (Son of the Father)

Son of the Irish god Dagda Eoin Ollachair (the Good God All-father). The Romans identified Lugh (Gaulish Lucos) with their own god Mercury, because of his many accomplishments, particularly in arts, crafts and magic. Caesar writes that the Gauls worship Mercury before all other gods and built him a sanctuary on the Puy de Dome in Auvergne.[16] The cities of London (*Lug-dunum,* Lugh's fortress), Leyden, Louvain, Lyon and many others are named after him. As Sun God he appropriated the month of August for his festival of *Lughnasadh* when the Celts celebrated their harvest festivals and summer fairs.

Lugh's favourite weapon was the fiery lance, still an important requisite in the Arthurian cycle. But his fiercest enemy, his giant grandfather Balor of the Evil Eye he kills with the sling, like David killed Goliath.

Lugh's epithet is *Samildanach,* meaning "the artful," the master of all trades. He is also known as *Lugh Lamfada,* Lugh of the Long Hand, referring to his ability to kill his enemies from afar. He assumes human form and helps the people of Ireland to overcome their worst enemies, the subhuman Fomorians. In Wales he is called *Llew Llaw Gyffes,* Lew Sure Hand, and his Welsh mythology is told in the *Fourth Branch of the Mabinogi* (see Chapter 7).

His father, the Dagda, meaning the Good God — "good" not in the sense of compassionate and merciful, but good and capable for any activity — stands in the biggest possible contrast to Lugh. He is a much older deity, a god of truly archaic times. Described as old, fat and ugly, he has an insatiable appetite for food and for women. He mates with the war goddess Morrigan and with the Boann of the River Boyn who bears him Angus or Oengus, the Irish god of youth, of (male) beauty and sexual love. The Dagda is omniscient and always intent on furthering the wellbeing of his people. He carries a huge club with which he can kill all his enemies, but can also revive all dead warriors to new life. He is the prototype of every Celtic tribal god, the original Toutatis.

The Insular Celts have also a sea god, Mannanan mac Llyr, Mannanan Son of the Sea. His realm is the Irish Sea and the Island of Man which bears his name. In the *Third Branch* he has been euhemerized into a wise Celtic chieftain who is not grasping for land and riches, and for this very reason he achieves the liberation of the goddess and her son from captivity (see Chapter 6).

Another complex Celtic deity is met with in the *Second Branch:* Bran, the God of the Head, who as far as we know was only worshipped in Britain. During the early centuries of their history the Celts believed the head to be the seat of the soul and their warriors collected the heads of their slain enemies as war trophies. In the *Second Branch of the Mabinogi,* Bran is styled as a giant and "High King of the Island of the Mighty" (Britain). He leads his army against Ireland to rescue his sister from a disastrous marriage but is killed in battle. Yet his severed head remains alive and uncorrupted, continuing to live and to provide for his followers (see Chapter 5).

In the following chapters we shall explore the lives and mythologies of these gods, together with another, more obscure deity, who entered the Celtic pantheon during the Anglo-Saxon invasion: Gwydion *alias* Woden. The relationships of these gods with the Goddess in her various manifestations will be central to this study. It should throw light on the complex religious ideas of the Celts during their millennial history.

The goddesses of Ireland and Britain

The oldest stratum of Celtic goddesses can be found in the pseudo-historic *Lebor Gabala* or *Book of Conquests,* relating the history of the settlement of Ireland. Here we meet with the pan-European mother goddess Dana (Danu) or Ana (Anu), whose ancient name is later changed into Don and finally masculinized. But the *Book of Conquests* reports that she is the goddess of the most distinguished tribe of Irish settlers, the *Tuatha de Danaan,* that is the Tribe of the Goddess Dana. So advanced was this tribe compared with the previous inhabitants, that its members were regarded as gods. In the time-honoured pattern of patriarchal mythology Dana is married to the Dagda and after the victory of a new wave of invaders, the Iberian Milesians, she is gradually forgotten. Yet she is the mother of a whole family of godlings, the Children of Dana, whose story was preserved by Irish emigrants who settled in North Wales and we find it as the *Fourth Branch of the Mabinogi* (see Chapter 7).

The Book of Conquests may not be strictly historical, but it tells us that Ireland was settled by several waves of different Mediterranean peoples who brought their deities with them. However, the Goddess who is identified with the land, Lady Sovereignty, always holds centre stage and she often appears in her triple manifestation: Eriu, Banba and Fodla, the Three Morrigans (plural Morrigna), or the Three Machas. It was Eriu who welcomed the Milesians to the island, after their bard had sung her praises, and it was she who cursed one of their chieftains for offending her, so that his ship sank and he drowned with all his clan.

In times of war the Irish war goddess Mor Rigan (Great Queen) appears under her three forms: as a seductive woman who promises victory to her favourite battle leader, in the form of the carrion eating crow (the Babd) and lastly as the battlefield itself, which was seen as the Earth goddess in her bloodthirsty aspect. This gruesome image seems to rationalize the death of warriors in battle as human sacrifice, and the fertility of the Earth depending upon the blood of fallen warriors. Yet this is but one side of the goddess, and just as the devout Hindu recognizes and worships the man-eating Kali, so the Irish warrior accepted the negative side of his goddess as a necessary part of Life.

The goddess meets her chosen hero and introduces herself under the name of Eriu, the Sovereignty of the Land. Then she offers him a ring of betrothal and a chalice filled with a red liquid, signifying blood, thus initiating him into her service. In later stories it is the god Lugh who orders her to offer the chalice to the chosen hero, a significant change in mythological symbolism.

Before his initiation can take place however, she tests the hero thoroughly. Only if he can accept the ugly and repulsive side of Life together with the good and pleasant, is he worthy to enter her service and become king. This is shown in the story of King Niall Noighiallach. The young prince went hunting with his brothers and together they killed a boar. As they sat around the campfire they felt very thirsty, but the nearby spring was guarded by an ugly crone who demanded a kiss for a drink of water. None of his brothers was prepared to pay the price, but Niall kissed the old woman and slept with her. In the morning she was transformed into a beautiful maiden, who told him that she was the Sovereignty of Ireland and promised him the kingship of Tara for himself and his progeny.[17]

Of all the Celtic goddesses Brigid was perhaps the best loved. Like Dana, with whom she may have been identical, she was worshipped all over Central and Western Europe. In Britain she was known from ancient times as Brigantia, which gave the island its name. In Wales her name was Bride. In the formerly Celtic countries of Switzerland, Austria and South Germany she was *Frau Perchta* or Bertha. Here we must remember that "Brigid" is not a name but an appellation, meaning "the Shining, the Splendid, the Exalted One." The cities of Bregenz on Lake Constance, Brescia in Lombardy and Brigantium in ancient Portugal all bore her name, testifying to her widespread veneration.

Brigid was the protectress of mothers, especially during childbirth, and the home fire was sacred to her. In Christian times mothers of stillborn babies secretly worshipped her as the protectress of unbaptized children. Like the Indian Lakshmi she is credited with the invention of Celtic writing (the Ogham alphabet), of poetry, of medicine, of smith craft and metalwork. Her priestesses at the sacred oak grove of Kildare took it upon themselves to perpetually tend her sacred fire. In Christian times they became nuns and declared a quasi-historical St Brigid to be their founder and spiritual mother. It was left to the Protestant iconoclasts under Henry VIII to extinguish their sacred fire and disperse their congregation. In Irish hagiography St Brigid lives on as "Our Lady's midwife" and her *vita* is one of the most colourful of all Celtic saints.

Then there is Mebd/Maeve (the Intoxicating One), the powerful protagonist of the Irish epic *The Tain* or *The Cattle Theft of Cooley.*

The monks who recorded her story were at pains to describe her as a reckless, amoral nymphomaniac, whose intrigues and war ruined two Irish kingdoms. They could not deny however that she united supreme beauty with high intellect, strategic competence and military prowess. Like the Etruscan Tanaquil she was a kingmaker. We learn this from the "pillow talk" with her husband, king Aillil. Here she tells him why she chose him to be her husband before all her other suitors. He was free of jealousy, free of cowardice and free of greed. These qualities are the same which Georges Dumézil enumerates as the virtues of the Roman gods, namely serenity as the function of the priest, courage as the function of the warrior and generosity as the function of the provider. In formerly Celtic countries these qualities are still the royal virtues *par excellence* and all a man should strive for.

Epona (the Great Mare) or Rigantona (the Great Queen) is a relatively late Celtic goddess. According to Robert Graves she has much in common with the Greek Demeter Phoreia,[18] the mare-headed Demeter. She is the only Celtic goddess who was admitted into the Roman pantheon, because she was the protectress of the élitist Celto-Roman cavalry squadrons. She was also the protective deity of all travellers, carriers, couriers and merchants throughout the empire.[19] As the horse is the fastest animal on Earth so the sun is the fastest star in the sky, and therefore she was also worshipped as sun goddess. Because of her zoomorphic form as a mare with foal, she was seen as a mother goddess and identified with the Great Mother, Matrona (Welsh Modron). In the First and Third Branches of the *Mabinogion* she appears as Rhiannon (see Chapter 4).

The Goddess and her suitors

It is well known that the change from matriarchal to patriarchal mythology was often characterized by a heavenly marriage of the god of the victorious tribe with the regional goddess of the conquered people. As happened in Ireland, so in Gaul. In Roman times the Gauls erected statues of their deities after the manner of the Romans and we usually find one of three divine couples gracing their altars. These are: Rosmerta and Lugh/Mercury; Nantosvelta and Sucellos/Dispater; Sirona with Apollo, who as god and goddess of healing appear usually in the vicinity of medicinal spas.

From these steles we can conclude that the most popular goddesses in western Gaul were Rosmerta and Nantosvelta, whereas in the East and along the Rhine the preferred goddesses were the Three Mothers *(Tres Matrones)*, followed by Epona. The name "Rosmerta" signifies "Great Provider" in Gaulish and "Nantosvelta" is usually translated with "Running Water." Hatt comments that the sanctity of water is here personified as goddess and has nothing to do with her divine spouse Sucellos.

These three female deities are by no means the only goddesses known in Gaul, and archaeology has found a multitude of "mothers of the country" whose name was only locally known. We may conclude that at some stage a compromise between male and female deities was reached, but it may have taken generations before it was generally accepted. It seems that the images on the Gundestrup Cauldron (see above) represent just such a period of transition and there are generally three motifs indicative of such changes: firstly, the wandering of the goddess and/or her champion between this world and the dimension called the Otherworld (Underworld) in Celtic religion; secondly, the war of the gods for the possession of the goddess; and thirdly, the fight of the human champion of the goddess to secure her freedom and integrity.

It is unfortunate that the Druids, as the religious leaders of the Celtic people, steadfastly refused to write down the stories of their gods and goddesses, leaving us only rare artefacts like the Gundestrup Cauldron, steles, altars and minted coins to piece together their religious beliefs. As sworn enemies of the Romans the Druids suffered cruel persecutions. Many had to flee and seek refuge outside the Empire in the endless Germanic woods, in Caledonia or in Ireland. The last of the mighty order took their secrets with them to the grave.

In the nineteenth century a number of druidic manuscripts came to light. Unfortunately Iolo Morganwg, the man who published them under the title *Barddas* (Bardic Teachings), was suspected of forgery and the manuscripts were never taken seriously. It would appear however from several Irish and Welsh stories, as well as from the content of *Barddas* that many Druids ignored the goddess or found that her service disturbed their power structure. This attitude can also be gleaned from some of the *Mabinogion* stories.

We can do no better, therefore, than to analyse and interpret what medieval Irish and Welsh monks have written down for posterity, the last remnants of sagas about gods, goddesses and heroes still circulating during the early Middle Ages among the Celtic-speaking people of the British Isles. In this way we have come to know the Irish *Book of Conquests,* the story of the *Cattle Theft of Cooley,* the Ulster and the Finnian saga cycles. They can tell us much about the gods and goddesses of Ireland and Wales, about the pagan beliefs and ancient Celtic Law.

CHAPTER 2

The Status of Celtic Women

Goddess worship does not necessarily entail a privileged position for women. We have but to think of the magnificent temple of Athena at Athens and the suppression of women in Ancient Greece, or of the cathedrals dedicated to Our Lady during the Middle Ages, at a time when thousands of women were burnt alive.

Much has been written about the status of Celtic women, yet authors have not reached agreement. This is understandable if we consider that Celtic culture spread over most of Europe and lasted from about 500 BC to the height of the Middle Ages and beyond. During this time it underwent considerable changes too divers and complex to be studied here in detail. Being a hierarchical society, there were always great differences between slaves, freeborn women and women of noble birth. Moreover, religious beliefs, tribal customs as well as regional usage and laws differed according to their geographical and political situation. Last but not least the indigenous populations which the Celtic tribes superseded still exercised their influence.

Earliest descriptions of the *Keltoi* by Greek writers are sketchy and misleading. Archaeology, which reaches much further back in time, has difficulty in pinpointing the beginnings of Celtic culture, but it is agreed that they first manifested as a disturbing element in a well organized commercial network spanning across Western and Central Europe during the so-called Hallstatt culture (*c.* 800–500 BC). The sumptuous graves of Celtic princesses discovered in south-eastern France and south-west Germany bespeak the Etruscan influence in the luxurious life style of élite women in the sixth pre-Christian century. But it is not clear if these people can already be classed as Celtic or rather belonging to the pre-Celtic population of the Hallstatt culture, comprising Illyrians in the East and Ligurians in the West. In any case these were the graves of women of high social standing. Doubtless, there were great differences between rich and poor, between mistress and slave, and we can be sure that the life of women of the lower classes was hard, harsh and short.

Yet historians hardly ever discuss the life of women, whether high or low born. Only occasionally we find vignettes concerning women, hidden away between the greater events. So we are told, for instance, that Cyrus the Great, king of the Persians, was killed in open battle by Tomyris, queen of the Massagetes, to avenge her son, whom the Persians had murdered in captivity; or that Hannibal, on crossing the Alps, had appointed the *matrones,* that is, the wives of local chieftains, as arbiters in disputes arising between his troops and the indigenous population.

One thing is certain: in classical antiquity Celtic women, particularly those of royal blood, fought at the head of their armies. They had the right to choose and divorce their husbands, to choose their own profession (including that of priestess, bard, midwife and healer) and they had the right to own private property and conclude contracts. Had they known, Roman and Greek women would have been very envious of their barbarian sisters.

History has recorded the lives of two Celtic queens in Britain: Cartimandua, who betrayed her husband to the Romans, and Boudicca who very nearly succeeded in chasing the Romans from British soil. Boudicca's rebellion had been provoked by the unspeakable cruelty of Roman tax collectors, who had the queen flogged and her teenage daughters pack-raped. Her vengeance was swift, and it must be said, even more cruel, particularly to Roman women. But as queen of the Iceni, Boudicca was also their high priestess and felt that her treatment was an unforgivable insult to their goddess Andraste. Significantly, in her prayer before the decisive battle, she addressed Andraste "as speaking from woman to woman." Then she sacrificed a hare by letting it run free and gave the signal to advance against the battle-hardened Roman legions. When the battle was lost she took poison.

A century later, Tacitus, a kind of roving reporter in the land of the Celts, praised both Celtic and Germanic women as a shining example to the women of Rome. He wrote:

> Their marriage rites are most commendable. They do not expect a rich dowry from the bride, but from the groom. Yet his gifts are not jewels and ornaments, but a pair of yoked oxen, a saddled horse, shield, sword and spear. So the woman understands that she too can strive for great deeds in life. She is reminded that she is the man's partner for good or ill and that she is to stand by him in war and peace ...
>
> In every family the children grow up naked, with sturdy limbs. The mother breastfeeds them herself and never entrusts them to nurses or servants ...
>
> The warrior shows his wounds to his mother and she does not shrink from counting them ...
>
> All tribes have a great devotion to the Mother of the Gods. They firmly believe that she takes an interest in the fate of men and regularly visits the tribes who trust in her protection ... This is a time of great rejoicing and festivities, and wherever she arrives she is greeted with joy and jubilation ...[1]

> The tie that binds sisters is sacred, and the children of the sister are loved more than one's own.[2]

The French Celticist Jean Markale writes at length about the sexual freedom of the Celtic women, but he limits himself largely to the customs of Ireland.[3]

And indeed, the women of Ireland seem to have enjoyed more freedom than their counterparts in all other Celtic countries. This may have been the result of the fact that Ireland was never exposed to Roman influence and further, as linguists tell us, Ireland had been settled, in part at least, from Spain and North

Africa, where in pre-Christian and pre-Muslim centuries women had always been regarded as equal to men. In any case, Ireland can boast of the first European love literature. In the stories of Deirdre and Naoise, Grainne (Grania) and Diarmuid, Tristan and Isolde, we possess the first erotic tragedies of world literature. Deirdre and Grainne choose their lovers, even against their will, force them to forsake their loyalty towards their king and share their lives as outlawed fugitives, living in the wilderness. Deirdre ends her own life when her lover is killed. Indeed, just as modern women fear to become sex objects to men, so Irish men feared to become sex objects to women. In some Irish sagas, women ask men to undress to show off their physique, whereas female nudity was taboo "because it weakens warriors."

In the Irish *Book of Conquests,* a pseudo-historic description of the successive waves of settlers in Ireland, we read that the leader of the first immigrants, Partholon, "died because of an excess of women." No wonder that Irish men feared women as harbouring demonic forces. But the case of Ireland must be seen as an exception rather than as the rule in Celtic realms. By contrast, in Wales women were expected to keep quiet for the sake of modesty, and sexual intercourse before marriage was strictly forbidden.

The antiquity of Celtic social structure can be gleaned from the fact that both Indian laws and Insular Celtic law tracts show great similarities in terms of marriage arrangements. As is the case in India, the old Irish and Welsh law manuscripts provide for eight different kinds of marriage, the main differences being of an economic nature. There were arranged marriages, love marriages, trial marriages for seven years or just "for a year and a day," marriages by abduction and "by right of the warrior." This last form of marriage still figures in the story of *Culhwch and Olwen* contained in the *Mabinogion* (see Chapter 8).

Usually marriages were arranged by the families, particularly by the fathers of the two young people and the couple's mutual contribution towards the common household was important: regardless of gender it was always the richer party who had the power of decision making. We hear about this at the beginning of the Irish epic *The Cattle Theft of Cooley,* during the famous "pillow talk" between Queen Medb (Maeve) and her partner, King Aillil. Their property is equal in everything, except that the king owns a magnificent bull, which the queen's herd is lacking. Overtures to the King of Ulster for the loan of a bull of equal worth led first to friction and then to open war between Ulster and Connaught. In spite of its trivial beginnings the literary impact of the saga has been compared to the *Iliad.*

The Celts had no special word for "wedding" or "nuptials." Nor did they have special rites to legitimize marriages. We notice this in the *Four Branches of the Mabinogion,* which is a sequence of four different, yet sometimes tragically connected sexual unions. In these stories all we hear about the conclusion of marriages is the description of royal banquets with often dramatic dialogue, followed by a laconic: "And then (the two partners) slept together."

The Celts regarded marriage as a civil contract and consequently easy to dissolve. In case of divorce each partner took what he or she had brought to the common household, together with half of the accrued profits, usually cattle. This sounds fair enough, yet it was to the disadvantage of the woman, who according to Celtic Law could not own land. In a society in which land was the only source of production and income, the lack of it could leave the woman destitute if she had no family to return to. The reason for this seemingly unfair law is to be found in the ancient Celtic belief that woman, like the Goddess, is inextricably tied to the land: "he who has the woman (whether queen or farmer's wife) has the land," a slogan prevailing in rural Europe until modern times, reflecting the fact that the production and preparation of cereals was almost entirely in the hands of women. Ownership of land had to be continually defended against attackers, and as women were not always in a position to defend themselves, they and their land could become a mere prey for landless (and lawless) man. The ancient lawgiver tried to address the problem by forbidding women to own land. In this endeavour he even went so far as to order widows off their deceased husband's property within nine days from his death. Yet where she was to go is nowhere stated.

In Wales a daughter could inherit land only if she had no brothers. In Ireland she could inherit land, but had to fight in case of war or had to find a man to fight for her. This rule was abandoned when the Church introduced the Adamnan Law, which forbade all military attacks on women and monasteries.

In case of divorce, children followed the parent of their choice. Small children stayed with the mother, but older children may have already been given in fosterage to relatives or friends of the family. Fosterage was an ancient Celtic institution. It consisted in an exchange of children between two families and it played an important part in the social structure. It strengthened the bond between related families, because foster brothers and/or sisters were usually much closer than siblings. On the other hand children were never spoiled as might have happened had they lived with their own parents. Foster parents were obliged to teach their fosterlings everything they would need in their future life and social status and parents had to meet the cost of their children's tuition according to their social standing. Generally speaking, though, children were seen as belonging more to the clan or the tribe than to their immediate family, and illegitimacy was never a problem, except in matters of heredity. Because of high infant mortality, women wished for many children. Yet medieval documents show that the Church frowned upon too many sons. As all sons had equal right to inherit land, the parcels of land shrank with each generation, and poverty was the inevitable consequence.

Wales was a poor country, with stockbreeding and dairy farming being the base of the economy. As it is still the case in the Alps, the Welsh practised transhumation: in summer they drove their cattle and sheep to higher pastures, and the hay harvested in the valleys was kept for winter fodder. Cereals and other crops were not extensively grown and food was often scarce, particularly in early spring. For this reason, the medieval Church introduced religious fasting during Lent, a measure designed to give starvation a spiritual meaning.

As happened in Celtic lands everywhere, the peasantry of Ireland and Wales suffered for centuries from the petty warfare of neighbouring tribes. In such cases the people fled with their goods and chattels into the woods, leaving their poor dwellings to be torched. These never-ending attacks were particularly hard on women. We get an idea of their tragic consequences in the Welsh epic *Canu Heledd,* the Song of Heledd, dating from the ninth century. This work of the bard Llywarch Hen (Llywarch the Elder) has been recorded in the *Book of Taliesin,* at least in its most moving, versified parts. It is the story of the tragic fate of a Welsh noblewoman, Heledd of Powys, whose brothers were killed in battle against Saxon invaders. Her lament has become a favourite Welsh folk song:

> My brothers are slain at one stroke
> Cynan, Cyndyllan, Cynwraith,
> Defending Tren, ravaged town ...
> White town between Tren and Trafar.
> More common was blood than the field's face.
> The hall of Cyndyllan, dark is its roof,
> Since the Saxon cut down
> Powys' Cyndyllan and Elfan
> It's not Ffrener's death that I mourn to-night
> But myself, sick and feeble,
> My brothers and my land I lament ...
> Heledd the Hawk I am called.
> O God! To whom are given
> My brothers' steeds and their land?
> (*Book of Taliesin* 949, 1022, 1063)

Sir Ifor William states that the stanzas of *Canu Heledd* which have come down to us are only the verses interpolated between the original prose text of the saga. The story itself was never written down and hence is lost. Had the full text been preserved, writes Williams, "these fragments would have rivalled the *Four Branches of the Mabinogi.*"[4]

The story of Heledd, as Williams reconstructs it, paints a grim picture of the life of a highborn woman after the military defeat of her family and the conquest of their land. One stanza in particular shows us the fugitive Heledd on the mountain side, scantily clad, driving her only remaining cow to safety. She calls to mind the happy days of old, her horses, her red robes and — of all things — the feathers on her hat, big yellow plumes,[5] perhaps a poetic symbol of former vanity. In another stanza she blames her overweening pride as having been the cause of the war and its tragic end: another proof of the fault-bearing role many authors like to give to women.

It was only in the eleventh and twelfth centuries that the Church succeeded in introducing Church marriages, which were strongly resisted initially. The letters of Celtic bishops to Rome are full of complaints about the immorality of their flock, and in particular about the frequency of incest. Many a Celtic hero was born from the love of brother and sister, as we read in the *Fourth Branch of the Mabinogi.* (see Chapter 7).

The problem of Celtic "matriarchy"

Some Celticists, like Jean Markale, are full of praise for the legal advantages which early Celtic women enjoyed, especially when compared to Roman women.[6] These however apply only to the daughters of landowning families. The question of so-called "Celtic Matriarchy" has occupied many writers, yet none has been able to give an unambiguous description.

One thing is beyond doubt: a "matri-archy" in the sense of "mother rule" never existed. There were however egalitarian societies wherever the economic contribution of both genders was equal and men and women respected each other. The German law historian Uwe Wesel, who rejects matriarchy in principle, has this to say:

> For Bachofen, the author of *Matriarchy [Das Mutterrecht],* it was clear that society had always been controlled by rulers. And if it was not controlled by men, then women must have done the ruling.
>
> Here Bachofen erred. Only recently has it been discovered that there are other possibilities; that there exist egalitarian societies, which are "an-archic" (rulerless), yet well organized. There are many who will never believe this and who reject the English *social anthropology* out of

> hand ... Yet if Bachofen had known about it, he would have written [his book on] *Matriarchy* differently.[7]

Wesel also admits that there is a certain stage of social evolution where we find women's societies.[8] These are characterized by matrilinearity and matrifocality. Similar social conditions may have obtained in the oldest strata of Celtic or pre-Celtic society, because many Celtic heroes are called after their mothers. In the *First Branch of the Mabinogi,* Pwyll, the newlywed husband, asks for special permission to take his bride to his home immediately after "having slept with her." This shows that the bride had the right to stay with her parents at least for some time after consummation of the marriage, doubtless a remnant of matrifocality. Wesel concludes:

> Matriarchy (in the sense of "women's rule") never existed. As a model of early matrilinear society with matrifocality we could quote the Hopi Indians. Among them women have an important voice within society — but they do not rule. It is a situation which is only imperfectly described by "egalitarianism." There is a social equilibrium which excludes gender imbalance and the rule of one gender over the other.[9]

Celtic society may have been similarly organized. Joseph Weisweiler, an author who is particularly interested in the status of Celtic women, summarizes his results in seven points:

- The customs in usage in gynocratic societies, such as polyandry, incest and promiscuity, can only be found among the Insular Celts.
- The reports about matrilinearity and matrifocality among the Picts cannot be proved.
- The sexual freedom of Irish women must be seen as an exception, a "secondary form of social organization."
- As far as religion and spirituality are concerned, the Insular Celts, and particularly the Irish, give women the preference. Their role in this realm is a consequence of their chthonic

(Earth derived) religion and has much in common with Bachofen's description of matriarchal conditions.

— Even if we have to deny matriarchy for Celtic realms in general, we have to admit that Celtic culture has its roots in maternal values which stem from earth-connected spirituality.

— It is true that the Celts know no matriarchy in the strictly legal sense as Bachofen understood it, yet their worship of motherhood is undeniable. It derives from the worship of mother goddesses in Gaul, in Ireland, in Wales and in Brittany.

— Most importantly: the myth of the Earth Goddess supplies the framework for the evolution of Celtic culture.[10]

Weisweiler emphasises the important part women play in ancient Celtic sagas as well as in modern literature and folklore. In particular, he notices that even in this century (writing in 1940) Celtic and Anglo-Celtic women see themselves as paradigms of Lady Sovereignty.

Welsh law concerning women

Weisweiler's description of the cultural importance of women is not reflected in medieval Celtic law tracts which, like law books everywhere, are conceived in the spirit of patriarchy, that is the rule of the father. While in contrast to Greek and Roman law, the free Celtic woman had the right to (moveable) property and could act judicially, even against her own husband, nonetheless she is always at a legal disadvantage, even if the Irish law tracts give women more rights than the Welsh ones.

The Welsh texts which have been collected under the title *The Rights of Women* date from the thirteenth and the beginnings of the fourteenth century. At that time the Church had considerable influence on their compilation, which was bound to be unfavourable for women. We find this influence already reflected in the Arthurian cycle, which dates from the eleventh and twelfth century. At this time women can no longer plead their own cause in court. In undecided cases they are obliged to find a representative or a champion who is prepared to submit to an ordeal, risking life and limb in a duel against her opponent.

In his comparison between Irish and Welsh legal attitudes to women, Christopher McAll emphasises the "market value" of the virginal girl, the various payments involved in the marriage contract, which in the Irish manuscript *Cubretha Caratniad* are referred to as "purchase of a wife"[11] and their economic implications, which apply equally to the Irish and to the Welsh marriage contract. In the same study Dafydd Jenkins states that "it has been mainly because of the property rights that the law has been concerned with marital relations at all."[12]

M.E. Owen informs us that "a woman in most traditional societies is dishonoured by a tainting of her sexual purity, whereas a man is not ..."[13] She goes on to explain that in spite of the inferiority of women before the law, Welsh legal texts, aphorisms and triads tactfully respect the female sensibility in sexual matters, usually circumscribed by the Latin word *pudor,* as stated in a triad found in the *Book of Colan:*

> The three shames of a girl are:
> One if her father tells her: "I have given you to a husband."
> The second is when she first goes to bed with her husband.
> The third when she first rises from the bed to the midst of the people.[14]

The Triad continues by rationalizing all payments due on marriage (whether due to the woman in question or to her overlord) as a prize payable in reparation for the women's offended *pudor,* and not, as the Irish law states, as the prize for "purchasing a wife." An equally serious offence to a woman's sensibility was marital unfaithfulness, which was one of the grounds for divorce. Other reasons for divorce included leprosy, halitosis, impotence and indiscreet talk about one's wife and the couple's intimacy.

Another scholar of Welsh law, R.R. Davies, explains the spirit of the law in medieval Welsh society:

> In a society where title to land depends on membership of a patrilineage and is restricted to the male members of a four-generation agnatic group, the woman has strictly speaking no role other than the bearer of male offspring. In terms of the descent and distribution of the major source of wealth, she is a non-person. She cannot, by definition, be an "heiress" and her attractions as a wife must depend on her charms and on the moveable goods she brings with her as a marriage portion.[15]

In the same article R.R. Davies points out the vital differences of legal status found between English and Welsh women in the Middle Ages:

> English women could inherit land and receive dower; and they did not have to pay *amobr* (the Welsh marriage fee due to the woman's overlord), which — at the rate of 7s 6d or 10s per marriage — was no mean imposition.[16]

> [By contrast:] The English widow took her dower as an interest in land, which could seriously embarrass her son, ... but at least ensured that she had where to lay her head.[17]

If there is one area where the Welsh law of Women seems to be on the side of the women, it is in the reparation provided for rape and in particular for the rape of a virgin:

> If a woman who is a virgin be raped, her attacker is to pay her marriage fee to her lord, a compensation for her loss of virginity, a morning gift according to her status, an honour price or face price for her loss of face and a special fine to the king, whose role it is to protect virgins. In the *Iowerth* text this fine is specified as being twelve kine, but elsewhere as being identical with the king's own honour's price: a silver rod and a golden plate and cup.[18]

Should the accused be unable to pay, the *Cyfnerth* text sentences him to castration. Fortunately for rapists however, the *Laws of King Hywel Da* (Hywel "the Good," who died in AD 950) overrule this drastic punishment by stating that "no man should be gelded for doing violence to a woman,"[19] which is fair enough in view of the fact that the barbaric law discriminated against the not so wealthy and in favour of the nobility: if the crime was committed by a nobleman (the only person able to pay such a multitude of fines), the defendant could clear himself of the charge "by the oath of fifty men, three of them being under vows against horsemanship, linen and women (monks)."[20] It is also unlikely that a common man or a retainer could have found so many oath helpers to clear his name.

Yet the Celtic law tracts had their serious inadequacies. The Welsh law was, by and large, a law for the land-owning class. Lacking a penal code it sought to administer justice through honour prices *(sarhaed)* and blood prices *(galanas, wergeld).* As law enforcement was largely non-existent, fines (with the exception of those due to the king or chieftain) were difficult to collect. Given the archaic state of Welsh society up to medieval times, it is not surprising to find law texts in which some attempt is made to protect women's sexual integrity. Of course in all Celtic law cases a woman's social status plays a decisive part. The difference between free woman and slaves is shown in the fixation of compensations for libel and injuries. In the *Laws of Hywel Da* we find the following specifications:

> The worth of a man's front tooth is twenty four pence.[21]

> [By contrast:] ...the *sarhaed* of a slave woman (no injury specified) is twelve pence if she be a servant, twenty-four pence if she be a needlewoman.[22]

Pregnancies of slave women were considered as a loss of labour to the woman's lord and had to be paid for to him:

> Whoever shall cause the pregnancy of a slave woman of another man, is to procure another woman to serve in her

> place; and after her delivery the father is to rear the offspring and if the slave girl is to die in giving birth, let him who caused the pregnancy pay her worth to her lord ...
>
> Whoever shall have intercourse with a slave woman without the consent of her lord, let him pay twelve pence for each intercourse.[23]

These and similar provisions open a window into a time of social dependency which we find hard to fathom. Then again we are reminded by Dafydd Jenkins that "at any given time the law of a nation may contain things old and new."[24] The lawgiver may well preserve social customs going back a very long time and their original meaning may be altered in the process. As an example we have mentioned the money payable to the king or overlord at the marriage (or any sexual union including rape) may be seen as purchase price for the woman. But originally it represented compensation to the women's kin for the assets the woman would have been able to provide: her prospective children and her workforce. Seen in this light the bride price points back to archaic times, when the husband joined his wife's family in a serving role, as Jacob served for Leah and Rachel. Far from devaluing her, it shows what high value her family placed on her person in early society.

The stories in the *Mabinogion* collection rarely speak of low-born women. Here we meet with former gods and goddesses who have entered the human dimension and submit to its rules. Welsh law historians tell us these stories provide a rare source of anecdotal material to illustrate the working of early medieval society. It is in this context that the gradual debasement of the goddess proceeds in tandem with the subversion of women of all social classes.

CHAPTER 3

Wales, its Bards and the *Mabinogi*

The language we call Welsh or Cymbric is one of the oldest in Europe. Within the family of Indo-European languages it belongs to the P-Celtic sub-group and it is more akin to Breton than to the Q-Celtic Gaelic. Ancient inscriptions found in the Leponto district of Northern Italy reveal that it is related to the Umbric-Foscian language of pre-Latin Italy, and indeed on hearing it spoken one is reminded of the speech patterns of rustic Italians.

Before the Germanic invasion of Britain, Cymbric was spoken throughout the island, with the exception of Scotland. Today it is confined to barely half a million people who still use it as their first language and who try to preserve it as their cultural heritage. Together with Ireland, Wales may be regarded as the cradle of early Western literature, containing the last vestiges of Celtic mythology in Britain. The island of Anglesey (Mona) has been dubbed by historians "the Rome of the Druids." The Roman legions had to conquer it twice before the last resistance of the mighty druidic order was broken.

The heritage of the Druids fell to the bards, who belonged to a lower order of the druidic hierarchy. They escaped the fierce persecution Rome visited upon the druidic priesthood and survived five hundred years of Roman occupancy as traditional teachers of truth and righteousness in Celtic lands. For centuries they remained the professional keepers of Celtic traditions, particularly in Britain, where monasticism was less energetic than in Ireland. It is said that a bardic centre flourished in the wilderness of Eriry in Snowdonia (North Wales), where as late as the twelfth century aspiring bards were initiated into the order of their goddess Ceridwen.[1]

The Bards

By the standards of his time a Welsh bard was a highly educated man. He called his art *cerd dafod,* "the art of the tongue," but above all he was a *gweledydd,* that is "a seer." Again and again we read in his verses the word *gwelais:* "I saw." The Welsh word for poem is *gwawd* and it has the same root as the Latin word *vates* which means a "seer of the future" — a prophet. The *vates* were a special class of the druidic order who had much in common with a shaman, whose inspiration can amount to frenzy. The muse of the bards was called *Awen,* a word still preserved in the English word *awe,* which originally had the meaning of "inspiration," "ecstasy."

Thus the true bard was basically a mystic, a man of superior spiritual gifts, who could foresee the future by synthesizing past and present: a man of higher knowledge and a wise counsellor. It was for this reason that bards always had their fixed place within the druidic hierarchy and in the political power game. This is how Sir Ifor Williams, the grand old man of Welsh literature, describes their function:

> A bard was an artist and as such he had a clear eye. He saw the warrior in his shining armour, the land in its beauty and the people with all their weaknesses. All this he shaped into poetic form after the strict rules of Celtic poetry which made use of the rhyme at a very early stage. Moreover he was a master harpist and hence a competent musician.
>
> A word about "bardic frenzy": here we have an element of the supernatural or daemonic which could border on mania and belongs to genius as much as to the charlatan. It is from this dark source that flows the great mass of Welsh poetry which we call *darogan* or "prophecies." Here the bard dons the feathered cloak of

> the Celtic seer and his prognoses have great authority for the people. They are thought to be orations inspired by the gods — equally sacred as the prophecies of the people of Israel. Merlin and Taliesin are the two great figures of this tradition, and some scholars believe that they are just two names for the same person.[2]

The professional training of the bard was long and arduous. It could take up to twenty years. The young postulants would present themselves to the old masters who had their schools deep in the forests of Wales, Ireland or Scotland. During the "dark time of the year," from November to May, the students lived at the expense of their family in those solitary colleges. During the summer months they would follow an experienced bard to the court of a tribal prince where they could earn their first wages by composing commissioned poems. The winter months were dedicated to intensive training. In these six months the young apprentices had to absorb an extensive syllabus. They worked for many hours a day, seven days a week, but always without pencil and paper. An enormous amount of material had to be committed to memory. In addition to the various poetic techniques it comprised the sagas of gods and heroes, geomancy, astronomy, astrology, genealogy, heraldry, tribal law and a huge repertoire of local tales which were arranged in special indices for easier memorizing.

After eight years of intense schooling the young postulant was initiated into the service of the goddess Ceridwen, the Bardic Order. He was then entitled to apply for a position as court bard with one of the many ruling families of Celtic lands. This position entailed the education of princes and young people of both sexes who aspired to higher learning. In short, the bards were the accredited teachers of the nation.

The bardic colleges reached their finest flowering in the pre-Roman and pre-Christian centuries. Roman occupation of Britain brought a cruel persecution of Druids and in the following dark era of continuous warfare much of the old wisdom teachings were lost or misinterpreted. Yet as the bards largely escaped Roman persecution their continuing activity was of great political importance for the resistance to foreign conquest in Wales. Again and again they inspired the men with heroic ardour, pleading with them to win back the land of their fathers. This struggle lasted till 1485, when a Welsh prince of the House of Tudor ascended the throne of England as Henry VI and called his firstborn son Arthur.[3]

A good bard was more than a poet and storyteller. He had to be fluent in Welsh and Gaelic, in later centuries also in French and Latin. As servant of a ruling family he had to know the genealogies of the country as well as all the heroic feats of their lords. Moreover a bard had to be a good lawyer, because the early Welsh and Irish laws were not written down, but composed in verse form and recited by the bard at court sessions. Above all bards saw their noblest task in the transmission of the mythic lore and the ethos of their tribe to the young generation. This explains the fact that the knowledge of Celtic gods and goddesses as well as Celtic moral teachings lived on in the British Isles for much longer than on the European continent. Robert Graves mentions the fact that Druids and Christian monks treated each other with exquisite politeness at their respective Glastonbury colleges.[4]

The bards never tired of telling stories about Modron, the great mother goddess and her beautiful son, Mabon (Maponos) a youthful god of Spring, healing and music. Indeed, the *Four Branches,* that is the four interlaced stories which appear under this name within the *Mabinogion* collection, represent the myth of Modron and Mabon retold in a veiled form under the names of Rhiannon and Pryderi. It is only to the *Four Branches* that the name of *Mabinogi* properly applies. Here we can see how the old pagan beliefs changed into magic wonder tales, the ancient gods and goddesses gradually assuming features of superhuman heroes, Christian saints and supernatural women or fairies. It was the bards and their successors, the medieval minstrels, who transformed the divine Mabon into the role model of the Western knight. As shall be shown, Mabon, Pryderi, Peredur and Perceval were originally the same character.

And what became of the Goddess? The Christian Church transmuted her into Mary, "the Woman whom God obeys." But in Wales the bards kept her image under the guise of Lady Sovereignty, that is the incarnation of the Land. Lady Sovereignty was held to be the divine spouse of the ruling king. She appeared under many different names and manifestations and was never forgotten in castle or cottage.

The travelling minstrels

Over the centuries the struggle against the English and Norman invaders decimated the ruling families of Wales. Llywelyn ap Gruffydd, the last king of Wales, ascended the throne in 1039. Over the twenty-four years of his reign he fought bravely against his enemies. But in 1063 he was betrayed and murdered, and his head was sent to King Harold as a peace price. The history of Wales as an independent nation seemed at an end. Yet when Henry I died in 1135, the Welsh regained their courage and their struggle for freedom continued, until finally all the great families had died out. Their end spelled also the demise of the bards, the "princes of song" as they had proudly styled themselves.

Their heirs were the untutored minstrels and travelling *conteurs* or storytellers, whom the bards had always despised as uneducated and illiterate. The bards had sung of the Goddess, who as Lady Sovereignty chose the best hero of the land as her earthly spouse. Now the minstrels took up this old myth and carried it among the common people as a challenge to stand against their enemies. This is why the heroes of the *Mabinogion* stories, and especially those of the *Three Romances,* are often represented as redeemers from oppression and social ills and as liberators of their people from unjust usurpers. The name Mabon was forgotten or even demonized (see Chapter 10). Yet it is no accident that of the three heroes of the *Three Romances,* both Peredur and Owain hail from the "Old Pagan North" where faith in the Goddess of the Land had been strongest. And it is indicative that all three men were called to their task and prepared for it by mysterious otherworldly women, who always came to their rescue when their strength failed. Who were these wise women with their mythical names? — such names as Rhiannon, Great Queen;

Arianrhod, Silver Wheel or Queen of the Silver Castle; the Lady of the Lake; Gwenhwyfar, White Spirit.

Scholars agree that these and many similar names (often misspelled or mistranslated by scribes) usually apply to the goddess in her many manifestations or to a priestess in her service. Many highborn women stand for Lady Sovereignty, the spiritual incarnation of the Land. As the Land and the Goddess were held to be identical in Celtic belief, every patriotic deed was seen as an exploit in her honour and no sacrifice was too great for her.

The achievement of the storytellers

When the independence of Wales was irretrievably lost, the minstrels and storytellers left for the sophisticated courts of France and Aquitaine. There the mythological themes were no longer understood and fundamentally altered. Now the hero's struggle for Lady Sovereignty became the inspiration of chivalry, the service of the knight for his chosen Lady and mistress, the quasi-religious ideal of *amour fin* in medieval literature. Yet intertwined with folkloric tales the ancient myths were still strong enough to carry this transformation. Thus it happened that the last vestiges of Celtic mythology became the court epics of the Middle Ages, the main content of the Matter of Britain and indeed the cornerstone of Western European literature.

It is true that the storytellers (Welsh *cyfarwydd*) lacked the rigorous training of the bards. But even a *cyfarwydd* had to have wide knowledge if he wanted to succeed at the courts of France and Aquitaine. According to his audience he recited his stories in Breton, medieval French or Provençal. But he also understood Old English and occasionally even Latin. One of the most famous among them was Master Bleheris (or Blaise), whom Chrétien de Troyes claimed as his teacher. Of him it is said that he brought the Grail legend together with the *Elucidation* to the Court of Aquitaine. The word *Elucidation means* "Explanation" and it stands as a preamble to the Perceval story titled *Li Conte du Graal:*

> Logres (England) was a magnificent country with deep dark forests. There was a healing well where beautiful maidens refreshed travellers with drinks from golden cups. Once a foreign king came to hunt in this forest. He and his men raped the maidens and stole the golden cups. Then the well and the maidens disappeared. Yet after a while some knights from Arthur's Court came into this forest. They found the maidens, who now lived with other men. King Arthur's knights challenged these men to single combat and killed them. Then they brought the girls to King Arthur's Court.[5]

What is the meaning of this strange tale? And why is it usually omitted in translations of Chrétien's Grail version? Could it be a vague memory of pre-Christian, even pre-Celtic times, reflecting a society which gave women greater freedom? Deep forests, springs, grottos, hospitable women who chose their own partners according to exogamic custom, these are images of the time before the arrival of the patriarchal Celts from continental Europe. Initially the women had fled the rapists and had found new partners. The Christian knights believed it their duty to liberate them. Instead they imprisoned them in the golden cage of the king's court.

This story is reminiscent of the tale of Thomas the Rhymer and the Fairy Queen, and also that of the German minstrel Tannhäuser and Lady Venus. Here linger conflicts pointing to the ancient clash of two different social orders: the gynocentric, goddess-oriented society of the pre-Celtic Brythons versus the patriarchal Celtic invaders of the fifth century BC, two social orders which had yet to achieve full integration.

The Normans adopt King Arthur

Wales had lost its freedom for ever. But as it often happens, the conquerors adopted the literature of the conquered. Thus the traditions of the *conteurs* lived on for centuries. Most importantly, the Normans discovered Arthur, the popular king, whose name is mentioned for the first time in the *Mabinogion* collection (see Chapter 8). Here they found the tradition of a ruler, however fictional, who was strong enough to stand beside the French Charlemagne and his paladins. What did it matter that nobody knew when he had lived? In Wales, in *Terre de Galles,* people were convinced that he was still alive, sleeping in a mountain cave until the dawn of a new time.

Thus Arthur became the shining hero of the West, the King of the Round Table and its brave knights, the Emperor who (according to the storytellers) had conquered Rome for Britain, the ruler who possessed the sword Excalibur, *Caled Fulch,* the "Strong Lightning," once the sacred weapon of the Celtic sky god Taranis. Best of all, Arthur had vanquished the Saxons, the very same that William the Conqueror had overcome at Hastings. So the hero tales centred around King Arthur and his knights became strong political propaganda in the hands of the Norman rulers. Besides, they forged a bond between the Breton and the Welsh knights in William's army. Later, when the realm of the Angevin kings extended from Scotland to the Mediterranean, the Knights of the Round Table became the exemplars of the Christian élite. The Quest for the Grail, originally a pagan Celtic theme, became the ideal of the *miles Christi,* the Christian soldier, and inspired all Christendom to immortal deeds during the Crusades.

The Mabinogion *collection*

The storytellers never forgot the old myths of the Goddess and her son Mabon. Originating in pre-Celtic times, they could not be found in the documents known as "bardic manuscripts." Their redaction is one of the enigmas of medieval literature: the bards had recited their stories from memory at the great occasions of ruling Houses: royal marriages, christenings or funerals. Yet they, the bards, had never actually written them down, and the minstrels who inherited the stories were usually illiterate. Only clergymen and noblewomen possessed the art of letters in those warlike centuries. Stylistically we can discern in these eleven stories (see Introduction) the hand of several very different authors. But who was the scribe who had committed them to vellum in the collections that became the *White Book of Rhydderch* (1300–1325) and the *Red Book of Hergest* (1375–1422)? They must have been important to their contemporaries, as their translator, Professor Gwyn Jones, once observed: "No Welshmen would ever have wasted expensive vellum on trivia."

For centuries these stories lay forgotten in Welsh castles. Then, in the early nineteenth century came the period of Celtic renewal. Whilst Europe swooned over Macpherson's Scottish Ossian ballads, Wales too remembered its legends of old. The *Four Branches* and the other stories were translated by two clergymen, John Jones and Thomas Price, and published in 1849 at the expense of Lady Charlotte Guest, the wife of a Welsh industrialist. To tell the truth, Lady Guest never recognized their mythological importance. She preferred to set the *Four Branches* at the end of the collection which she started instead with the *Three Romances.* These and the four other folktales she dedicated to her young sons in the mistaken belief that they were hero tales of the dragon-killer type, best suited as children's reading material.

Welsh scholars have argued long and hard about the title *Mabinogion.* The renowned Celticist Rachel Bromwich thought it originally referred to the sons and daughters of Celtic gods. But Gwyn Jones, one of the best translators of the collection, argues convincingly that the title *Mabinogi* refers strictly to the *Four Branches.* In the time honoured form of hero sagas everywhere, they relate the story of conception, birth, hero's night journey, return and sacrificial death of the Welsh tribal hero Mab ap Modron, who here is called Pryderi ('Sorrow').

In the *Three Romances* Owain, Peredur (= Pryderi) and Gereint whose stories are told under the title *Three Romances,* represent the three 'redeemers from oppression' whose adventures contain the last vestiges of Celtic pagan beliefs, rituals, symbols and legal usage. These three tales became the source for numerous court epics in continental Europe.

By contrast, the stories subsumed under the title *Four Independent Native Tales,* are a type of wonder tale with hardly any mythical implications. It would appear that they are destined to familiarize the audience with the loss of former glory and the deteriorating conditions of life in Wales. We find here two dream stories: *The Dream of Macsen Wledig* showing us how the Roman occupation of Britain is remembered and glorified in the figure of the Empress Elen of the Hosts (see Chapter 9); and *The Dream of Rhonabwy* which clearly describes the contrast between former greatness and present misery.

The tale of *Culhwch and Olwen* seems to be especially commissioned by a ruling family to show what a competent ruler such as King Arthur can do for his people. He is the monarch who protects his own and deals ruthlessly with his enemies. As King Arthur is here mentioned for the first time in written literature the story deserves a chapter of its own (see Chapter 8). It also opens a window to real life at King Arthur's court and the ruthless power politics of medieval aristocracy.

The story *Lludd and Llefelys,* which tells about the liberation of the country from demonic forces, is too short and obscure to be studied here.

A tale of bardic initiation

The American scholar Patrick K. Ford ignores the mythological connection of the *Four Branches* to the *Three Romances,* which he omits in his edition of the *Mabinogion.* Instead he inserts two much later stories: *The Tale of Gwion Bach* and *The Tale of Taliesin.* They are connected through the person of Gwion Bach ("Little Gwion") transmuting into the great bard Taliesin through the intervention of Ceridwen, the goddess of Bards (see Chapter 11). According to Ford this material describes in a veiled form the postulant's initiation into bardhood and therefore he ascribes it a far greater importance than all the other stories in the collection.

Scholars agree that the *Mabinogion* represents a unique source of Celtic law and lore in Britain, miraculously preserved from the first millennium to the third. The bards had deemed the *Four Branches* too sacred to be written down, and they were probably preserved through the memory of travelling storytellers who had heard them recited by a bard without understanding their full impact.

Seen in this light the *Mabinogion* stories, and the *Four Branches* in particular, are important documents tracing the passage from paganism to Christianity in the British Isles. In particular, they document the descent of the Celtic goddess from her exalted position of Lady Sovereignty, Great Queen and Mistress of the Bards, to the ambiguous roles of fairy, wise woman and dreaded witch. For the women of formerly Celtic countries this had serious consequences: on the one hand the aristocratic woman inherited the exalted position of Sovereignty over the land, a role still expressed in British queendom. On the other hand, as history showed, this privileged role made her vulnerable to fortune hunters, and a bait to ambitious men without moral integrity.

Submerged in the male unconscious, however, remained an unexplained fear of Woman and her life-giving power, a fear found at the root of every form of misogyny from medieval witch hunts to the politically inspired suppression of women through the centuries. It is the fear of what Jung called the negative anima figure.

The following chapters are an attempt to redeem this negative anima, and to return the Celtic goddess to her rightful place. For every fear that is made conscious will lose its threatening power and turn into psychic energy. Thus the tales of the Welsh storytellers can still help us to grow if we but try to understand their deeper meaning.

PART II

Reading the *Mabinogion*

CHAPTER 4

The First Branch: Rhiannon

The *First Branch of the Mabinogi* tells us about Rhiannon, about her spouse Prince Pwyll of Dyfed, and their son Pryderi. Pryderi is the tribal hero of Wales, and perhaps even the tribal hero of the pre-Celtic Priteni. His true mythological name is Mabon (Gaulish Maponos), an abbreviation of Map ab Modron, "the Son of the Great Mother."

Conception, birth and childhood of a hero were set-pieces in the bards' repertoire. In the *First Branch of the Mabinogi,* entitled *Pwyll Prince of Dyfed,* we are told how prince Pwyll is brought to the Otherworld by King Arawn and tested for his prowess and sexual integrity so as to fight in combat against Arawn's enemy Havgan. There he meets the fairylike princess Rhiannon, who has chosen him for her husband, but loses her to an unwanted suitor because of a thoughtless promise he makes at their wedding feast. Rhiannon coaches him in her magic and with her help Pwyll succeeds in winning her back. Later, in the second part of the story, the unwanted suitor takes his revenge by abducting Rhiannon's newborn son on the night of his birth. The mother is accused of infanticide and cruelly punished.

Pwyll's liegeman Teyrnon finds the child, rears him as his own and discovering at last his true parentage, returns him to his overjoyed mother, who calls him *Pryderi,* meaning "Sorrow."

All in all the story is a combination of several folktale themes with the *infantia,* the hero's conception, birth and childhood in the foreground. In the background, and perhaps unknown even to the narrator, we find a number of motifs from Celtic and pre-Celtic mythology, clustering around the figure of Rhiannon

(*Rigantona),* the otherworldly woman who is the main protagonist.

Most writers see in Rhiannon a euhemerized version of the British Epona, a goddess of the Sun and of Spring, the helper of mothers and the protectress of young children. She can also appear in her zoomorphic form as a white horse, the "Great Mare." Her title Rigantona, "Great Queen" connects her with the Gaulish Rigani, the deity Professor Hatt sees represented on the Gundestrup Cauldron.[1]

Here a few examples of the basic myths reflected in the story:

— The chosen Year King who in ancient times was sacrificed on a sacred mound. This sacrificial death seems to have been forgotten at the time of compilation, the ancient ritual being only alluded to by a combat to the death.
— The otherworldly woman (goddess or fairy) who chooses a mortal man for her spouse and the problems resulting from this misalliance. Here the woman acts against the wishes of her clan — an act of female rebellion unheard of in medieval Wales. Yet ethnologists know that in pre-patriarchal times girls had the right to chose their husbands from outside her tribe (exogamy). This relative freedom was lost with the introduction of the patriarchal social order, where women had to marry the man chosen for them by their father and within the tribe (endogamy). This change must have occurred in the early Neolithic with the introduction of agriculture, when land became valuable as a means of production. Endogamy prevented inheritance by husbands who were not members of the tribe.[2]
— Rhiannon represents the image of Woman as integral, wise and self-assured queen and mother of her people, the ideal of Lady Sovereignty. She stands in contrast to her rash husband, teaching him wisdom, moderation, and firmness in dealings with his counsellors. Moreover Pwyll's marriage with the otherworldly woman secures future dynastic legitimacy for the ruling House of Dyfed.
— The figure of Arawn can be identified with Cernunnos the Hunter, but also with Bran (see Chapter 5). His pack of white

hounds with red ears are the hunting dogs of Modron, the Great Mother in her manifestation as death goddess. Pwyll's stag hunt and transmutation into King Arawn's appearance amounts to a death experience, his journey to Annwn, the Celtic abode of the dead. Hence the special significance of Pwyll's new title *Pen Annwn,* Lord of the Underworld.

— The second part of the story parallels the myth of the suffering Earth Mother Demeter, who also lost her child to the Underworld. In an effort to force her daughter's return she withdraws her life-giving powers and the Earth becomes a "Waste Land," a seasonal myth typical in northern latitudes. By contrast Rhiannon loses her divine powers *(kynosis)* by her marriage to a mortal and therefore cannot resist her accusers and judges. Knowing this she willingly submits to her "penance," as it is said of many other "suffering gods" (e.g. Inanna in the Underworld, Woden on the World Ash-tree). In the *Third Branch* she becomes a prisoner of the otherworldly powers and this imprisonment turns Wales into a Waste Land.

Prince Pwyll of Dyfed and King Arawn

The first episode of the story shows us Pwyll's meeting with Arawn, his experiences at Arawn's Court, including the combat against Havgan and his return to Dyfed. Pryderi's prospective father has a telling name: Pwyll means "wisdom," "good counsel." But this is pure irony. Pwyll commits one rash act after the other, which lands him in ever deeper trouble, until finally his bride Rhiannon despairs of his so-called wisdom and has to resort to her own magic.

Like many Celtic myths, the story opens with a stag hunt. It is autumn in Dyfed, and the hunting season has begun. The hunt is a mythical image of death. In archaic times the hunter identified with his quarry. The stag itself was seen as psychopomp, the leader of the soul across the threshold of the Underworld or Otherworld.

An inner voice calls Pwyll to hunt in Glen Coch, the Red Forest. Forests like the sea are always a symbol of the unconscious, the world of the unknown. The name "Red Forest" emphasises the mystery of his experience, preparing us for a supernatural event.

Pwyll is drawn into this adventure with unescapable fatality, almost against his will. At first his hunting adventure seems to be an every day occurrence in the life of a huntsman: a stag is brought down, but another hunter claims the quarry. Pwyll should have known that according to Welsh law no quarry could be claimed before sunset. Yet being a prince he thinks himself above the law, not realizing that he has inadvertently crossed into the Otherworld. Now he finds himself in its power. The strange white dogs with the red ears should have warned him, because white beasts with red ears are spirit animals in all Celtic sagas: Pwyll has met with the pack of the death goddess, and the grey hunter who claims the stag introduces himself as Arawn, "a crowned king in the Otherworld."

Arawn tells Pwyll about his enemy Havgan (variously translated as "Summer White" or "Summer Song") who threatens his realm and whom he cannot overcome without Pwyll's help. In order to atone for the wrongly claimed stag, Pwyll is to spend "a year and a day" in Arawn's realm and fight against Havgan in Arawn's guise. With Arawn's magic the two men exchange their appearance, and while Arawn rules Dyfed in Pwyll's stead, Pwyll succeeds in overcoming Havgan. For a year he shares the bed of Arawn's queen, "the most beautiful woman," without ever touching her.

In pagan times however, the situation would have been different. As the chosen Year King, Pwyll would have also been the chosen lover of the goddess, after which he would have met with a sacrificial death and glorious afterlife. In this story the pagan prototype has been erased and Pwyll is merely tested for his prowess in his fight with Havgan (which he wins), and also for his sexual integrity with respect to Arawn's queen, in whom we may recognize Modron the Great Mother and Earth Goddess (*Magna Mater)*.

He returns unscathed and greatly honoured to his own realm, having acquired the title of *Pen Annwn,* "Chief of the Otherworld." This was a Celtic title of highest degree conferred only to severely trained and tested initiates, men destined for priesthood and kingship. Pwyll's new dignity, quoted in the story almost as an afterthought, is nevertheless of great importance to the petty kingdom of Dyfed. It means that Dyfed had its very own entrance to the Otherworld, comparable to the Sacred Grove of Diana at Lake Nemi, where the Sybil of Cumae showed Aeneas the entrance to Hades. By his exploits in the Otherworld Pwyll gave his country a ritual advantage which would have been the envy of its neighbours. Hereafter only princes of Dyfed would be able to find the way to the Otherworld and to the abode of the Goddess.

The connection to the Otherworld had also economic advantages. In the *Fourth Branch of the Mabinogi,* we read that Arawn gave Pwyll's son Pryderi a herd of breeding pigs, with the command "not to sell them before their number had doubled." Unfortunately, Pryderi disobeys this order and thus brings about his own tragic death (see Chapter. 7).[3]

Many Celtic sagas tell of a ritual combat to the death, which usually takes place at a ford. Here the name of his opponent, "Summer Song," tells us that Pwyll takes part in a seasonal fight between Summer and Winter. In Celtic imagination this combat takes place in the Otherworld, but it is of vital importance for Life on this side of the Threshold. The battle between Summer King and Winter King was dramatically enacted in rural regions all over Europe and survived in folklore until the nineteenth century.

Rhiannon and Pwyll

Pwyll's sojourn in the Otherworld and his adventures there are seen as a testing of the hero for his future role as spouse of Rhiannon who, in the opinion of some mythologists, is another manifestation of the Celtic Modron/Matrona, the Great Mother. She appears to Pwyll on the sacred mount of Arberth, riding a white mare, and nobody can overtake her. During two consecutive nights Pwyll tries to catch up with her. Finally, in desperation he begs here to wait "for the love of the man she loves best." Immediately she reins in her horse and turns to him. With her first words she rebukes him for having abused his mount in his wild chase — an admonition to control his impetuosity. When Pwyll asks for her name and intentions, she answers: "I am Rhiannon, a maiden from the Otherworld, and I ride in mine own errand." This reply reveals her as a woman of inner resources, who will always act according to her own insights, a woman who is at one with herself and follows her own initiative. Later on she steadfastly stands by her man, even when she sees his faults and weaknesses. Unfortunately her love and loyalty to a mere mortal call forth the revenge of the dark forces who originally wooed her.

Who was Rhiannon? As we have seen, the name seems to derive from Rigantona (Rigani?) "Great Queen," but in continental Europe she was better known as Epona, "the Great Mare" (see Chapter 1). In her manifestation as goddess of Spring she was also a bird goddess. In the *Mabinogi* we read that she owned three magic birds whose song could sooth the pain of the sick, ease death for the dying and resuscitate the dead to life.

Until Reformation times, Rhiannon/Modron was worshipped in Wales as St Madrun ("foster mother") and in that role she was represented as a woman on horseback, cradling a child in her arm and fleeing from some conflagration — an image reminiscent of Mary with the Baby Jesus on the Flight to Egypt. The events we read in the *First Branch of the Mabinogi* would justify this image of a protecting mother and in the wartorn history of the time it had a special significance.

The Welsh scholar W.J. Gruffydd was the first to recognize the fusion of Modron (Great Mother) with Rigantona (Great Queen) and Epona (Great Mare). Judging from the great number of Celtic coins carrying her image and altar steles erected in honour of this complex goddess, the fusion must have occurred before the Celtic migration to the British Isles. Robert Graves speculates that Epona's myth may have emerged from the story of the Greek Demeter Phoreia. In this manifestation Demeter appears in her dark aspect with the head of a mare. While searching for her abducted daughter, she had to flee from the unwanted attentions of Poseidon. In order to escape him she changed into a mare, but Poseidon rapes her in the shape of a black stallion. Rhiannon flees from Gwawl (Lugh?), an otherworldly suitor who wants to marry her against her will.[4] In both cases the wrath of the goddess causes a standstill in nature, the Waste Land, and both myths point to a conflict between a god and the goddess.

The myth of the mare-headed Demeter Phoreia precedes the Demeter myth of the Eleusinian mysteries, which may have been instituted to effect a compromise between matriarchal and patriarchal mythology. A thousand years later, Rhiannon, the former horse goddess, is confronted with a similar problem. Her father Hefeydd the Ancient wants to marry her against her will to an unwanted suitor. She however chooses Pwyll and proposes marriage to him — an act unheard of in patriarchal society. The punishment for her wilfulness is the loss of her newborn child, who like Persephone, is abducted by dark forces.

Through his impulsiveness Pwyll loses Rhiannon to Gwawl, the rejected suitor who appears at the wedding feast asking for a boon. Rashly Pwyll promises him on oath "everything that is in his power to give." Gwawl asks for Rhiannon and Pwyll is caught. Rhiannon has to recur to magic to get rid of Gwawl and return to Pwyll. She pretends to accept Gwawl's suit, but then turns the tables on him. A new wedding feast is arranged "within a year and a day," and this time it is Gwawl who sits beside Rhiannon as the lucky bridegroom. Pwyll appears disguised as a beggar, carrying a little bag with a potent magic. This bag was given to him by Rhiannon the previous year and she had carefully coached him in its use. Appearing before Gwawl he humbly asks for permission to fill it with food from the banquet table. But however much is put into it, the bag appears empty. When Gwawl angrily asks if it will ever be filled, Pwyll challenges him to tread its contents down with his feet. Instigated by Rhiannon, Gwawl complies, but is instantly caught in the bag. To add injury to insult, Pwyll's men play a cruel game with him, beating him as "the badger in the bag." To regain his freedom he is forced to release Pwyll from his oath and to swear not to take revenge. This part of the myth must have been known on the European continent, because at least on one altar Epona is shown with a menacing expression, holding a bag instead of the usual platter with fruit and bread.[5]

In the second part of the story Gwawl's friends avenge him by abducting Rhiannon's newborn son. As the nurses were sleeping instead of watching over the child, afraid of being punished they falsely accuse the mother of having devoured the baby in a fit of madness. Rhiannon is convicted of infanticide and condemned to stand for seven years by a mounting block, to confess her alleged crime to all comers and to carry them to the Court on her back — another allusion to her manifestation as a mare.

In the meantime, in another part of the realm, Count Teyrnon watches over his foaling mare, when a ghostly claw reaches through the window of the stable intent on stealing the newborn foal. Teyrnon fights off the attacker and then finds a newborn baby at the stable door. As his marriage is childless he adopts the boy and rears him as his own, but when he finally discovers the child's true parentage he returns him to his overjoyed mother, who calls her son *Pryderi,* "Sorrow."

Teyrnon's magnificent white mare which foals on May Eve represents Rhiannon herself in her equine form. It is the last time that we meet the goddess in her zoomorphic manifestation. But the equine mask never quite disappeared from folkloric games. It survives as the Mari Lwyd, the Hobby or Hoodening Horse or as the May Horse in Wales and rural England.[6]

The name Teyrnon (Tigernonos) means Great King, and is perhaps a pendant to Rigantona ("Great Queen"). W.J. Gruffydd speculates that Teyrnon may have been the original divine spouse of the goddess, perhaps an euhemerized Taranis, as the images of the Gundestrup Cauldron suggest.

But pre-Christian mythology saw it differently. In those archaic cultures with egalitarian (matriarchal) social structure, the goddess and her parthenogenically born son stood alone in the Cosmos, except for an Earth Spirit or Spirit of Vegetation such as Cernunnos. According to primitive belief, in order to make the Earth fertile she had to choose a mortal lover, the Year King, with whom she entered a *Hieros Gamos* or Sacred Marriage. At this occasion she may have been represented by the queen of the land as her priestess. The Year King was her champion from May to November and then died a sacrificial death to make way for his tanist, his "twin," who would succeed him the following year.

The Arberth, where Rhiannon chose to meet her future spouse, was a sacred place, a *Nemeton,* perhaps a tumulus such as Silbury Hill. In the Pwyll story we read that the man who dared to spend one of the holy nights of the year on its summit could expect "wounds or a wonder."[7] This obviously means that the Arberth was the place where the tribe came together to celebrate its religious rites, and where the Year King was chosen, enthroned and sacrificed.[8]

We may ask: was the narrator still aware of these old rituals? Perhaps he may have had a glimpse of them, as in those days people had very long memories. But the sacrifice of the Year King had long been abandoned and the myth as well as the corresponding rite had to be changed accordingly.

We know from Irish sagas and from coeval reports[9] that in order to be enthroned as the rightful monarch of a tribe, the future king had to enter into a symbolic marriage with the goddess of the land. She alone was the true sovereign — Lady Sovereignty — and the role of the king was that of her protector "with life and limb." For this important role only the best man of the tribe was good enough. In Celtic lands royal succession was not based on primogeniture as under Latin law, but elective. The future king had to be perfect in mind and body and sexually potent. The slightest physical imperfection or character flaw disqualified him, and he had to abdicate in favour of another contender. For this reason kings were hedged about with a number of taboos, later developed into "royal protocol." In compensation his divine spouse taught him the royal virtues of wisdom, courage, generosity and moderation. The name Pwyll means "wisdom, good counsel," but we have seen that the young king was sadly lacking in these virtues: his rashness at the stag hunt, his vain pursuit of Rhiannon on horseback and finally his thoughtless promise to Gwawl at his wedding feast clearly show that he needed tuition and Rhiannon was always prepared to help him. At last, when she stands falsely accused of infanticide and bereft of her former powers, she shows greatness in defeat. Realizing that the women who accuse her are acting from fear she is prepared to forgive them. But rather than wrangling with them, she accepts the verdict of the druidic judges whom she herself had convened and submits to her "penance." In the end she is saved by Teyrnon, who by his vigilance and courage shows how Pwyll should have acted as king and spouse of the Goddess.

As mentioned before, the *First Branch of the Mabinogi* relates the *infantia,* that is the story of conception, birth and childhood of the tribal hero Pryderi. Through phonetic changes his name was later transformed into Peredur.[10] On the European continent, Chrétien de Troyes changed this name into *Perceval,*[11] which becomes *Parzival* in Wolfram von Eschenbach's court epic, the first German *Bildungsroman.*[12] It was Wolfram who found a fitting name for Parzival's mother: *Herzeloyde,* "Heart's Sorrow." This name would also fit Rhiannon in her deepest humiliation, grieving for her lost child and doing penance at the mounting block.

The story of Rhiannon in the *First Branch* is the last Celtic story describing a woman of such exalted position in the fullness of her power and wisdom. A teacher and counsellor of men, she always acts with love, understanding and true compassion, except in the case of Gwawl who attempts to force her under his will. Here she permits a cruel revenge.

In a "feminine reading" of the *First Branch* one would note that this is first and foremost the story of an exceptional woman's life: her conflict with her family and her unwelcome suitor, her brave initiative in choosing her own husband (unheard of in patriarchal Wales), the loss of her child; her submission to an unjust verdict, and the joyous reunion with her son. These are classical motifs common in any woman's life and Rhiannon's example can inspire any female reader.

If it is true that gods and goddesses are the projection of people's ideals, then Rhiannon may well be the image of the ideal Celtic wife and mother. It is important to note however, that she is the only woman in the *Mabinogion* who comes close to this ideal and is free to act according to her own initiative. In the stories that follow, the women, whether euhemerized goddesses, otherworldly fairies or heroines, will appear as either helpless or ambivalent females, often with a negative influence on men's character and destiny, women whom Jung describes in psychological terms as negative anima figures. Only the story of Rhiannon preserves the memory of the powerful Celtic goddess, *Brehines Nef a Daear ac Uffern,* the queen who ruled the Heavens, the Earth and the Underworld. Sadly, as we shall see later, her exalted status is lost in the *Third Branch,* where she is reduced to merely human dimensions. Totally bereft of her former power, she falls an easy victim to Gwawl's revenge (see Chapter 6).

CHAPTER 5

The Second Branch: Branwen, Daughter of Llyr

Following the usual structure of hero sagas, the *Four Branches* may be seen as the four-part saga of Pryderi's predestined "hero's journey," that is, his conception and birth, his heroic exploits, his captivity and his sacrificial death. However, in the *Second Branch* his "heroic exploits" in Bran's campaign against Ireland, the traditional enemy of the Brythons, are left to the reader's imagination. Pryderi's involvement in the campaign (its aim being the liberation of the princess Branwen, who had been humiliated by her husband, king Matholuch) is only revealed at the end when his name is mentioned among the seven survivors.[1] In the same campaign the Brythons tried to reconquer the fabulous *Pair Dedani,* the Cauldron of Rebirth, which had been part of Branwen's dowry.

The image of the goddess is hard to discern in this story. As far as we know Branwen ("White Raven"), does not come from the Otherworld like Rhiannon. However, her whole family is of divine origin: Branwen and her brother Bran "the Blessed" *(Bendigeidfran)* are the children of the Irish sea-god Llyr and the Irish queen Iweridd. As *Iweridd* (Iberia) is the Welsh name for Ireland, we may suppose that Bran and Branwen are, in this story at least, the children of the Irish Lady Sovereignty, the mother goddess of Ireland.

Later their father, Llyr "of the Foreign Tongue," brings them to Britain, where he weds queen Pen Arddun,[2] daughter of the divine couple Beli and Dana. She bears him Manawydan (see

Chapter 6), but has two sons, Nissyen and Evnissyen, from a mortal father by the name Eurosswyd. About these two sons it is said that "Nissyen was a good youth and could make peace between the most hostile of forces; Evnissyen however, would bring about fighting between the most loving of brothers."[3]

Bran is introduced as "crowned king" of Britain, his sister Branwen as one of the "three matriarchs" of the island.[4] The story begins at the Castle of Harlech in Ardudwy, where Bran liked to hold court. The ancient name of Harlech Castle was "Branwen's Tower." This would indicate that the castle (and probably the land) were originally in the possession of his sister Branwen. Was Branwen the regional goddess of Ardudwy? By contrast, Bran's spouse, the mother of his son Caradoc, is nowhere mentioned.

Here is a short summary of the *Second Branch.*

King Bran had married his sister Branwen to Matholuch, High King of Ireland. According to matriarchal inheritance right, which went from maternal uncle to sister's son, Branwen's son would have become High King of Britain after Bran.

But the story reveals that this old inheritance right is about to be abandoned in favour of patriarchal inheritance from father to son. This is the basic conflict of the story, but it is only alluded at towards the end. It is Bran's secret wish to see his son Caradoc as future king. Therefore Matholuch's suit for his sister's hand is much to his liking, although he does not mention his secret thoughts. The marriage of Matholuch and Branwen is a purely political one, as one of Matholuch's follower's admits: "He (Matholuch) wishes to unite the Island of the Mighty (Britain) with Ireland, so that they become the stronger."[5]

For Branwen's half-brother Evnissyen this marriage is not only a break with old British inheritance rules, but a deadly insult, because he had not been consulted. During Branwen's wedding night he mutilates Matholuch's horses, which is not only a crime against the guest and new brother-in-law, but also an insult to the horse goddess. Bran is highly embarrassed, and to save the peace he offers Matholuch a royal honour's price in gold and silver, adding to it the legendary *Pair Dedani,* the Cauldron of Rebirth.

This cauldron had originally belonged to the Irish earth goddess/giantess Cymidei Cymeinfoll, who had brought it to Britain on her flight from Ireland. It had the property to resuscitate dead warriors to new life, except for the faculty of speech. Cymidei was incredibly fertile, bringing forth a fully armed warrior every six months. Embarrassed by her numerous offspring, the Irish thought how they could rid themselves of the woman, her partner and her clan. As these people knew neither iron nor intoxicating drinks, the Irish invited them to a party in an iron house, made them drunk and lit great fires around the house, until it was glowing white hot. Cymidei's children perished, but her partner Llasar Llaes Gyfnewid managed to break through the iron wall and save her together with the Cauldron of Rebirth. They fled to Britain, where Bran received them graciously and put their warrior sons to good use in guarding the shores of the island against invaders, thus showing at once compassion and political wisdom.

Yet by bestowing Branwen, one of the "three Matriarchs of Britain," on the Irish king, and thoughtlessly adding the Cauldron of Life to her dowry, Bran has sealed the fate of his dynasty.

In Ireland queen Branwen does her duty and bears a son to the king and an heir to the throne. They call him Gwern.[6] Unfortunately, Evnissyen's crime has become known in Ireland. And just as Rhiannon as queen from a foreign land had aroused suspicion in Dyfed, so too Branwen is mistrusted and hated in Ireland. The king's counsellors demand that he divorces her. More than that: Branwen is to be completely crushed. Banned to the kitchen as a scullery slave she is regularly beaten by the butcher. Alone and abandoned she tames a starling, and through that little bird sends a message to her brother.

Thus alerted, Bran immediately musters his army and fits out a fleet to free his sister and to avenge her sufferings. The Irish sue for peace. Branwen is not vengeful. All she wants is to be given her child back and to return to Britain with her brothers.

Yet such a peace is too cheap for Bran. The Irish are prepared to recognize Branwen's young son as their king, which would effectively unite both islands under the British rule. But Bran is now eager to become king of Ireland himself and leave both countries to his son Caradoc.

While he is hesitating, Branwen suggests that the Irish build her brother a house big enough to hold him, because Bran is a giant and no house had ever been big enough for him. The Irish follow Branwen's advice and build "the great house." But on each of the hundred columns supporting its roof, they fasten a bag, in which they conceal a warrior in full armour. Evnissyen discovers the treacherous plan and kills the warriors one by one, just before the beginning of the feast that should see young Gwern enthroned as King of Ireland. Branwen is overjoyed to be reunited with her son, but as the boy is to meet his uncles, Evnissyen commits another shocking crime. As he hugs his young nephew, he lifts him up and hurls him headlong into the fire which burns in the middle of the hall.

A horrible carnage follows, in which the British are at first victorious. However, the Irish resuscitate their fallen warriors each night by dropping them into the *Pair Dedani,*, so that next morning they are alive and ready for battle again. Finally the British are in a desperate situation, and Evnissyen, realizing his guilt, decides to atone for it. He joins the Irish fallen warriors and when he is thrown into the cauldron, he stretches himself out in it, breaks it with superhuman strength and dies in the effort.

The breaking of the cauldron causes a terrible conflagration which ends all fighting. Of the British force only seven men survive: Bran, his brother Manawydan, Pryderi, Taliesin the bard and three others. However, Bran has been wounded in the heel by a poisonous spear and feels close to death. He orders his head to be struck off, to be taken to Britain and buried in the White Mound of London, from where it would protect Britain at all times.

On the return journey, as they reach Anglesey, Branwen looks upon Ireland and Britain. And as she realizes that the two islands had been laid waste because of her, her heart breaks and she dies. The company of survivors with the Head of Bran leading them, spend seven years at Harlech, entertained and fed by Bran's severed Head and by the singing of Rhiannon's marvellous birds. Then they spend another "fourscore years" at the island of Gwales in Penfro, always enjoying "the hospitality of Bran's Head" and forgetting the horrible battle and the sufferings they had endured in Ireland.

When this pleasant time comes to an end, they discover that Caswallawn, King Beli's son, had donned a mantle of invisibility, and had killed the seven chieftains left behind for the protection of Britain. Bran's son, young Caradoc, had escaped, but had died of shame, because he had not been able to defend the chieftains. Caswallawn son of Beli is now the undisputed king of Britain according to patriarchal succession and a new era is about to begin.

As in the Rhiannon story, *Branwen Daughter of Llyr* follows the folktale tradition of the "calumniated wife."[7] Yet there is much in the *Second Branch* recalling the Germanic *Lay of the Nibelungs:* the brothers who seem to care for their sister, but are her worst enemies; the arranged marriage that serves her brother's political interests; the murder of the young crown prince before the eyes of his mother; the carnage in the banquet hall and the total annihilation of two royal Houses.

Like the wicked Hagen in the *Lay of the Nibelungs,* so in this story it is Bran's half-brother Evnissyen who drives the story to its tragic conclusion. He is motivated partly by his hate for the Irish, partly by injured pride because he was not consulted at Branwen's marriage. Another motive for his indignation may be the fact that he foresees Matholuch's secret scheme to acquire Britain for Ireland by right of (matriarchal) succession and feelings of jealousy because of his own inferior paternity, a fact that points to the growing importance of the father in inheritance rights. In any case the narrator leaves us in no doubt that the basic conflict is to be sought in the change from the old matriarchal order to the new patriarchal succession, a change which both Bran and Matholuch hope to exploit, and which eventually Beli's son Caswallawn achieves for himself by magic and murder.

Yet comparing the heroines of the two stories we notice an enormous difference between Branwen and Crimhild. In the opinion of critics Branwen's love of peace and her conciliatory attitude is unworthy of a British princess. Professor Mac Cana (Dublin) writes that "beside the other heroines of the *Four Branches,* Rhiannon, Arianrhod and Blodeuedd, she appears like a Cinderella, "colourless, apathetic and apparently born to suffer."[8] His criticism is not entirely valid however, because even in her deepest humiliation Branwen never loses her innate dignity or her initiative. Even as a kitchen maid and suffering daily abuse, she still retains power over her totemic bird, the starling, whom she trains "at her kneading trough," and through it regains her freedom.

Further, Mac Cana points out that the other heroines of the *Four Branches* — Rhiannon, Arianrhod and Blodeuedd — are mythological figures, shaped by centuries of narrative tradition, whereas Branwen appears nowhere in Celtic mythology prior to the redaction of *The Four Branches.* Only in later Welsh poetry is she celebrated as the "Welsh Aphrodite." We must assume therefore that the storyteller invented her story with the express purpose to justify Pryderi's journey to Ireland, to connect him with Bran and to explain the change in British royal succession from the old to the new system, from Bran to Beli. In typical Celtic narrative style these main objects are concealed until the last moment. Only when the seven survivors prepare to return home are we told that Pryderi is among them.

At the beginning of the story we are told that "Bran was the crowned king of this island." Here the god Beli, an important god of the Sun and of Summer in most Celtic realms, is related to him only in so far as he is the father of his (step)mother Pen Arddun (Head of the Shining Ones), and it is not clear whether Bran has inherited the crown from or her or won it by election. He is shown as a model of kingly virtues, the very opposite of his opponent Matholuch, who is described as weak and dependent on his counsellors.

In the *First Branch* we see Rhiannon constantly advising her husband, Pwyll. By contrast, Branwen can only make her voice heard in council when she has long been separated from the king and the British stand victorious before Matholuch's fort. Now the king's counsellors tremble before her, but Branwen is not out for revenge. Although she never hides her disdain for the king and his court, her call for peace and reconciliation is not a sign of weakness, but of true concern for the land. During the peace negotiations everything the Irish did to pacify Bran "was due to the pleading of Branwen, who feared that otherwise the land would be laid waste."[9] Here we perceive once again the true role of the queen as Lady Sovereignty, the goddess who *is* the land. The land is the foundation of all Life, both in Ireland and in Britain. If it is laid waste, Life cannot continue.

Bran the Blessed

In the *Four Branches* we meet three British divine dynasties: Dyfed (Pembrokeshire), Gwynedd (Venedotia, Snowdonia), and the Children of Llyr — the Irish Sea God — whose origin is to be sought in Ireland. The story of the Children of Llyr is clearly connected to Ireland and tells us much about Irish myths and customs, nonetheless we have to see in Bran (here styled as Son of Llyr) an ancient god of Britain. If we can believe Robert Graves, Bran is one of the oldest gods of Europe, sharing his identity with the Titan Cronos/Uranos/Saturn.[10] Graves also sees parallels with Orpheus, whose severed head continued to sing and preach — doubtless mythological shorthand for the continuation of his cult after his death.

Another possible prototype of Bran (according to Graves) could be Phoroneus, the legendary founding father of the matriarchal Pelasgians.[11] In the druidic tree alphabet Bran's attribute is the alder. He can therefore be regarded as the Alder King, the original *Erlkoenig* of folklore. In this context it is perhaps significant to mention that the alder, together with the aspen and the cypress, is the tree of resuscitation.[12]

We could dismiss Robert Graves' assumption that Bran is the Titan Cronos banished by Zeus to the Underworld (or the Celtic Otherworld), if it were not for his gigantic size. Neither house nor ship can contain him. On his journey to Ireland he wades through the Irish Sea, while his fleet sails beside him. At the same time he carries his musicians on his back, which would show that he is also a god of music like Orpheus. When the Shannon stops his progress he utters one of those gnomic sayings which are still quoted in Wales: "Let him who would be chief be the bridge!" He stretches himself across the river and his army marches over him to the other shore.

The Celtic worship of Bran is shown by his epithet "the Blessed" (*bendigeidfran),* in spite of the fact that according to the *Mabinogion* his power politics brought ruin to his family and to the whole of Britain. There was even an attempt to ascribe to him the Christianization of Britain, but this fiction met with little success.[13]

Anne Ross emphasises that British archaeology is particularly rich in images of "the God of the Head" and this predilection is carried on in Christian iconography where many saints are represented as carrying their head in their hand.

We can also refer to the gruesome beheading game which we meet both in Irish and Arthurian sagas. Authors of classical antiquity are agreed that the early Celts were passionate head hunters, who used the severed heads of their enemies to decorate their horse trappings and their houses. They regarded the head as the seat of the soul and the cult of the head "was spread over the whole of Britain."[14] It appears that in Britain at least, Bran was the original "God of the Head" as the story of Branwen avers: his gigantic severed head is carried along with the seven survivors of the campaign, leading them and providing food and drink for them in the episode called "the hospitality of the wondrous Head." Only after eighty-four (twelve times seven) years does decay set in. The sojourn of the returning warriors at Harlech at first and then on the island of Gwales in Penfro, can be likened to the Norse Valhalla, a heroes' paradise. Here they can enjoy for a whole lifetime a well earned rest after the murderous battle with the Irish ghost army. The episode is an important clue to the Celtic beliefs in an afterlife which most probably included reincarnation after a sojourn in the Otherworld.

Is there a deeper meaning to the Second Branch?

In the convoluted style of the Middle Ages, the *Four Branches* present us with marriages and partnerships, both happy and unhappy. This does not mean that the happy marriages are free of tests and problems. But in the end the couples who keep their pledge will overcome all difficulties. This is shown in the First and the Third Branches. However if the couple is separated by selfishness, misunderstandings and disloyalty, then tragedy follows.

Branwen Daughter of Llyr is a case in point. Branwen is sent to Ireland by her brother Bran who is following his own political agenda: he wants to avoid her children becoming rivals to his son Caradoc for the throne of Britain.

She accepts his decision without objecting, even if she must have been aware of her role as *prifrieni/genitrix* of the future kings of Britain. If she really loved Matholuch (which is nowhere mentioned) she gave her love to an unworthy man. Or was it perhaps the memory of her mother Iweridd, once Lady Sovereignty of Ireland, who attracted her to the Green Isle? Then she was ill informed, as the times of the Irish Lady Sovereignty were past, and the present king evidently means to end matriarchal succession. The author of the *Four Branches* mentions none of these possibilities. But we can assume that his audience may have been aware of them and of many other pagan relics which were still known in medieval times, such as the following examples.

The episode of the "Iron House" in which the Irish goddess/giantess and her children are to be burnt, is symbolic of the Great House which the Irish built for Bran, and in which the British were to perish.

The earliest settlers of Britain and Ireland did not know iron nor intoxicating drinks and this ignorance was their downfall. Memories of such genocides are preserved in our fairy stories, where "the Little People" are afraid of iron and intoxicating drinks.

Nissyen, the peaceful of the two brothers is often described by commentators as a superfluous appendage. Graves disputes this and cites a whole litany of semi-divine twins in Classical mythology. It seems that in some regions they acted as the Year

King's double. When he died his pre-ordained sacrificial death (as Evnissyen in this story), the second brother took on his role for the second part of the year.[15] They both function as champions of the goddess and stand to Branwen as the two Dioscuri stood to Helena.

More important is the constellation of the goddess (here represented by Branwen) between two contenders: Bran — Branwen — Matholuch — and back to Bran. This is one of the many symbols for the yearly cycle of the goddess, and as we shall see, the constellation is repeated in each of the *Four Branches.* It re-emerges in the Arthurian cycles but by then its mythological context is forgotten and therefore misinterpreted. Sacred Marriage becomes adultery, the great theme of Guinevere and Lancelot, Tristan and Isolde.

Further, Bran's death and Beli's ultimate victory must also be seen as the annual victory of the Summer King (Beli is a sun god, and therefore a god of Summer) over the Winter King Bran, a god of the Otherworld and of the dead, a Celtic Saturn like the Gaulish Dispater.

In this context the Cauldron of Rebirth is of great interest. Originally in the possession of a primeval Earth Goddess, the cauldron is the symbol of transformation *par excellence.* It stands for the womb of the Earth, which receives the dead and brings them forth again to new life. The catastrophic consequences of its misuse read like an apocalyptic warning to our own generation. A similar cauldron of resuscitation is found in the story of *Peredur Son of Efrawg.*[16] But in this case the vessel is in the hands of women and its resuscitating properties are totally benevolent, underscoring the life preserving role of women. Both cauldrons can be seen as pre-figurations of the Grail.

The Arthurian connection

In one of the last sentences of the Branwen story the bard Taliesin is mentioned as one of the seven survivors. This would not be of much consequence, were it not for two dark poems in Welsh medieval literature which are both ascribed to Taliesin and which both show parallels to the *Second Branch.*

Much has been written about Taliesin, and he has been likened to the Welsh Homer in the scope of his poetry, but he remains an enigmatic figure about whom very little is known. The events of the *Second Branch* are alluded to in two of his most famous poems: *Cad Goddeu* or *The Battle of the Trees*, and *Preiddeu Annwn* or *The Spoils of Annwn.*

In *The Battle of the Trees,* Bran and the tree goddess Achren are fighting against the gods Amatheon and Gwydion. Bran and the goddess cannot be overcome as long as his enemies do not know his name. But clever Gwydion guesses it from the alder twigs which Bran, the god of the Alder, holds in his hand. Amatheon, the god of the ploughmen, wins the battle. Robert Graves' book *The White Goddess* is largely dedicated to the analysis of this obscure poem. If we can believe him, the Battle of the Trees is the veiled narrative about the conquest of an ancient (neolithic?) oracle shrine (Avebury?) and its secret tree alphabet by Celtic Brythons.[17] This mythological battle is also mentioned in the Welsh Triads as one of "three frivolous battles," because 71,000 warriors lost their lives on account of three animals: a lap dog, a roebuck and a lapwing. However, as S. and P. Botheroyd point out, much more important things than three animals were at stake.

> Amatheon, the ploughman and farmer, can only cultivate the earth successfully, if the powers of the Otherworld (the Earth Goddess) are engaged on his side. Knowledge and technology alone are not enough ... It seems that Amatheon stole the (sacred) animals from the Goddess as a pledge to negotiate her help. In the battle with his otherworldly opponents he succeeds in overcoming them.[18]

In this mysterious story, it seems that here too Bran, cast as protector of the goddess, loses her battle: another indication that like Saturn or the Winter King he can never win.

Finally a word about another important poem by Taliesin: *Preiddeu Annwn (The Spoils of Annwn).* Here the poet tells about a journey to the Otherworld undertaken by King Arthur with a shipload of chosen heroes. The aim of the campaign is the capture of the magic treasures of the Otherworld including the Cauldron of Life. The fortresses his warrior have to conquer are all symbolic of otherworldly places. Here as in Bran's Irish campaign of the *Second Branch,* Taliesin is one of the few survivors to tell the tale, and if Arthur did indeed bring back any treasures they were dearly paid for, as each stanza ends with the lament: "Only seven did return." Taliesin (or the bard who adopts this name) identifies King Arthur and his men with Bran and his seven survivors. He presents both kings as superhuman heroes, who dared to go where no man went before to combat against the invincible powers of the Otherworld, and both lost.

Another mythological connection of Bran with the Arthurian cycle is found towards the end of the *Second Branch* in the episode of the final battle. Just as the horrible carnage is about to begin one of the Brythons warns the Irish with the battle cry: "Dogs of Gwern, beware of Pierced Thighs!"

"Dogs of Gwern" means the Irish warriors, whose new king, Bran's nephew, is called "Gwern." But "Pierced Thighs"? None of the translators has ventured to explain the word, except in a superficial way as a proper name or as a connection to Bran's future wound on the heel. The Welsh word *Morddwyn Tyllion* clearly means "pierced thighs," but not even the narrator has dared to spell out the real identity of the man so called. Perhaps a verbatim quotation of the episode will show the pathos behind these words:

> When Branwen saw her son burning in the fire, she made as if to leap after him from where she was sitting between her two brothers, but Bran seized her with one hand and his shield with the other. Everyone in the house sprang up, and there arose the greatest commotion ... as everyone reached for his arms.
>
> This was when Pierced Thighs said, "Dogs of Gwern, beware of Pierced Thighs!" As each man went for his weapons Bran protected Branwen between his shield and his shoulder.[19]

It seems that in the heat of the moment the author reveals a closely guarded secret: *Morddwyn Tyllion* ("Pierced Thighs") is none other than Bran himself, who in this moment of high pathos betrays his fatal wound, the wound which disqualifies him not only from kingship but from partnership with the goddess forever. The giant Bran (whom Graves identified with Uranos) is the Wounded God. Made impotent, he can no longer celebrate a sacred marriage with the goddess after the fashion of Celtic kings. He is a widower plotting the "new" patriarchal succession for himself and his son, hence not one but *two* Waste Lands, and hence his secret desire to disengage himself from the goddess and her rule of succession. His tragedy is revealed in this passage only for those "who have ears to hear," that is for initiates into (pre-)Celtic mysteries.

Sylvia and Paul Botheroyd have understood the underlying problem when they write:

> Bran is the wounded god. Surely, his wound on the foot is a euphemism ... an image which connects him with the Fisher King (Bron!) of the Grail saga. The Waste Land is a consequence of his wound.[20]

Is he the "wounded god" who has the power to heal? And is it because of this that he is called "the Blessed"? The concealment of his "wondrous Head" at the White Mound of London in order to protect Britain from invaders would allude to this. According to the triads, this interment was disturbed by King Arthur, as he alone wanted to have the glory to defend Britain from invaders — another identification of Bran with the medieval king.

Here, Sylvia and Paul Botheroyd see the Waste Land, emblematic of the European winter, as a consequence of Bran's wound, associating him with Bron the Fisher King. But the originating cause of the Waste Land can be seen differently. For instance in the classical Demeter myth it is definitely the goddess who brings all life on Earth to a standstill. Again, in the *Second Branch* Branwen holds herself responsible for the devastation of Britain and Ireland, while in the *Third Branch* we are told that the desolation of Dyfed was caused by Rhiannon's rejected suitor as an act of revenge.

I am inclined to argue that the Waste Land motif was originally seen as being caused by the grief of the goddess and/or her absence from the land, or by her displeasure at the impotence of the king as her earthly spouse. Only after the advent of Christianity, and particularly in the Grail stories, was the Waste Land seen as a direct consequence of a king's genital wounding that rendered him impotent.

All considered it seems that the *Second Branch* with its plain and naïve storyline takes us back to a primeval "time before time," into the centuries before the Celtic invasion of Britain, and later when Celtic mythology first coalesced with the archaic beliefs of Old Europe. We will never decode all its secrets. One thing is clear however: the central conflict here is the battle for male supremacy and patriarchal succession in Britain. Bran and Matholuch who fought the battle royal — even to the extent of usurping the mysteries of Life in the shape of the Cauldron of Rebirth — have both lost it. Branwen, the priestess of the Goddess, saw her son murdered, and died of a broken heart. Was it because she had not been strong enough to resist the arranged marriage — as Rhiannon had done? The clear winner is Beli the Sun God who secures patriarchal succession for his son. Henceforth royal succession in Britain will be unequivocally patriarchal.

CHAPTER 6

The Third Branch: Manawydan, Son of Llyr

The murderous war in Ireland had ended and Branwen had died of a broken heart. The author of the *Four Branches* avoids the description of bloody battles and gory details. Yet we are given to understand that the explosion of the Cauldron of Rebirth was an event of cosmic dimensions: in Ireland only five women had survived it. The resettlement of the island is told with lapidary brevity:

> In Ireland, meanwhile, there was no man left alive, only five pregnant women in a cave in the wilderness, and these women all bore sons at the same moment. The boys were reared until they grew into big lads; their thoughts turned to women and they desired to take wives, so each one in turn slept with his companions' mothers.
>
> They lived in the land and ruled it and divided it among the five of them, and because of that division the five parts of Ireland are still called fifths.
>
> They scoured the land wherever there had been battles; they found gold and silver and became wealthy.[1]

Here the role of the founding mothers is clearly shown. But the future rule of men and the importance of wealth through booty is just as clear.

In the meantime the seven surviving Brythons, Pryderi among them, arrive home to a totally changed situation. Beli's son Caswallawn sits on Bran's throne and rules as High King of London. The old matriarchal succession, which would have given Branwen's son Gwern the crown of Britain, has ended.

A last sacred duty remains: according to Bran's wish they bury his head at the White Mound of London, "where it will protect Britain against all enemies." According to the Welsh Triads this was one of "three fortunate interments."

Now Manawydan, the last of the Children of Llyr, feels the full weight of his loss. According to the matriarchal succession, he would have been the rightful heir, but he has no strength left to fight for his right, and here the author cites a poignant dialogue:

> Manawydan looked at the town ... and felt an immense sadness and longing. "Alas, almighty God, woe is me!" he said. "Among all those here I alone have no place for the night."
>
> "Lord, be not so heavy-hearted," said Pryderi. "Your cousin is king over the Island of the Mighty, and if he has wronged you, still you have never claimed land or property — you are one of the Three Ungrasping Chieftains."
>
> "Even though the king is my cousin," answered Manawydan, "it saddens me to see anyone in my brother Bran's place, and I could not be happy in the same house as Caswallawn."
>
> "Then will you listen to some more advice?"
>
> "I need advice. What is yours?"
>
> "The seven cantrevs of Dyfed were left to me," said Pryderi, "and my mother Rhiannon is there. I will give her to you, along with authority over the seven cantrevs, ... Though the title of the land is mine, let it be you and Rhiannon who enjoy it."[2]

It is clear that the victory in Ireland had been a Pyrrhic victory for the Children of Llyr. Branwen's son Gwern, last hope of the matriarchal succession, had been murdered, her brother Bran killed in battle. His son Caradoc, Bran's hope for his own succession, had "died of shame" when he could not hinder Caswallawn's murder of the chieftains. Manawydan, the last of his family, is too weak (or too wise?) to fight for his heritage.

Pryderi, the son of Rhiannon, the "second British Matriarch," is already inured to patriarchal thinking. His mother, once a goddess, or at least an otherworldly woman with magic powers, has now become a powerless dowager widow. We have seen that according to the Welsh Law of Women, widows had to leave their husband's property within nine days of his death (see Chapter 2). Perhaps Pryderi, the "Son of Sorrow," does his mother a favour for bestowing her on his comrade in arms, as this at least allows her to stay in her own land. Fired by his plan, he even praises her fading charms, should his friend hesitate. He makes Manawydan a generous offer in the person of his mother and his land: note that the woman and the land are still legally inseparable. But Rhiannon, who once braved the wrath of otherworldly powers in order to marry the man of her choice, is never asked for her opinion.

From the masculine point of view Pryderi's offer is proof of his friendship. It shows the comradeship binding the two warriors, but completely ignores a woman's feeling. What counts here is sheer pragmatism. The thought that it may degrade the woman, even a former goddess, would never enter these men's heads. Pryderi, tribal king and hero of Dyfed, is showing his greatness not by heroic deeds in combat, but by his generosity and friendship. He gives his friend his most sacred possession — his land. In this deal his mother has become merely an adjunct. Besides Pryderi's solution is a clever move: for the moment it guarantees peace in Britain and thus secures the survival of the present generation. In the further unfolding of the story the alliance with Manawydan will prove the salvation of Dyfed.

From a woman's point of view, this deed of friendship has all the weaknesses of the "new Order." On the one hand, woman is still bound to the tillable land. On the other, it is this very union with landed property which makes woman a bait for men in search of land, and land was the only means of subsistence. Woman has become property and like property she can now be disposed of according to the intentions of her "guardian" — whether father, brother or son. Just like the Greek Penelope, the Celtic Rhiannon has been degraded to the status of the rich and therefore desirable widow. She has no choice but to acquiesce.

Manawydan, who in London was lamenting his sad fate, is a different man in Dyfed. The ladies, Rhiannon and Pryderi's wife, have prepared a rich banquet for the men's homecoming; and as they are feasting, Manawydan, in high spirits, says to his friend: "I accept your offer!" When Rhiannon asks: "What offer was that?" Pryderi answers: "Lady, I have given you as a wife to Manawydan Son of Llyr."[3] Fortunately Rhiannon rather likes this "ungrasping chieftain":

"I accept that gladly," she says with wise restraint. Yet we are left to ponder Manawydan's reply: "God reward the man who gives me such true friendship." Not a word of homage, devotion, or just plain gratitude to Rhiannon. It is the most "unromantic" transaction and shows that chivalry and "romantic love" is still far in the future. But at least Manawydan was honest. And it will be shown that by accepting Pryderi's offer, he also accepts the duties and commitments.

Yet well may we ask: where is that Rhiannon who met Pwyll on the Arberth and proudly declared: "I ride in mine own errand!" Where the woman who had her unwelcome suitor, the demigod Gwawl, caught in an uterine bag and forced him to release her lover from his oath? The answer is clear: in the *Third Branch* Rhiannon has changed because she understands that this marriage is for the best of the land. This is clearly shown in the next episode:

> Before the feast ended, then, the couple slept together.
> "Continue with what remains of the feast," said Pryderi, "while I go to England to offer my submission to Caswallawn son of Beli."
> "Lord, Caswallawn is now in Kent," said Rhiannon. "You can continue with the feast and wait until he is nearer."
> "Then we will wait," said Pryderi.[4]

This is the last time that Rhiannon has occasion to show her political wisdom.

Pryderi knows that he must do homage to the new king in order to preserve the peace. To this end he is prepared to leave the feast before it has ended. After all that has happened, Rhiannon understands how hard this act of submission must be for him. Yet she is convinced of its necessity, as Dyfed, while sheltering Caswallawn's enemy, is in no position to oppose the High King. Well informed about the king's movements, she knows his whereabouts and how long it will take Pryderi to reach him. Her unspoken advice is not to show undue speed in the dealings with Caswallawn, as not to hurt her son's pride and give the usurper reason to humiliate him. She is aware of the importance of good timing in political matters. Her son obeys her without argument, and goes for a royal circuit instead. And just as his father Pwyll had found his realm well cared for by Arawn, so Pryderi can be pleased:

> (He) had never seen a more delightful land nor a
> better hunting ground, nor one better stocked with
> honey and fish.[5]

Later Pryderi's act of homage is successfully accomplished: "...Pryderi went to see Caswallawn at Oxford, where he was received joyfully and thanked for his act of submission." Peace for the land is secured and Rhiannon's advice sets the scene for the further cooperation of mother and son. In spite of the legal transaction that was her marriage to Manawydan, Rhiannon remains the power behind the king. Pryderi's spouse is not mentioned in the first part of the story. She plays a rather subordinate role, her most important attribute being her impeccable pedigree: she is "Cigfa (Kigva),[6] daughter of Gwynn the Splendid, daughter of Gloyw Wide Hair son of the ruler Casnar, one of the nobles of the land."[7]

The difference between the two women is clearly shown by implication: Rhiannon is the woman of clear mind, born to rule. Cigfa is the woman chosen for her pedigree, the "breeder." She is good-natured, if occasionally given to overbearing family pride.

The foursome now enjoy a period of idyllic country life and their friendship and loyalty deepens. "Such friendship arose between the four that none of them wished to be without the other day or night."[8] But it was not to last:

> They began to feast at Arberth, since that was the chief court where their celebration began, and after the evening's first sitting, while the servants were eating, the four companions rose and went out to Gorsedd Arberth taking a company with them. As they were sitting on the mound they heard thunder, and with the loudness of thunder a mist fell, so that no one could see his companions. When the mist lifted it was bright everywhere, and when they looked out at where they had once seen their flocks and herds and dwellings, they now saw nothing, no animal, no smoke, no fire, no man, no dwelling — only the houses of the court empty, deserted, uninhabited, without man or beast in them; their own company was lost too, and they understood only that the four of them alone remained.[9]

In their happiness, the four, even Rhiannon, seem to have forgotten the threat of the otherworldly powers, even the mystery of the *nemeton,* Gorsedd Arberth, where according to the old saying a man may experience "wounds or wonders." Perhaps their walk took place on May-day eve, when the doors to Otherworld stand wide open and anything may happen.

They had to pay dearly for their carelessness: like the poorest of their subjects they had to live off the land; hunting, fishing and gathering became their only means of survival. But no matter how well Dyfed was stocked with "game, fish and honey," without shepherds, farmers and servants it was a hard life.

"They passed one happy year thus, and then another. At length they grew weary." Manawydan takes the initiative: "God knows, we cannot go on like this. Let us go to England and there seek a trade in which we can support ourselves."[10]

This is a complete break with mythology and the heroic age,

where trades were unknown, except for the magical knowledge of metalwork. We have reached the Christian Middle Ages.

Manawydan's idea pays off. The two aristocrats go into saddlery and their products are excellent. The other saddlers resent their competition and plot against them. Rash like his father, Pryderi would kill them all, but Manawydan advises against this. They leave for another town and make shields, and again they are chased by the shieldmakers. They try their luck making shoes, and the same thing happens. Again they return to Dyfed living off the hunt, when misfortune strikes again. In spite of Manawydan's warnings, Pryderi follows his dogs which have flushed out a "shining white boar" into a great fortress they had never seen before. Inside the castle he finds a fountain, and beside it a golden bowl suspended from above "on four chains extending into the air and he could see no end to them."[11] While Manawydan has seen all the warning signs, Pryderi is obviously blind to them. "Ecstatic over the beauty of the gold and the fine craftsmanship," he grasps the bowl — and becomes stuck to it.

Prudently, Manawydan did not enter the castle. He waited for the return of his companion, and at nightfall he returned home without him. On hearing his story, Rhiannon is outraged: "You have been a bad companion, and lost a good one!" she says and in spite of his protestations leaves to seek her son. She finds him in the castle, mute and stuck to the golden bowl, and as she tries to pull him away, grasps the bowl and is stuck too.

> And with that, as soon as it was night, lo! a peal of thunder over them and a fall of mist, and thereupon the caer vanished and away with them too.[12]

Here Rhiannon is completely euhemerized. The mother instinct has taken over and she is inaccessible to reason. Yet one sign of her divinity remains: with her disappearance, Dyfed becomes a Waste Land, an uninhabitable desert. This is the irrefutable proof that the "Waste Land" phenomenon is not a direct consequence of the king's wound, as most authors assume, but follows the absence of the Goddess from the Land.

Manawydan and Cigfa remain alone in the wilderness. The

young woman fears that her father-in-law will now pursue her with unwanted attentions — the constant fear of woman. Manawydan reassures her: never would he betray her and his friend's trust. Like Pwyll at Modron's court, he knows what becomes a gentleman. The episode reflects the morals of the time.

The two of them, now completely destitute, journey to England once again and work as shoemakers with the same result as before. They decide to return to Wales, but this time Manawydan buys three sacks of seed grain, to try his luck as a crofter. The "ungrasping, landless chieftain" has sunk to the lowest social class, which is however the only one to guarantee his survival.

We have reached the turning point of the story, and with it a change in style. The "heroic tale" becomes a humorous farce, similar to the medieval tales where a simple crofter tricks the clever devil.

Manawydan's has sown three fields of wheat. They grow well and he can look forward to a good harvest when a mouse plague threatens to ruin it. But Manawydan does not give up. Just as Lord Teyrnon once watched over his foaling mare, so he now decides to watch over his wheat — a service to the Goddess in her manifestation as the Corn Mother. He succeeds in catching one of the mice, and just as Pwyll caught Gwawl into his magic bag, so Manawydan now ties the mouse into his glove, a bargaining chip for future negotiations.

On the following morning he takes the mouse to the Arberth, the Mount of Destiny. He is now fully aware of the importance of the place and proceeds to hang the mouse on this spot, a sign that the place of pagan sacrifice has become a place of human justice, the gallows. Cigfa thinks he is mad. As a former princess she reminds him that the job of a hangman is beneath his dignity. He remains unmoved and prepares to build a small gallows. Then things begin to happen.

At short intervals a travelling clerk, a priest and a bishop with full retinue appear and attempt to stop him from killing the mouse, offering higher and higher sums for its release. Manawydan, who has not seen a living soul in Dyfed for years, knows who these men are. Putting the noose around the mouse he springs the trap: the life of the mouse for the return of Rhiannon, Pryderi and the end of the desolation of Dyfed. And he wins his game: Rhiannon and Pryderi reappear, and the land returns to its former life.

Manawydan hands the bishop the mouse — and it immediately changes into a beautiful young woman, the "bishop's wife." "And she was pregnant, or you would not have caught her." The bishop is none other than the magician Llwyd son of Cil Coed, Gwawl's friend, still intent on avenging his friend's humiliation at Rhiannon's behest. Manawydan, the wise old sea god, has overcome him, and the Desolation of Dyfed has ended.

The captive Goddess and her Son

At first glance the story of *Manawydan the Son of Llyr* appears to be the weakest of the Four Branches. But on closer investigation we can see that the narrator has succeeded in bringing a kind of order into the old mythological motifs and reassembled them in a complex structure for the needs of the time. Here starts the feudal changeover of matriarchal values.

First inversion: Rhiannon has lost her divine aspect and simply appears as a noblewoman in difficult circumstances. In contrast to Manawydan she seems to have forgotten her higher knowledge: she no longer heeds the warning signs of evil magic and runs heedless into the trap her enemies have set for her. Yet on the other hand, by her very entrapment she fulfils her ancient mythological role as the captive goddess in the Otherworld.

Second inversion: Celtic scholars have written much about the "Desolation of Dyfed" as the classic Waste Land motif, and connected it with the story of Demeter and Persephone. In both cases the goddess goes on a desperate search for her child and in both cases the grief of the mother goddess causes a standstill in nature. But what in Greek myth is represented as an act of the goddess herself intended to force the return of her daughter, is here described as an act of revenge directed against her and beyond her influence. She is herself captured together with her son and imprisoned in a realm we can only describe as another dimension.

As it is often stated, the capture of the goddess and the rape of Persephone are characteristics of the change from matriarchal to patriarchal mythology. In Celtic mythology the goddess is abducted by a rival from her divine spouse[13] (here Manawydan) together with her son. In another version of the myth the Son is abducted at birth. Of course this capture and imprisonment, like so many abductions and ritual murders of heroes and divine sons/lovers throughout mythology, typically occurs during the hunting season which announces the arrival of winter and the death of vegetation. Pryderi who stands for Mabon/Maponos, a god of Spring and of the growth of vegetation, is captured in pursuit of a magic boar. Therefore his captivity during the winter months accords with the cycle of nature in temperate latitudes.

Scholars agree that in spite of the altered names and circumstances the *Third Branch* is the story of the captivity of the goddess and her Son in coeval setting. As we shall see, the myth of Mabon's captivity is also told in the story of *Culhwch and Olwen* (see Chapter 8) and in Taliesin's famous poem *Preiddeu Annwn* (The Spoils of Annwn):

> The prison of Gwair was prepared in Caer Sidi
> After the manner of the telling of Pwyll and Pryderi.
> None before him was sent into it,
> Into the heavy grey chain which bound the loyal youth.[14]

In both versions Pryderi/Mabon is described as imprisoned in a dungeon "under the earth" (to which the vegetation growth has gone). Only higher powers will be able to liberate him. In *Culhwch and Olwen* this deed falls to the best of Arthur's men and, significantly, is initiated by the "oldest animal," the wise Salmon of Llyn Llyw.[15]

Manawydan

Manawydan himself, Rhiannon's second husband, is originally the Irish sea god Mannanan, Lord of the Isle of Man, euhemerized into a much feared magician and seducer of women. Yet in the *Third Branch* nothing is left of this role but deep magic knowledge and wisdom, combined with relentless tenacity.

His divine pedigree has also been changed: he is now the son of Llyr (also a Sea God) and Pen Arddun, daughter of Beli and Dana. His victory over the wizard Llwyd son of Cil Coed ("the Dark One from Behind the Woods") proves his superior magical knowledge. But in contrast to most Celtic gods, whose forte is martial prowess, Manawydan excels in patient and painstaking scheming. P. Mac Cana argues convincingly that the character of Manawydan was modelled after St Eustache (Eustachius), a popular French saint in the Middle Ages.

St Eustache was a first century Christian martyr whose life story must have given much comfort to impoverished noblemen. According to legend, Eustache (significantly called Placidus before his baptism) was a Roman general who had lost not only his troops, but also his family and his possessions. Refusing to fall on his sword, he survived for many years as a farm labourer, until he was discovered by his soldiers, reinstated into his former dignity and reunited with his family. According to legend Christ appeared to him in the guise of a magnificent stag (a typical Celto-Roman myth) and persuaded him to become his follower. St Eustache is by no means the only saint thus favoured by Christ.

We may speculate that he was perhaps a Gaulish chieftain destined for the royal sacrifice usually enacted during a stag hunt. By becoming a Christian he may have avoided death as a human sacrifice, but did not avoid martyrdom. He was martyred under Hadrian in AD 118.

The author of the *Four Branches* must have known this legend. What may particularly have attracted him in this life story of a Celtic chieftain was his patient submission to the blows of destiny and his determination to survive under harsh and humiliating circumstances. Such an attitude is totally opposed to the ideal of the Celtic warrior who preferred death with honour to life in serfdom. As survivor of Bran's Irish campaign Manawydan had given ample proof of his proficiency as a warrior. In the *Third Branch* he is tested in a different way. His is the royal test of "the kiss granted to the hag," that is to say of accepting the Goddess in her repulsive aspect and to choose life before death under any circumstances. His service consists in suffering, enduring repeated trials and failures, yet never wavering from his final goal.

Did the author wish to present his audience with a new ideal of man? Neither the brave warrior nor the solitary monk seemed able to solve the problems of the time. What the land needed were men like Manawydan who could bide their time suffering all kinds of hardships, yet using their knowledge for new solutions, men who preferred survival to vainglory.

Manawydan is put at the helm of an impoverished family. Knowing that fighting would cause further trouble, he halts Pryderi's aggression. He warns him not to pursue the magic boar and silently suffers Rhiannon's scolding. He reassures Cigfa and secures her survival in extreme poverty. Her reproaches and fears for his sanity cannot move him. He alone seems to know the reason for the family's misfortunes and he alone works out a plan to overcome them. In the end he wins.

A poem in the *Black Book of Carmarthen* addresses Manawydan as "the god of deep and wise counsel" (*oet duis y cusil).*[16] The author may have known the poem and it may have caused him to present his hero as a model of wisdom, tolerance and moderation. These are the very virtues the warrior caste was lacking and which had caused the tragedy of Bran and Branwen. In the figure of Manawydan the author seems to have consciously created an anti-hero: a sorely tested man who, notwithstanding the blows that rain upon him and his family, wins through with patience, pragmatism and compromise. He is the first redeemer from the curse of the Waste Land, the "Desolation of Dyfed." Celtic scholars may miss in him the passion, the rashness, the deep feeling as well as the laconic wit of the traditional Celtic hero. Yet even in this Christianized and thoroughly medieval Celt the old structure of the King and

Lady Sovereignty holds good: Manawydan is no monarchic ruler, but still the champion and defender of the Goddess, the hero whose lot it is to free her from persecution and captivity.

The figure of Manawydan, steeped in virtues so uncharacteristic of the time, also suggests the hypothesis that his author may have been a woman, perhaps an aristocratic lady who had lost patience with the martial prowess of her contemporaries. Beside moderation, patience and tolerance, the author praises the virtues of friendship and loyalty as preconditions for the smooth running of family and community. Women are at the centre of this little community and their safety and survival is always paramount — even in the case of the pregnant mouse.

Finally we must not forget that the story was written at a time when Wales, a small and poor country, was constantly threatened by English and Norman invasions and rent by tribal warfare. In this situation princes of vision and diplomacy might have achieved more than the most accomplished war leaders. This is the lesson of Manawydan.

Nomen est omen. Scholars have asked why the old name of Mannan was replaced by Manawydan, and here again there were suggestions that the change was due to a scribe's error. But it makes sense when we realize that on occasion the hero has to earn his bread as a saddler and shoemaker. These are trades which use the awl as their most important tool. The name "Manawydan" sounds very much like the Welsh word for "awl," *mynawyd.* It seems that the main weapon of Manawydan is no longer the sword, which is never mentioned here, but rather a humble tool indispensable for penetrating thick skins: in Celtic parlance "to solve hard problems." No doubt, Manawydan "the Awl" is the hero of the new time.

CHAPTER 7

The Fourth Branch: The Children of Dana

The first three Branches of the *Mabinogi* are set in South Wales and comprise the conception, birth, hero's journey and imprisonment of Pryderi, the tribal hero of Dyfed. The fourth and last Branch is set in the north of the country and relates the events leading up to his heroic death in mortal combat with Gwydion, the son of the goddess Dana, and the birth of Llew, the Sun Hero of the North. Here we meet with another family of gods which may be much older than that of Rhiannon/Epona.

Dana was one of the names of the pan-European Earth goddess, the "mother of the gods."[1] According to the *Lebor Gabala Erenn,* the Irish Book of Conquests, one of the tribes that settled in Ireland, (perhaps the first Celtic settlers) called themselves the *Tuatha de Danaan,* the Tribe that serves the Goddess Dana.

The north of Wales is called Gwynedd (Venedotia) and was inhabited by a tribe called after the White Goddess,[2] probably the same deity. Irish settlers had taken up land on the north west coast of Wales and may have brought the myth of Dana's Children with them. The region had been fought over by Brythons and Gaels for centuries and the hate against the Irish, so prominent in the *Second Branch,* emerges again in the Fourth, but the possible Irish origin of the cult of Dana is not mentioned.

If we can believe Robert Graves, Dana's son Gwydion, the main protagonist of *The Fourth Branch,* is an Anglo-Saxon interloper in this ancient family of Celtic gods: Gwydion is the Celtic name of Woden/Odin.[3] And indeed, Gwydion has many features of this complex Germanic god, whom the Romans identified with Mercury.

His nephew/son Llew (or Lleu) is the last pale epiphany of the mighty Celtic Gaulish/Gaelic Sun Hero Lugh of the Long Arm, who had his Gaulish sanctuary at the Puy de Dome in Auvergne and gave his name to many great cities, including London and Lyon. In the Celtic pantheon it was Lugh, and not Gwydion, whom the Romans identified with Mercury. The Irish called Lugh *Samildanach,* the All Skilful and celebrated him as the redeemer from the oppressor Balor of the Baleful Eye and his Fomorians.[4] The death of Lugh and that of the Welsh Llew are remarkably similar: both are betrayed by their wives and killed by their rival. In other words, their death is caused by the eternal triangle: the goddess between the gods.

The *Fourth Branch* is entitled *Math Son of Mathonwy,* and Math is introduced here as the brother of the goddess Dana, whilst the goddess herself is described as the spouse of the Sun God Beli. The fact that her children are named after her and not after Beli, bespeaks her great antiquity, but she has no active role in the story. The names Math and Mathonwy have their origin in Mathgen (son of a Bear), an old Irish god of whom only the name is known. Math has been euhemerized into an ancient king of Gwynedd and a mighty magician.[5] He functions as guardian to Dana's sons Gwydion, Gofannon (a god of smithcraft), and Gilfaethwy as well as to her daughter Arianrhod (Aranrhod), a name which means "Silver Wheel" and connects her to the moon. Like her brother Gwydion, Arianrhod is a complex figure and the ambivalent relationship of brother and sister is at the centre of the plot.

Here is a summary of the story:

At the time when Pryderi ruled in South Wales, Math ap Mathonwy was King of Gwynedd. He was of hoary age, very wise and a great magician. He had the peculiarity that his feet had always to rest in the lap of a virgin and only in times of war was he free of this obligation. The king's footholder was called Goewin and she was so beautiful that Gilfaethwy fell deeply in love with her. She however did not return his feelings and only cared for her duty towards the king. As Gilfaethwy was pining with unrequited love, his brother Gwydion thought how he could help him. It occurred to him that if his uncle had to go to war, his brother would have a chance to win her. It was not difficult to find a *casus belli.*

Arawn had given Pryderi a herd of breeding pigs, which were a great novelty in Britain, and he had ordered him not to sell them until their number had doubled. Gwydion planned to steal the pigs and so to start a war between Dyfed and Gwynedd. Disguised as bards, he and his brother visited Pryderi, and Gwydion's stories pleased the king so well that he offered him any gift that was in his power to give. Gwydion asked for the pigs, and when Pryderi hesitated, he made him a counter offer of twelve horses with golden saddles, twelve hounds with golden leashes and twelve golden shields. All this he had created by magic from toadstools and dry leaves. Pryderi was duped and gave him the pigs, which Gwydion's companions drove northward in great haste. On the next morning horses, hounds and shields had changed again into toadstools and leaves and Pryderi saw that he had been tricked. Enraged, he mustered his army and marched on Gwynedd. Mathonwy had to call together his forces, leave his court Caer Dathyl, and offer battle. During his absence the two brothers returned to his court under a pretext, and Gilfaethwy raped Goewin on Mathonwy's couch. Then they followed their uncle's war band.

The two armies clashed. There was a bloody battle and Mathonwy was victorious. Pryderi sued for peace and sent hostages to Gwynedd, but he could not hinder his men to continue the fight. To avoid further bloodshed he offered to fight Gwydion in single combat. In this fight he was overcome and killed, "not by strength and valour, but by Gwydion's magic."

The war was ended, Math returned to his court Caer Dathyl, whilst his two nephews went on a circuit of the realm. When Goewin told Math about the crime committed against her, he was outraged and deeply hurt, but could not take revenge against his own nephews.

To compensate Goewin he made her his queen and "gave her authority over all of Gwynedd." Then he ordered that nobody should give his nephews food, drink or shelter, so they had to give themselves up to him. His punishment fitted their crime: as they had behaved like animals, he changed them into wild beasts. They had to live one year as a stag and hind, one year as a boar and sow and another year as wolf and wolf bitch. In these animal forms they produced a young each year, which Math changed into boys, and these children grew up to be heroes. After the third year Math pardoned his nephews and accepted them back at court.

But again Gwydion thought of mischief. When Math was looking for a new footholder, Gwydion suggested his sister Arianrhod. He brought her to Caer Dathyl and Math asked her if she was a virgin. "I know not but that I am," she answered. Math bent his magic wand into a circle and asked her to step over it. As she did so, she dropped a healthy baby boy, and "another small thing, which Gwydion wrapped into a silken cloth and hid in a box beside his bed."

Arianrhod fled in shame, but Math had the boy baptized and named him Dylan. As soon as Dylan was dipped into the water he swam away like a fish.[6]

One morning Gwydion was wakened from the crying of a child in the box near his bed. He took the babe to a wet nurse and, like Pryderi, he grew twice as fast as other children. At the age of four he was old enough to go to court and Gwydion became his foster father. At the appropriate time he took the boy to Arianrhod's castle and introduced him to his mother. But Arianrhod did not want to be reminded of her shame and rejected her son. When she heard that the boy had no name yet, she swore that he should never have one. Again Gwydion thought of a ruse: he took the boy to her castle, disguised as a shoemaker. Arianrhod wanted to buy his shoes and came to have her measure taken. While he did that, the boy shot a wren through the sinew of its foot and Arianrhod remarked: "A sure hand has the little fair one!" At that Gwydion answered: *"Llew Llaw Gyffes!* The Fair One with the Sure Hand! You have given your son a good name!" And he dropped his disguise. Again Arianrhod was furious and swore that the boy should never receive any weapons from her, as was a mother's right. And again Gwydion tricked her: disguised as a bard he took the boy as his apprentice to Arianrhod's castle, which was on an island in the sea. Then he conjured up an illusory fleet intent to attack her castle. Startled and fearful Arianrhod asked for his help. He armed himself and asked that she arm the boy too. As soon as this was done, the fleet disappeared, and laughingly Gwydion told Arianrhod that she had just armed her son. This time Arianrhod's fury knew no bounds and she swore "that Llew shall never have a wife of the race of man." Gwydion answered that "she was a wicked woman, but a wife he shall have."

To this end he asked Math for his help. Together the two magicians created a beautiful woman from oak flowers, furze, meadowsweet and six other blossoms and called her Blodeuedd, the "Flower-daughter." They gave her to Llew as his wife, together with land and property in the region of Eyfynyd and Arduddwy. Llew built himself a castle and called it Mur Castell. There he lived happily with Blodeuedd and all the people praised his rule.

One day Llew went to visit Math at Caer Dathyl and Blodeuedd remained alone at home. In the evening a young lord, returning from a stag hunt, passed by. His name was Gronw (Goronwy) Pebir, Lord of Pen Llyn.[7] As it was getting late, Blodeuedd invited him in and the two fell in love. They plotted against Llew and on his return Blodeuedd persuaded her husband to tell her the secret of his death. His death was virtually impossible to achieve: he was to be pierced by a magic spear while he was just emerging from a bath in the open, with one foot in the bath tub and the other on the back of a goat. Blodeuedd asked him to "show her" how all this was achieved and as he did so, Gronw her lover, lying in wait, hurled the magic spear at him. With a great cry Llew changed into an eagle, his totem bird, and was not seen again. Then Gronw moved to Mur Castell and he and Blodeuedd lived happily together.

News of this reached Math and Gwydion at Caer Dathyl and they were greatly aggrieved. Gwydion asked Math's permission to go in search of his nephew. He searched for him all over Britain. After a long time he came to a farm called Menawr

Bennard. There the swineherd told him about a magic sow which ran away every morning and he could never find her. Gwydion followed the sow and came to a glen which is called Nantlleu. There stood a great oak and Gwydion saw the sow rooting in the ground and eating worms and rotten flesh that dropped from above. He looked up into the oak and on its top he saw an eagle. Then he knew that he had found Llew. He sang three magic verses, and gradually the eagle flew down and sat on his knees. Gwydion touched him with his magic wand and changed him back to his human likeness. Llew was more dead than alive and only skin and bones. Gwydion took him back to Caer Dathyl and called the best physicians in the country to cure him. When he was healed Gwydion and Llew went together to punish Blodeuedd and Gronw Pebyr. Llew killed his rival with the same magic spear that Gronw had used on him, and thus achieved his revenge.

But when Gwydion found Blodeuedd, he realized that he could not kill her, because she was not a real woman but an artificial creature. He changed her into an owl, a bird who shuns the sun and is forever attacked by the other birds. Then Llew took possession of his land again and ruled it with good fortune, until finally he became lord of the whole of Gwynedd.

Here ends the *Fourth Branch.*

The fourth is perhaps the most complex of the *Four Branches.* Two things are clear however: Pryderi is dead and the power of the goddess has been taken over by Math and Gwydion his nephew.

W.J. Gruffydd has written an in-depth analysis of the *Fourth Branch,* in which he traces most of its motifs to their Irish origins and explains at least some of its riddles.[8] He comes to the conclusion that the *Fourth Branch* is the Brythonic form of the Irish myth of Lugh, here called Llew or Lleu. Like Mabon and Pryderi, Llew is a son of the goddess, but in his case his mother Arianrhod, to judge by her name, is a goddess of the moon. This puts Llew in contrast to Pryderi, the son of Rhiannon, who has a solar aspect.

Math is the Welsh counterpart of the Irish giant Balor of the

Baleful Eye. He is one of the many rulers to whom it was foretold that their daughter's son will kill them. Therefore the daughter is locked up in a tower and forbidden any contact with men.[9] Inevitably, a suitor gains access to her and she conceives a son who fulfils the prophecy. In this story the usual prophecy is missing, but typically, according to Welsh folklore, Arianrhod lives in a tower on a lonely island in the Irish Sea.

The motif is typical for the changeover from matriarchal to patriarchal succession. During matriarchy, paternity was unimportant and often hard to establish. Therefore the mother's brother, the *avunculus,* became the most important man and focal point in the family. Here too the succession goes to the mother's brother: here from Dana to Math, from Math to his nephew Gwydion and from Gwydion to his nephew and son Llew. But now the important point is that, as his nephew is also his son, Gwydion succeeds in achieving full patriarchal succession for his son. Llew's succession follows both matriarchal and patriarchal rules — but at a price.

There is an inconsistency in the fact that it is Goewin who is raped, but Arianrhod who bears twins, namely the usual divine twins, which we find so frequently in mythology. By comparing the *Fourth Branch* with a number of similar Welsh folktales Gruffydd is able to prove that the episode of Goewin is a late interpolation. Originally Math seems to have chosen his niece Arianrhod to be his footholder, to be able to keep her under constant surveillance. As Gwydion wanted to succeed Math together with his brother, he provoked the war to separate Arianrhod from the king and then raped her. For various reasons the author has made significant changes, but on reading between the lines we understand that Llew is the child of Gwydion and his sister Arianrhod, although this is never clearly spelt out. Is this incest the reason why Arianrhod rejects her son and makes his life impossible by putting him under heavy taboos? Hardly.

True, W.J. Gruffydd writes that Celtic women (of presumably the pre-Christian period) exposed children born from incest or handed them to foster parents. But in mythology brother/sister unions are frequent and the incest taboo does not apply.

And why would Arianrhod lie and declare to be a virgin, when she knew that nothing could be hidden from all-knowing Math? Jean Markale speculates that she must have misinterpreted the word *morvyn,* meaning "maiden" or "virgin." Like the Latin word *virgo* the word is ambivalent in Welsh, or at least its meaning has changed over time. Originally it meant a woman who lives alone and independent of men, regardless of any sexual relations she may have. According to Markale, Arianrhod understood the word in this sense and therefore answered the question in the affirmative, whereas Math understood the word in its more recent, physiological sense.[10] Markale may be right, but his theory leaves other questions unanswered.

To clarify the situation let us take a glance at the structure of the story. It is composed of three distinct parts, which Gruffydd designates as MSM *(Math Son of Mathonwy)* I, II and III:

— Gwynedd's victory over Dyfed and death of Pryderi. In veiled form this part also contains the obscure conception and birth of the new tribal hero Llew. (MSM I)
— Llew's initiation into manhood, in spite of the objections of his mother and his marriage to Blodeuedd. (MSM II)
— Blodeuedd's betrayal of Llew, his murder and resurrection. Gwydion's punishment of Blodeuedd and Llew's revenge on his rival Gronw Pebir. (MSM III)

Llew is the son of Arianrhod and Gwydion, both the children of the Mother Goddess Dana. In Celtic mythology Dana becomes the spouse of Beli, a Sun God on the European continent and in Britain. In Ireland Dana was married to the Dag Da, whereas Beli in Ireland is called Bile and is a god of Death. If we compare the First Branch with the Fourth, the following emerges:

— Between the two families of gods in north and south a power struggle has erupted, in which the family of Dana is victorious.
— This victory is also a victory of the "motherless" Son of the Father, Llew (or Lleu) over Pryderi/Mabon, the Son of the Mother.

— Llew owes his victory to his two maternal uncles Math and Gwydion, a feature characteristic of the change from matriarchal to patriarchal succession.

Irish origins and matriarchal motifs

According to W.J. Gruffydd, MSM I and MSM II are repetitions of the Irish myth of Balor and his grandson Lugh, the Irish sun hero, whereas MSM III is the age-old myth of the Sun Hero's faithless wife — a motif also contained in the Lugh-Balor myth.

In Irish tradition, Lugh is the grandson of the giant Balor of the Evil Eye, king of the Fomorians. He hides his daughter Ethniu from the eyes of men, but the hero Cian, son of Dian Cecht, gains access to her and she bears him Lugh. In the battle against the Fomorians, Lugh kills Balor, not with his spear, but by hurling a sling stone into the giant's eye. This is a motif of great antiquity, which we also find in the fight between David and Goliath.

The original identity of Lugh and Llew is also proven by the form of death of the two heroes: the Irish Lugh's wife betrays him and he kills her lover Cet. In revenge, Cet's three sons, Mac Cuill, Mac Cecht and Mac Greine kill Lugh with his own spear. In the Welsh counterpart, Llew, he too is betrayed by his wife and killed with a magic spear, but brought back to life by Gwydion. He then kills his rival and murderer, Gronw, with the same magic spear that Gronw used to kill him.

What is missing in the Welsh saga is the motif of liberation. In Ireland Lugh is celebrated as the redeemer from Balor's oppression. By killing his grandfather Lugh liberates his people from a long and bitter servitude to the Fomorians, a primeval race representing the forces of Chaos. By contrast, the Welsh Llew never liberates anyone, but is himself in great need of salvation: first from the curses of his mother, then from death through the betrayal of his wife. This is a startling difference in treatment and signals the weakening of the Sun Hero in Britain.

If, admittedly, Llew is a weak hero, by contrast the women in the story are very strong. Yet they are both negative figures. Arianrhod, the woman who rejects her child, is described as an unnatural mother. Blodeuedd, if anything, is even more unnatural: created artificially from flowers to please the erotic dreams of a young man, she falls for the first man who appears during her husband's absence. Soulless and hence devoid of deeper feelings she pursues her murderous scheme with relentless cunning, whereas Llew for his part is so guileless that he fulfils her demands with unforgivable carelessness.

It seems that in the *Fourth Branch* the relationship of the sexes has become fundamentally flawed. The relationship of Blodeuedd and Llew seems lifeless from the start, that of Blodeuedd and Gronw is built on murder and the relationship of Arianrhod and Gwydion is everlasting warfare. The ancient icon of divine Mother and divine Son has been shattered. But among the debris Gruffydd finds two remnants of old traditions: the relics of matriarchal succession and divine incest. He writes:

> Indeed one of the distinguishing marks of the *Four Branches* is the great prominence given to the social position of the nephew/niece. It is due, of course, to the existence of some form of inheritance other than the usual one of a son succeeding the father; there is little doubt that the state of society denoted by this form of inheritance was matriarchal, where the position of son and daughter was occupied by nephew and niece.[11]

This is the only time Gruffydd mentions matriarchal social order and, of course, we find no mention of it in the medieval Welsh law tracts. The form of succession mentioned here contradicts medieval usage, which was inspired by Latin law and the canons of the Church. It follows that the stories of the *Mabinogion,* or at least the motifs making up their structure, are much older and here at least the usage of the matriarchal period has been preserved.

In the emerging patriarchy (which was long established at the redaction of these stories) the succession from mother's brother (Math, Gwydion) to sister's son (Llew) cedes to patriarchal succession from father (Gwydion) to son (Llew). Therefore the ambiguous paternity of Llew is of great interest here. We must remember however that the *Fourth Branch* reflects only the archetypal pattern and not the medieval reality.

A further pointer to ancient matriarchal conditions is the initiation of the son by his mother. Here we can conclude that it had once been the privilege and indeed the duty of the mother to name her son, to arm him and to find a wife for him. Even Math and Gwydion, euhemerized gods and great magicians that they are, cannot circumvent her ancient rights and have to resort to magic. These maternal privileges in Celtic tradition lasted for a long time and are proof of the ancient belief that it is the mother who gives a young man his strength and valour.

As to the alluded incest motif, the following points must be made. Arianrhod's "shame" which causes the conflict of mother and son is not caused by Llew's illegitimate conception and birth, as some authors believe. The rights of illegitimate children were fully recognized in Celtic society. They even had inheritance rights if the father wished it. True, children conceived by incest were often rejected or even exposed by their mothers, but Gwydion and Arianrhod, as children of the goddess Dana, were not subject to the incest taboo.

Modern authors have different opinions about Llew's conception. Some write that Arianrhod's sons were born parthenogenically, like Maponos and other divine sons. Others think that Dylan and Llew were created on purpose by the touch of Math's magic wand to ensure the succession of the maternal line. This is the usual explanation of anthropologists who know of the importance of the maternal line in certain tribal societies. Gruffydd even suggests that Gwydion may have created Llew from the placenta of Dylan.

Could there be other ways to solve the riddle? Here we could ask the following questions: Why does Gwydion invite his sister to Math's court, when he knows that her virginity would be tested and he was aware that she was no longer a virgin? Could it be that he did it for this very reason: that he wanted to be sure that he and no other man was Llew's father?

Considering the sexual freedom of Celtic goddesses, it may be that Arianrhod does not reject her son because he is proof of an incestuous relation with her brother. Her relentless fury betrays a much deeper trauma which had its roots in Gwydion's betrayal of her sexual integrity. Under patriarchy the last and only prerogative of Woman was that she, and she alone, knew who was her child's father: *Mater semper certa est.* Gwydion succeeds in circumventing this last female privilege, in order to prove his paternity to himself, in spite of the sexual freedom enjoyed by Celtic goddesses (and, we may add, women in gynocentric societies in general). If he has begotten a son with Arianrhod, why does he bring her to Math's court, when he must know that Math will soon find out that she is no longer a virgin? He does it to be quite sure that Arianrhod believes herself to be a virgin: "I know not but that I am." When Math proves to her that she is not, what follows for Gwydion? That he and no other is the father of her child — because Arianrhod believes herself to be virginal and knows nothing of his sexual relations with her. This is the real reason for Arianrhod's outrage: that he made her a mother without her knowledge and consent; that he raped her in her sleep;[12] that he did not hesitate to embarrass her as a liar in front of Math, and that he did all this to be sure of his own paternity. No doubt, this was a great victory for Gwydion the technocrat, who also succeeds in keeping his prematurely born son alive.

When Math changed Gwydion into three different animals, including female animals, he experienced the mysteries of pregnancy and motherhood and used his knowledge against his sister. He became a father at Arianrhod's expense, proving himself to be the master of women's mysteries. Henceforth a woman's decision for or against motherhood has become irrelevant. She is reduced to the role of incubator, the mere "vessel of man's seed." In this veiled narrative we have the Celtic equivalent of the Greek Oresteia — the mythical triumph of the Father over the Mother.

From the begetting of a son without the consent of the mother to the creation of a woman from blossoms it is but a small step. Yet the beautiful Flower-daughter has a long mythological history. According to Graves she is no other than the goddess herself in her seductive aspect. She overwhelms the young hero with her charms, only to hand him to his sacrificers at the end of the year. This is not a specifically Celtic, but a pre-patriarchal, pan-European myth described by many writers.[13] However, if the author of the *Four Branches* saw Blodeuedd as the goddess in her death aspect he does not mention it. For him she could not act otherwise because she was not a real woman, but only a creation of male fantasy, a negative anima figure in Jungian terms.

When Gwydion wants to punish her by death, he discovers that he cannot kill his own creation. Blodeuedd will live on in another form, in this case as an owl. Why an owl? There are several reasons. With her silent flight and uncanny night vision, the owl is a symbol of "intuitive or night wisdom." Therefore this bird has always been represented as an attribute of the goddess in her dark aspect.[14] But in Wales there is also a linguistic reason for Blodeuedd's transformation into an owl: in Welsh the word for "owl" is *tylluan (tyl huan)* meaning "fleeing the sun." Since Llew is the "light, shining" sun hero, she has every reason to flee him. Secondly, Welsh is perhaps the only language where the owl is sometimes called "flower-face" because of its feather-encircled eyes resembling flowers. There may also be a connection with the ancient "Eye Goddess" frequently represented on petroglyphs which resembles an owl.

The Owl Blodeuedd reappears in later Welsh poetry, where the poet takes her voice and sings her lament in persuasive verses.

Llew's return

In the last part of the story the goddess appears once again in her darkest aspect as the Death Goddess, "the sow that eats her fallow." In the wake of pre-Celtic monotheism which knew only one Goddess, the Celts believed that every goddess could appear in her death aspect, because they understood the close connection of Life and Death. At the end of the *Fourth Branch* the goddess appears in the shape of a magic white sow. Pigs were animals connected with the moon and we recall that Arianrhod's name "Silver Wheel" makes her a moon goddess. Further, swine are notable for producing more young than other quadrupeds, but also for occasionally eating them. In the episode of Nantlleu the goddess in her zoomorphic aspect eats Llew's flesh. Yet, as we shall see in the story of Ceridwen and Gwion Bach (see Chapter 11), she does it so that he can be reborn from her womb. Here again Gwydion intervenes and disturbs her magic of transformation. Seen in this way we understand the symbols of the Celtic myth, which never shrinks from the darkest and most abhorrent aspects of Life.

Gwydion may have begotten his son against Arianrhod's will, but to bring him back to life he still needs her. In the shape of the "white sow of Menawr Bennard" she leads him to *Nantlleu,* the "Valley of Llew" (or the Valley of the Moon) where his son awaits resurrection in the shape of his totem bird, the eagle. He perches on an oak, which the bard Taliesin has called the "stout guardian of the door."[15] Did the poet see the oak as the tree separating this world from the Otherworld? Perhaps because more than any other tree, the oak most readily attracts lightning, the bridge between heaven and earth?

But Gwydion's revivification of his son remains futile: Llew never accomplishes heroic deeds like the Irish Lugh or the Welsh Pryderi. And Arianrhod's curse is literally fulfilled: Llew never finds a wife "of the race that is now on earth."[16] Although he eventually rules all of Gwynedd, he never achieves his people's liberation like his Irish counterpart. By arrogating her life-giving mysteries, Gwydion has overcome the Mother Goddess, but like Bran's campaign in Ireland, his triumph remains a Pyrrhic victory. If the era of the Mother Goddess and her Son are gone forever, it remains to be seen if the future of the Father God and his Son holds more promise.

Who is Arianrhod?

The name "Arianrhod" or "Aranrhod" is rarely mentioned in Celtic mythology. Triad 35 informs us that she is the daughter of Don (Dana) and Beli and in Triad 78 she is called "One of the most beautiful maidens." This would make her also a sister to Caswallawn, the magician and usurper of the throne in the *Second Branch.*

As W.J. Gruffydd explains, it was originally Arianrhod who filled the office of the king's footholder, because Math wanted to have her under constant surveillance. Odd as it may sound today, the office of "royal footholder," together with his rights and duties, is minutely described in the Welsh law tracts, and particularly in *The Laws of Hywel Da.* It was an office with largely ceremonial duties and always held by a man. But according to Jean Markale it must have been held originally by a maiden, especially when the king was old, sick or impotent. Markale explains that in this case the virgin footholder was literally the agent of the goddess, who strengthened the king and protected him from a violent death through his successor.[17]

Gruffydd and Markale agree that in the original version of the story it was Arianrhod and not Goewin who held the office. Perhaps the author of *The Four Branches* replaced Arianrhod with Goewin because he considered the position as unworthy for Arianrhod's status. Even if she was largely euhemerized in the story, her very name "Silver Wheel" identifies her with the moon, and she was indeed worshipped as a moon goddess.

The name "Arianrhod" too could have a different meaning by changing its spelling: if the name is spelt *arian-rath* it signifies "Silver Hill," in Latin *Argentoratum,* which is to this day the Latin name of the city of Strasbourg. The name designates the presence of royal burial sites, because Celtic royal graves were covered with quartz stones, which gleamed in sun- or moonlight with a silver reflection. Therefore the spelling "Arianrath," which we find occasionally in the manuscripts, would make her the goddess of royal gravesites, perhaps identical with the Irish *ban-shee.* But that is not all. Taliesin reveals that Arianrhod owns a glass castle in the constellation Corona Borealis. At the court of King Maelgwn he sings a song in which he boasts: "I was three times prisoner in Arianrhod's castle" (see Chapter 11). This means that he had died three times and each time he was held imprisoned in the constellation of the Northern Crown. This is her revolving Glass Castle, "the Prison of the Dead" where kings, poets and heroes await reincarnation.

Robert Graves goes even further. He makes a direct connection between Arianrhod and the Cretan Ariadne, quoting

E.M. Parr, the renowned researcher of Sumerian antiquities. According to Parr the name has nothing to do with *arian/aran* = silver. In Sumerian *Ar-ri-an* means "high Mother of Heaven," namely the goddess who turns "the wheel of heaven." Graves continues: "If Parr's etymology is correct, then Arianrhod would be the (northern) counterpart of the Cretan *Ar-ri-an-de.*"[18] This shows that the image of a revolving castle in the dome of heaven is very old. W.J. Gruffydd makes the point that a most unusual expression is used to describe Blodeuedd's movements in her castle Mur Castell just before Gronw Pebyr appears on the scene:

> When Blodeuedd found herself alone after Llew's departure, it is said of her that ... she turned within the court ... (*troy o vywn y llys a wnaeth hi.*) There seems to be no particular reason for this extraordinary phrase ... I have failed to find the phrase elsewhere in Welsh; certainly the usual word for "moving about" would be the reflexive form *ymdroi,* and not the active *troi.* I suggest that we have here the vestiges of some phrase which describes her as being kept in her husband's revolving castle, and when he had gone, she turned it round so as to be able to go out.[19]

Gruffydd interprets the episode as that of a "locked-up wife" who "gets out" in spite of her husband's precautions. But if we revert to the image of the "Great Queen who turns around the wheel of Heaven," we gain quite a different impression. If, as Graves tells us, Blodeuedd is Arianrhod in another guise, then we are entitled to see in her also the manifestation of that cosmic force that "moves Heaven and Earth and the other stars."[20]

In 1977 a book by James Vogh set out to prove that the Celts had a thirteenth zodiac called "the Spider."[21] Situated between Taurus and Gemini, that is between May 16 and June 13, it appears as the constellation of Auriga, otherwise known as "the Charioteer," which because of its shape, can also be interpreted as a spider. According to Vogh it is an interesting fact that many of the stone circle observatories on the British Isles are aligned towards Capella, the brightest star in the constellation of Auriga. Could the rider Rhiannon be identical with Arianrhod the charioteer? — and the Sun Goddess Rhiannon of the *First Branch* with the Moon Goddess Arianrhod in the *Fourth Branch?*

For Graves and Markale there is no doubt that Arianrhod was the triple Queen of Heaven and a much older goddess than Rhiannon. In the story of *Math Son of Mathonwy* she appears in her triple manifestation, but not in the usual sequence: first as Arianrhod the mother of the hero, then as Blodeuedd, his flower bride, who betrays him and has him killed by his successor, and finally as the death goddess Ceridwen, *Hen Wen,* "the Old White One," who prepares his rebirth. Grave comments that in Triad 107 Arianrhod appears as "the silver encircled daughter of Don." Her identity is clear to anyone who knows the numerous variants of this myth. She is the Mother of the divine (fish-) child Dylan, who, after having killed the wren in winter, is changed into Lleu Llaw Gyffes, the "Lion with the Sure Hand." He is the Sun Hero who always has his twin beside him. Arianrhod now takes the shape of the love goddess Blodeuedd who, as usual, betrays the Sun Hero to his successor and causes his death. Then she changes into the Owl of Wisdom and finally into "the Sow that eats her fallow."[22]

The meaning of the Four Branches

Caitlín Matthews is another writer who sees in *Math Son of Mathonwy* one of the many myths of Eternal Return. For her Mabon/Llew is the "miraculous child," "the *puer eternus,*" a symbol of renewal, standing in vivid contrast to the Titans of age and stagnation (Bran, Math). And indeed, all the Mabinogion stories are structured on the pattern of continual renewal.[23] Matthews is in agreement with Graves, but gives more importance to the hero, whereas Graves emphasises the power of the goddess. For him there is no doubt that Arianrhod is the same goddess that she was as Rhiannon at the beginning of the *First Branch.*

Reviewing once again the goddesses we have met with, we notice that, in the relationships of Rhiannon, Branwen,

Arianrhod and Blodeuedd, each of them stands between two male protagonists who either woo her or want to bring her under their influence as brother, uncle or avenger (as in the case of Llwyd), but never as her father, as in the story of *Culhwch and Olwen* (see Chapter 8). Therefore we find five triangles:

Pwyll	Rhiannon	Gwawl
Bran	Branwen	Matholuch
Manawydan	Rhiannon	Llwyd is Coed
Gwydion	Arianrhod	Mathonwy
Gwydion	Blodeuedd	Llew Llaw Gyffes

We shall meet with the same pattern again in each of the other stories of the collection, whereby the gradual loss of power and status of the goddess will continue. We witness the gradual eclipse of her image, which Taliesin tried in vain to halt.

But the hero too loses power and prestige: Pryderi does not really die to save his tribe, but in an attempt to avenge himself. Llew does not kill, like the Irish Lugh, the tyrannical oppressor of his people, but his rival for a woman. We also notice that the tie between mother and son, originally so strong in Celtic society, is weakening. It gradually dissolves and the negative aspect of the stepmother appears, as in the story of *Culhwch and Olwen.*

CHAPTER 8

Culhwch and Olwen

The story *Culhwch and Olwen* is one of the *Four Independent Native Tales* which make up the middle part of the *Mabinogion* collection. Here King Arthur is mentioned for the first time in Celtic literature, appearing as a British king of the heroic age, far removed from chivalry, *courtoisie* and all the trappings of knighthood as represented in the twelfth and thirteenth centuries. The story was written around the year 1100, but is much older. It shows a typical Celtic petty king surrounded by his warriors, as he may have lived in Wales around the sixth century. In other words the author describes him much closer to historic reality than later court poets.

Culhwch and Olwen is not a ramshackle, whimsical Celtic ruin, as some readers might think on first impression. Rather, according to Stephen Knight, it is "a wide-ranging and complex narrative, a central ideological text of the tribal élite."[1] The threats to the royal family alluded to in the story are those that would have been perceived by members of the group. The values offered and the results achieved are ones which would have seemed both real and consoling to them. Knight adds that there can be little doubt that such a family would be the patrons for an extended prose story of this sort and the fact that it was recorded in writing well before other Welsh prose stories indicates that it was held in special esteem by its audience.[2]

If Arthur ever lived, he was probably a Celto-Roman warlord *(dux bellorum),* a commander of Roman-trained cavalry squadrons who beat the Saxons in several decisive battles and halted their advance in Britain for about a generation. In the

Culhwch story he is the ruler of the whole of Britain: *Pen teyrnedd yr ynys hon,* "the most powerful prince of this island," the monarch of all Brythons, as opposed to their enemies, the Saxons.

In the second half of the first millennium the Welsh — that is to say the former Celtic élite of Britain — had been obliged to retreat from the advancing Angles and Saxons to the west of the island. Leaving the fertile regions of Britain, they found themselves in a relatively poor country. The soil is infertile, therefore tillage did not pay and animal husbandry became the most important pursuit. Besides hunting, the nobility resorted to cattle rustling and raids into neighbouring territories. For these enterprises an adequate war band was an absolute necessity. Such bands and their leaders were praised by the bards and popular storytellers carried their deeds among the common people.

Under those conditions women's role was limited to that of bearers of the sons required for the armed enterprises of the family. The greatest concern of the clan chiefs was female infertility, or worse, the dying out of the family for lack of male heirs, as indicated at the beginning of this story. The spiritual influence of Woman, as perceived in the *First Branch of the Mabinogi,* has long ended. If Rhiannon, the woman from the Otherworld, was able to advise her husband or take the initiative, the women in this story have no such chance. Here we have an absolute monarchy, where the will of the king is law and the fists of his men his power.

Culhwch's family

The first part of the story gives a vivid impression of the reality of a woman's life in the Middle Ages and tells how an extraordinary wooing comes about. We hear that King Cillydd's wife, queen Goleuddydd ("the Light, Shining Day") fell pregnant and that during that time "she went mad" and kept away from human dwellings. But when her time drew near, her right senses came back to her and she returned among people. Nevertheless her son was born "where a swine herd kept his swine." The child was given to a wet nurse and because he was born in a pig-sty they called him Culhwch (pronounced "kil-lich"), "the piglet." Far from being derogatory, this name had the significance of a totem, because among Celts and Teutons swine were sacred animals, and many a Celtic chieftain had the boar in his shield.

One of the greatest adventures in the story is the hunt of the Twrch Trwyt (pron. Toorc trooit), the "Boar of Boars." For this hunt only the best of Arthur's men were good enough. We hear that Twrch Trwyt had once been a king, but had been changed into a boar — yet that he had he had never given up his spite and wickedness. The story of the Twrch Trwyt is symptomatic: here a king became a pig. In Culhwch's case a young "Piglet" is destined to become a king. It seems that the author intended the structure of a heroic tale in the vein of Perceval, but with inverted signs: if Perceval is the fatherless mother's son who spends his childhood in the forest, Culhwch is the motherless father's son, who spends his first years in a piggery. He too will grow up to become a mighty boar just as his Uncle Arthur, who was called "the Boar of Cornwall."

To return to the story:

Soon after her delivery the queen sickened and died. But before dying she told the king: "I am going to die of this sickness and thou wilt wish for another wife. And these days wives are dispensers of gifts, but it is wrong for thee to despoil thy son. I ask of thee that thou take no wife till thou seest a two-headed briar on my grave."[3]

Cillydd promised it. Then Goleuddydd called her confessor and asked him "to strip the grave each year, so that nothing might grow on it."[4] And the confessor promised it too. But after seven years he forgot his promise, and when the king visited the grave while on a hunting excursion, he saw a two-headed briar rose flowering on it. So now at last he could marry again. Overjoyed, he immediately consulted his counsellors where he might find a new wife. One of them said: "I could tell a woman would suit thee well. She is the wife of king Doged." They decided to seek her out. And they slew the king and the wife they brought home with them, and an only daughter she had along with her; and they took possession of the king's lands.[5] This laconic report of murder and wife stealing stands like a leitmotiv for things to come. The feelings of the raped queen are only hinted at, as far as the action permits:

> Upon a day, as the good lady went walking abroad, she came to the house of an old crone ... Quoth the queen: "Crone, wilt thou for God's sake tell me what I ask of thee? Where are the children of the man who has carried me off by force?" Quoth the crone: "He has no children."
>
> Quoth the queen: "Woe is me that I should have come to a childless man!"
>
> Said the crone: "Thou needst not say that. It is prophesied that he shall have offspring. 'Tis by thee he shall have it, since he has not had it by another. Besides, be not unhappy, he has one son."
>
> The good lady returned home joyfully, and quoth she to her husband: "What reason hast thou to hide thy child from me?"
>
> Quoth the king: "I will hide him no longer."[6]

Culhwch is sent for and brought to court. At once his stepmother plans to marry him with her daughter. When Culhwch refuses, she curses him by telling him that he will never have a wife unless he marries the Chief Giant's daughter. Considering the difficulties of winning such a maiden, his stepmother has condemned him virtually to death or at least to childlessness. But what the queen had pronounced as a curse, Culhwch accepts as his destiny. Without ever having seen her, he falls in love with the giant's daughter immediately. The problem is how to win her. But Culhwch is well connected. The king tells his son that his mother was King Arthur's sister. He should therefore go to Arthur's court "to get his hair cut by him" (that is, to place himself under Arthur's protection) and ask him for his help. Thus begins Culhwch's journey into adventure and it is worth quoting in full:

> Off went the boy on a steed with a light-grey head, four

> winters old, with well-knit fork, shell-hoofed,[7] and a gold, tubular bridle-bit in its mouth. And under him a precious gold saddle, and in his hand two whetted spears of silver. A battle-axe in his hand, the forearm's length of a grown man from ridge to edge. It would draw blood from the wind ...
>
> A gold-hilted sword on his thigh, and the blade of it gold, and a gold-chased buckler upon him, with the hue of heaven's lightning therein, and an ivory boss therein. And two greyhounds, white-breasted, brindled, in front of him, with a collar of red gold about the neck of either, from shoulder swell to ear ...
>
> (Culhwch wore) a four-cornered mantle of purple, and an apple of red gold in each of its corners; a hundred kine was the worth of each apple. The worth of three hundred kine in precious gold was there in his footgear and his stirrups, from the top of his thigh to the tip of his toe. Never a hair-tip stirred upon him, so exceeding light was his steed's canter under him on his way to the gate of Arthur's court.[8]

The special mention of Culhwch's hair shows how elegantly this pig prince rides off "to get his hair cut by Arthur" and this is the author's intention. During the whole narrative he finds occasion to mention hair cuts, hair style, hair combs — anything to do with hair, to underscore the importance of hair care and hair fashion at Arthur's court. To this we may add that in the Middle Ages only free men were entitled to wear their hair long, and "shorn" hair was a sign of serfdom. Therefore the ritual of haircut which Culhwch asks of Arthur has also the meaning of offering his service to the king.

Could this preoccupation with hair imply a concealed criticism or satire? A hint that in this society superficialities such as hair are more important than strength of character? Stephen Knight denies this. He believes that, on the contrary, the author wants to show that the prince is in absolute control of nature, "to the tip of the hair," a quality which has always been expected from the warrior caste.[9]

Arriving at Arthur's court, Culhwch shows his mettle with the greatest possible arrogance. As he arrives late, the porter refuses him entry. But Culhwch threatens not only to bring dishonour to the court, but also to "raise three shouts that every woman that is in that court shall miscarry, and such of them that are not with child their wombs shall turn to a burden within them, so that they shall never bear child from this day forth."[10] It seems that Culhwch has control even over women's fertility.

When he is finally allowed into Arthur's presence, he disdains to dismount and enters the banquet hall on horseback. Arthur is duly impressed and offers him the best of his hospitality. But of course, Culhwch "is not come to wheedle meat and drink," but to ask for more important things, namely "to have his hair cut by Arthur." The king graciously complies and while he is thus occupied "he asks who he was." Culhwch reveals that he is Arthur's nephew (not his cousin as the texts says) on his mother's side, and immediately Arthur "grows tender towards him." We recall the special relationship between the *avunculus* (mother's brother) and sister's son. Arthur feels fatherly pride towards this new nephew, and assures him of his protection. Then Culhwch, invoking a whole litany of excellent referees, comes out with his big request: Arthur's help to win the giant's daughter. Arthur immediately agrees and the winning of Culhwch's bride is now a point of honour for his extended family, his court and his war band. A search party is sent out to find the maiden, but when the men return after a year without having found her, Culhwch grows impatient. Again he threatens to bring dishonour on Arthur and his court if he will not get what he wants.

This time Cei and Arthur's best men offer to take him on a second search, and he agrees. This quest for the giant's daughter is his only contribution to the winning of his wife Olwen. Everything else is done for him by Arthur and his men. Each one of them can boast of a special miraculous gift or quality and the list of the handpicked participants fills seven pages. Beside well known knights of the Round Table like Cei and Bedwyr, it contains heroes of Greek and Irish mythology such as Achilles and Conchobar, and a great number of figures born of the author's fantasy, whose names enounce their bearers' qualities in humorous exaggerations: Nerth Son of Gadarn, "Powerful Son of Strong"; Clust Son of Clustveinydd, "Ear Son of Listener"; and so on.

Out of this illustrious company Arthur picks the best to accompany Culhwch on his quest. And what at first was not achieved in a year is now accomplished in a day. They see a great castle from afar, and meet a wild, fear-inspiring shepherd tending his flock. This shepherd is a well known mythological type. As the "Lord of Animals " we shall meet him again in the romance of *The Lady of the Fountain.* Originally the ancient partner of the goddess, Cernunnos, but now in medieval guise, he functions as the guardian of the threshold to the Otherworld. Therefore this meeting signals the company's entry into the world of the Giant, where normal standards no longer apply. The shepherd's name is Custennin ("the Faithful one"), a name that inspires trust. And indeed Custennin is full of good will towards the expedition because, as he tells them, the giant is his sworn enemy. He robbed him of his land and killed twenty-three of his twenty-four sons. It is not clear how the enmity began, but Custennin blames his wife for it, and the whole episode recalls Balor's oppression of Ireland.

Predictably, Custennin earnestly advises Culhwch's party to turn back: "Whew men! God protect you! For all the world do not that! Never a one has come to make that request that went away with his life."[11] But of course, his warning goes unheeded.

Culhwch rewards Custennin with a gold ring which Custennin hides in his glove, and later gives to his wife. Surprised, she asks him how he got it, and he tells her he found it on a body washed up by the tide. As she does not believe him, he admits that Culhwch, the son of king Cillydd and Goleudydd, has come to ask for the giant's daughter. Comparing this episode with parallels in Irish and British sagas, Caitlín Matthews concludes that the ring was a token Goleudydd had left her son, so that he could be recognized by her sister and obtain her help.[12] And indeed, Custennin's wife immediately recognizes in Culhwch her sister's son, because like Arthur, she too is a sibling of Goleudydd.

The shepherd's wife is an interesting figure, a matriarch in the vein of the ancient Earth Goddess. A sister of queen Goleudydd, she has obviously married beneath her and fallen on hard times. But instead of sickening and getting mad in "high society" like her sister, she retained her good health and bore twenty-four sons. Unfortunately the wicked giant had killed most of them, so that only her youngest remained, and it is because of this loss that she immediately decides to help her nephew. Her primeval strength is shown in a typical episode: at the arrival of the company at her homestead, she hurries outside to welcome the guests. But instead of yielding to her embraces, Cei holds a log of wood in front of him, which she squeezes between her arms to "a twisted withe," whereupon Cei tells her in his rough manner: "Woman, had it been I thou didst squeeze in this wise, there were no need for another to love me ever. An ill love, that!"[13]

She opens a box near the hearth fire, and a fair haired boy jumps out. "He is all that is left," she says. "Three-and-twenty sons of mine has Ysbaddaden Chief Giant slain, and I have no more hope of this one than of the others."[14]

Cei promises to protect him, and, as another of Arthur's nephews, he is destined to become one of the best of Arthur's warriors, and to share the spoils of Culhwch's victory.

In the episode at the shepherd's home, the protocol of Celtic hospitality is strictly observed: although Custennin's wife knows the reason for the strangers' arrival, she only asks them about it, "after they have eaten." Like Custennin, she too warns them not to risk their lives in such a dangerous adventure, but after some hesitation, promises to introduce them to Olwen. She seems to be a foster mother to her, and the maiden visits her every Saturday, to wash her hair, and pays for the service handsomely with her rings. It would appear therefore, that Olwen is frustrated in the father's castle and yearns to get out. Yet her liberation can only be achieved at the cost of her father's life.

As Custennin's wife does not trust her nephew nor Arthur's men with the fair maiden, she demands a solemn oath "that they will not harm her." Only after that reassurance is Olwen sent for and makes her grand entrance:

> And she came, with a robe of flame-red silk about her, and around the maiden's neck a torque of red gold, and precious pearls therein and rubies. Yellower was her head than the flower of the broom, whiter was her flesh than the foam of the wave; whiter were her palms and her fingers than the shoots of the marsh trefoil from amidst the fine gravel of a welling spring. Neither the eye of the mewed hawk, nor the eye of the thrice mewed falcon, not an eye was fairer than hers. Whiter were her breasts than the breast of the white swan, redder were her cheeks than the reddest foxgloves. Whosoever beheld her would be filled with love for her. Four white trefoils sprang up behind her wherever she went; and for that reason was she called Olwen.[15]

Unless the author intends to underline Olwen's ancient background, her wearing of a torque, the old Celtic neck ring, would make her a priestess or even identify her with the goddess — an impression emphasised by the trefoil (again the figure three) which springs up under her every footstep.

Naturally Culhwch immediately declares his love for her and wants to abduct her without further ado. She however resists his haste, objecting that she has promised her father never to marry without his consent. While not opposing his suit, she asks him to see her father and to formally ask for her hand in marriage and to this Culhwch agrees.

What follows is Culhwch's "formal visit" to Ysbaddaden, which the author describes with grim humour.

> Then they arose to go after her, and slew nine gatemen who were at nine gates without a man crying out, and nine mastiffs without one squealing.
>
> And they went forward to the hall. Quoth they, "In the name of God and men, greeting unto thee, Ysbaddaden Chief Giant."
>
> "And you, where are you going?"[16]
>
> "We are going to seek Olwen thy daughter for Culhwch son of Cillydd."

> "Where are those rascal servants and those ruffians of mine?" said he. "Raise up the forks under my eyelids that I may see my future son-in-law." That was done. "Come hither tomorrow. I will give you some answer."
>
> They rose, and Ysbaddaden Chief Giant snatched at one of the three poisoned stone-spears which were by his hand, and hurled it after them. And Bedwyr caught it and hurled it back at him, and pierced Ysbaddaden Chief Giant right through the ball of his left knee. Quoth he: "Thou cursed savage son-in-law! I shall walk the worse up the slope. Like the sting of a gad-fly the poisoned iron has pained me."[17]

In keeping with the tradition of folk tales, this scene is repeated three times. Each time the giant throws one of his spears and each time it is hurled back at him But what ought to have caused lethal wounds to a mere man, is only an annoyance to the giant, who seems to be indestructible.

At the second visit they are delayed by the answer that Olwen's four great-grandfathers and four great-grandmothers have to be consulted about the match. At their third visit the giant again hurls a spear at them, which this time Culhwch returns and "pierces the giant's eye, so that it came out through the nape of the neck." This recalls Lugh's killing of the giant Balor with a sling stone into his eye. But Ysbaddaden is made of sterner stuff. He says: "Thou cursed savage son-in-law! So long as I am left alive, the sight of my eyes will be the worse. When I go against the wind they will water, a headache I shall have, and a giddiness each new moon."[18]

At last, at Culhwch's fourth visit, Ysbaddaden names his conditions: a veritable catalogue of no less than thirty-nine tasks (*anoethu,* "impossible tasks") are to be accomplished by the young suitor, each of which demands herculean strength, superhuman ability and sometimes sheer magic. Only fourteen of them are achieved, and they are all in preparation for Olwen's marriage feast: a fine linen wedding veil, food, drink and music for the celebration have to be provided. Tasks 15 to 39 require the assembling of men, horses, hounds for the hunt of the boar Twrch Trwyth, and his double, Ysgithrwyn.

Task 28 comprises the freeing of Mabon's cousin Eidoel ap Aer as a preliminary to finding Mabon himself, of which more later.

In Task 32 Ysbaddaden demands that the hunter Gwyn ap Nudd (an ancient British god perhaps identical with Arawn) be found and brought to take part in the boar hunt. But this task is delayed, because Gwyn is fighting with Gwythy ap Greidawl over possession of the maiden Creiddylad, daughter of Ceridwen.

At the background of this dispute is again the fight between Summer king and Winter king. Here it is resolved by Arthur who rules that every May Eve the two champions shall fight for her, but none shall win until Judgment Day: a clever way of dealing with heathen beliefs and Christian teaching alike.

As far as the other tasks are concerned, Arthur's men are up to every one of them and Culhwch's help is never required. Only three of them, the most interesting and most dramatic, are described in greater detail: the liberation of Mabon from imprisonment, the hunt of the Twrch Trwyth throughout Ireland and Britain and the slaying of the Black Witch daughter of the White Witch, "from the Valley of Grief in the uplands of Hell." The last two adventures are so difficult that they can only be achieved by Arthur himself.

As Mabon is represented as a great hunter, his liberation is a precondition to the great boar hunt, and the liberation of his cousin Eidoel son of Aer is in turn a precondition of finding and liberating Mabon. The latter task is an adventure at which Custennin's youngest son distinguishes himself and gains his warrior name Goreu, "the Best."

The king boar Trwrch Trwyth carries between his ears a comb and a pair of shears, which Ysbaddaden has asked for to shave his beard and to comb his hair for his daughter's wedding. (We note that even the savage giant is preoccupied with hair care, in a fruitless imitation of his enemies.) Arthur and his men win all the precious trophies asked for, but of Twrch Trwyth they can only rip the shears from between his ears. The boar himself flees into the Severn and hence into the sea. He disappears in the direction of Ireland and is never seen again. Stephen Knight suggests that this gigantic boar symbolizes the constant danger perceived as coming from Ireland.

Equally, the battle with the Black Witch is harder than anticipated. Celtic witches, whom we shall meet again in the Peredur story, were probably priestesses of the old religion and champions in martial arts. They recall Scatach and Aife, who taught the Irish hero Cuchulainn. After the witch has defeated four of Arthur's servants (obviously his warriors thought themselves too grand to fight with mere women) Arthur himself has to go and deal with her in her cave. He throws his knife at her, cutting her into two. Caw of Scotland collects her blood, which Ysbaddaden had asked for to dress his hair and beard for his daughter's wedding.

The killing of the witch is typical for a patriarchal kingdom, where strong women living independently of men, like Amazons or priestesses, are a constant threat to the male order. We shall find a similar adventure in the romance of Peredur of Efrawg, where the hero kills his teachers and benefactresses "because it was prophesied" (see Chapter 10).

In the end Culhwch together with Goreu, the whole company, and "and every one that wished ill to Ysbaddaden," reappear at the giant's court. The giant admits defeat, making the point however, that the victory is Arthur's and not Culhwch's.

> And Cadw of Pridein came to shave his beard, flesh and skin to the bone, and his two ears outright ...
>
> And Culhwch said, "Hast thou had thy shave, man?"
>
> "I have," said he. "And is thy daughter mine now?" "Thine," said he. "And thou needst not thank me for that, but thank Arthur who has secured her for thee. Of my own free will thou shouldst never have had her. And it is high time to take away my life."
>
> And then Goreu son of Custennin caught him by the hair of his head and dragged him behind him to the mound [i.e. the rubbish heap] and cut off his head and set it on a bailey-stake. And he took possession of his fort and

> his dominions. And that night Culhwch slept with Olwen, and she was his only wife as long as he lived ...
>
> And in this wise did Culhwch win Olwen daughter of Ysbaddaden Chief Giant.[19]

The generally satisfying happy end has thus been achieved. Culhwch takes Olwen more like a war prize than a beloved bride; his cousin Goreu, the shepherd's youngest son, inherits the giant's castle and dominions, and King Arthur emerges as the hero who turned his nephew's curse into a family blessing.

Two matriarchal traditions however are still in force: the duties of the mother's brother (here Arthur) towards his sister's son, and the love of the mother's sister, Custennin's unnamed wife, for her nephew. These two persons act as Culhwch's true parents — proof of the strength of the maternal line, even in patriarchal society.

Olwen is the symbol of tamed nature. Her fertility is precious and control of nature for the benefit of all is the constant justification of patriarchal attitudes. Given that Woman's fertility is counted among the gifts of nature, control of her sexuality and fertility is seen as justified. This is the double victory of Arthur for his nephew Culhwch the Pig Prince.

With all that it was not possible to erase the triple goddess completely. We find her in the three sisters in the background of the story: Eigr or Ygraine "the Sunlike," Arthur's mother, who does not appear in this story but is important to establish the family relationship; the poor queen Goleudydd, Culhwch's mother, and above all the earthy strength of Custennin's unnamed wife, whose youngest son Goreu ("the Best") succeeds in liberating Mabon and his kinsman from captivity and thus is forever assured of a place in Welsh sagas.

Finally a word about King Arthur, the great patriarch. The storyteller continuously emphasises how "civilized" Arthur's men are. The task which they achieve however are all accomplished by violence, cruelty, ruse, trickery and outright murder. Yet this attitude is presented as acceptable, desirable even. The question of ethics or knightly honour is carefully concealed and glossed over. The lesson for the audience seems to be that this is the way to deal with giants, local tribesmen and women. To question these methods would be "politically incorrect" and endanger the community.

We are forced to agree with Stephen Knight: the story of Culhwch and the concomitant glorification of Arthur is a subtle piece of ideological propaganda for the *realpolitik* of the men in power. If there had ever been an "old order" built on honour, fairness, truth and decency it seems to have disappeared, and a new order of "might is right" has taken its place.

Before closing this chapter, however, let us look for a moment at tasks No 18, 26 and 28 which lead us back to the oldest Celtic myth and into the realm of Celtic spiritual beliefs: the imprisonment and release of Mabon.

The freeing of Mabon

The freeing of Mabon, task No 26 (together with that of his cousin Eidoel ap Aer, task 28, as a preliminary) is one of the "impossible tasks" set by the giant. It must have wakened age-old memories and is told here with truly mythological grandeur.

We have seen that Mabon, a god of Spring, music, healing and hunting, is the Son of the Goddess and shares with her the imprisonment of Nature's abundant life during the northern winter. He also shares solar qualities with Apollo and was identified with him particularly during the five hundred years of Roman occupation.

In her study *Mabon and the Mysteries of Britain* Caitlín Matthews has attempted to identify Pryderi as well as Culhwch and his cousin Goreu as reincarnations, parallel figures or "aliases" of this youthful deity and archetype of Eternal Return.[20] Far from explaining the Culhwch story as originating in the economic problems of eleventh century aristocracy as Stephen Knight does, she treats it on a different level: as an initiation into the spiritual Brotherhood of Celtic leadership or Pendragons.

To prove her point she underpins the story with the little known collection of British Triads,[21] with Taliesin's poem *The Spoils of Annwn* and with W.J. Gruffydd's study *Mabon and Modron*.[22] It may be remembered that Mabon (or *Mab ap Modron)* is not a name, but an honorific meaning "the Son of the Great Mother." For Mabon's real name Gruffydd proposes none other than *Pryderi,* who, as we have seen, has his *vita* woven as a red thread through the *Four Branches,* and whose imprisonment is described in the *Third Branch.* In this story it is his friend and comrade, "the ungrasping chieftain Manawydan" who achieves his liberation by his intelligence, patience and obstinacy. Yet it could be argued that in the spiritual realm "the liberation of the god" is an achievement every one of us is called upon.

Matthews bases her argument on Triad 52:

> Three Exalted Prisoners of the Island of Britain:
> Llyr Halfspeech, who was imprisoned by Euroswydd,
> And second, Mabon son of Modron,
> And third Gwair, Gwair Son of Geirioedd.
> And one [prisoner] who was more exalted than the three of them
> Was three nights in prison in Caer Oeth and Anoeth,
> And three nights imprisoned by Gwen Pendragon.
> And three nights in an enchanted prison under the Stone of Enchymeint.
> This exalted Prisoner was Arthur.
> And it was the same lad who released him from each of these three prisons —
> Goreu, son of Custennin, his cousin.[23]

This chimes with the poem *The Spoils of Annwn* where we read:

> Perfect was the captivity of Gweir in Caer Sidi
> According to the tale of Pwyll and Pryderi.

Whilst it is impossible to identify the other prisoners named in this Triad we may deduce from Taliesin's line — "I was three times prisoner in Arianrhod's Castle" — that all these imprisonments ultimately mean periods of death between lifetimes. For the Celts, who believed in reincarnation, all the dead are prisoners awaiting "liberation," that is rebirth. Matthews contends that there must have been certain "exalted prisoners," whose rebirth was more important than that of others. In this sense then, Mabon, the Son of the Great Mother, may have been a divine dispensation, whose release from captivity was of immense importance, if not for all mankind than at least for the Welsh at that particular time of their history.

In the *Culhwch* story we have a unique opportunity to see how the narrator imagines the release of this immemorial prisoner, Mabon the Son of Modron, "who was snatched from his mother's bed when he was but three nights old" (see Chapter 4).

As the mythological birth of Mabon happened aeons ago, nobody could possibly remember it. To find Mabon it is therefore necessary to ask the five oldest animals of Britain: the Blackbird of Cilgwri, (Gwri's Retreat[24]) the Stag of Rhedinfr (Fernbrake Hill), the Owl of Cawlwyd (the Wood of Caw the Grey), the Eagle of Gwern Abwy (Alder Swamp), and finally the Salmon of Llyn Llyw (Lake of the Leader). Here the figure five would indicate the sacredness of these animals, which represent the archetypes of their species, and therefore are particularly powerful helpers in this quest.

The four men appointed to search for the Mabon are the aforementioned Eidoel ap Aer, a kinsmen of Mabon, Gwrhyr Interpreter of Tongues, who knew the language of birds and beasts, and finally Cei and Bedwyr. With the help of their interpreter they ask the animals one by one, until the Eagle leads them to the Salmon, who is the oldest and wisest of them all. And the Salmon gives them the information they seek:

> "As much as I know I will tell. With every tide I go up along the River (the Severn) till I come to the bend of the wall of Caer Loyw (Castle Gloucester); and there I found such distress that I never found its equal in all my life; and, that you may believe, let one of you come here on my two shoulders."
>
> And Cei and Gwrhyr Interpreter of Tongues went upon the salmon's two shoulders, and they journeyed until they came to the far side of the wall from the prisoner, and they could hear wailing and lamentation ...

> Gwrhyr said, "What man laments in this house of stone?"
>
> "Alas man, there is cause for him who is here to lament. Mabon son of Modron is here in prison; and none was ever so cruelly imprisoned as I; neither the imprisonment of Lludd Silverhand nor the imprisonment of Greid son of Eri."
>
> "Hast thou hope of getting thy release for gold or for silver or for worldly wealth or by battle and fighting?"
>
> "What is got of me will be got by fighting."[25]

As Mabon can be freed only by fighting, Arthur and his men attack the castle, while the heroic Salmon, taking Cei on his back, "broke through the wall of the castle and Cei took the prisoner on his back; and still he fought with the men. Arthur came home and Mabon with him, a free man."[26]

We recall the image of the Gundestrup Cauldron (see Chapter 1), where a little man is represented riding on a dolphin. This image, Professor Hatt explains, represents "a man's soul riding on a dolphin to the realm of the Blest."[27] In the same way, Cei's ride on the Salmon into Caer Loyw and his freeing of Mabon is not a happening of earthly reality, but a heroic deed in the Otherworld. And this, Matthews concludes, is the crux of the matter: like the tasks of Hercules, the adventures of Culhwch (and by implication those of Arthur's men), are "initiatory deeds in the Inner Planes" winning the heroes' access to the secret brotherhood of champions of their people, who were the champions of the goddess Sovereignty in the older belief system. Matthews is an esoteric, and her ideas can be inspiring. One question, however, remains to be answered: if, as Matthews states, Mabon's liberation is an heroic feat achieved in the Otherworld, why is the castle from which he is liberated firmly placed on British soil: Castle Gloucester on the river Severn? Could the author possibly allude to the situation of Wales in its coeval political context?

A similar episode in the romance *Peredur Son of Efrawg* (see Chapter 10) seems to prove it. Peredur is called upon to kill his benefactresses, "the Witches of Gloucester" who are revealed as the enemies of his family. In the study *Peredur and the Welsh Tradition of the Grail,* Glenys Goetinck sees in the Witches of Gloucester a code name for the political enemies of Wales.[28] Gloucester, situated in the border region between Wales and England, could well have been a strategic rallying point of invading forces. Goetinck's central theme is the motif of the Sovereignty of Wales. The figure of Peredur can be identified with Pryderi son of Rhiannon and hence with Mabon son of Modron. These three names merge into one, the Son of the Goddess, herself the beleaguered Sovereignty of Wales.

Here Mabon functions as a collective figure, representing the youth of Wales. We may speculate that in the fierce battles between invaders and defenders many a young warrior was caught and imprisoned in the dungeon of Gloucester Castle, awaiting his release "by ransom or by fighting." This is the political reality behind "the wailing and lamentation at the far side of the wall." It represents the loss of the Sovereignty of Wales which must be regained, not only in the otherworldly, spiritual realm, but rather by brave political action, as exemplified by Arthur's warriors.

The freeing of Mabon can therefore be regarded as an encoded message to an audience who had the Sovereignty of Wales at heart and was readily understood by all listeners as a rallying cry to renew the fight for freedom, and for the freeing of contemporary prisoners.

Whether we choose Knight's and Goetinck's political reading, or Caitlín Matthews' esoteric interpretation, the tale of *Culhwch and Olwen* proves once more the multilayered technique of the Welsh storyteller. He may describe harsh times and desperate struggles, yet he never fails to inspire his audience.

CHAPTER 9

Elen of the Hosts

The most important of the *Four Independent Native Tales — Culhwch and Olwen* — is preceded by *The Dream of Macsen Wledig.*[1] The two other stories are *Lludd and Llefelys* (not discussed here), and *The Dream of Rhonabwy.* It is significant that the first and the last of these four "wonder tales" are dream stories.

The fourth and final "Native Tale," *The Dream of Rhonabwy,* gives a description of the hardships of life encountered by the storyteller in medieval Wales. It speaks of the suffering of the people, particularly of the women, during the continuous tribal warfare, of hunger, dirt and vermin, and "thereupon, lo, a storm and rain that it was not easy for any to go out and relieve himself."[2] From this miserable reality the storyteller escapes into blessed sleep and dreams about the marvellous world of King Arthur and his men. The dream visions captivate him completely, so that he does not wake up for three nights and three days.[3]

The Dream of Macsen Wledig offers a complete contrast to this harsh reality. It tells of a Roman Emperor who literally meets his beloved in a dream. On a hunting expedition he falls asleep and dreams of Elen, his woman of destiny. Here again a wonderful (divine?) bride must be won. But whilst prince Culhwch woos the daughter of the wild giant, the suitor in this story is none other than Maxentius, Emperor of Rome, and the bride is the British princess *Elen Luydanc,* Helen of the Hosts or Helen of the Highways. This Helen shares no more than a name with the Greek Helena: it may be that the storyteller knew about Helena's status as Selena, the moon goddess and alludes to her during the dream phase of the story. But as we shall see, his model was a historic personality, namely Helena, the mother of Constantine the Great, in the guise of Lady Sovereignty, not only of Britain but of the whole Roman Empire.

Here is a summary of the tale:

Once upon a time Maxentius [Maxen], the Emperor of Rome, went hunting in the Tiber Valley. Towards noon, as the sun grew hot, he got tired and fell asleep. He dreamed that he left the valley, scaled the highest mountains, passed over a plain and reached the sea. He went aboard a ship that took him on a beautiful island. He crossed it until he reached a mountain range where a river ran into the sea. At the mouth of the river he saw a huge fortress. Its gates stood open, he entered and came into a magnificent hall. He saw a worthy old man who carved chess pieces and two boys who played a board game. And on a golden throne sat the most beautiful woman he had ever seen. She arose and led him to the throne, inviting him to sit beside her. He put his arm around her, but as he wanted to kiss her — he awoke.

This dream caught the Emperor's soul. He forgot his duties, neglected the empire and only thought of the beautiful lady of his dream. His counsellors thought how they could help him, and they sent out messengers in all directions, hoping to find her. As their efforts failed the Emperor returned to the same spot where he had had the dream, and sent his scouts in the same direction that he had wandered. This time they succeeded. They found the old gentleman, the two boys and the beautiful woman. They went down on their knees and did homage to her as the empress of Rome. Then they invited her to go with them to become the spouse of the Emperor. But she replied:

"Gentlemen, I can see that you are noble men and you carry the badges of messengers. Why then do you mock me?"

"Lady we do not. The Emperor of Rome has seen you in a dream and now life and being and existence have left him. We will give you a choice: you may come with us and be made empress of Rome, or else the Emperor will come here to make you his wife."

"Men," she answered, "I do not doubt what you say, but I do

not believe it overmuch either. If it is I whom the Emperor loves, let him come for me."[4]

And so it was done. Led by his messengers, the Emperor went to Britain and reached the fortress of Aber Seint (Segontium). He entered the hall and saw the two brothers Kynan and Avaon, their father Eudav son of Caradoc, and the woman of his dream on the golden throne. He greeted her and said: "Hail to you, Empress of the Romans." He embraced her and kissed her. And in the same night he slept with her.

On the next morning she asked for her maiden fee as he had found her a virgin: the island of Britain for her father, and the three islands of Wight, Man and Anglesey for herself as Empress of Rome. Further she wanted three fortresses to be built for herself, namely Arvon, Caer Lion and Caer Vyrddin.[5]

Then she had built roads to join her fortresses, and these roads are called Sarn Elen, Helen's Roads. She herself was called Helen of the Roads; only because she was a British princess were her people prepared to build them.

For the Emperor she had brought soil from Rome, as it was healthier for him to walk on Roman soil.

The Emperor lived with her in Britain for seven years. Then the Romans elected a new Emperor and Maxen had to go and fight him. On the way he also conquered France and Burgundy. Then he laid siege to Rome. He beleaguered the city for ten years but could not conquer it. But Elen's brothers had followed him with a small army, and they stormed the walls and succeeded in conquering Rome. They killed the false Emperor and all his supporters. Only then did they allow Maxen to enter the city in triumph. Now Maxen sat again on the throne of Rome and the people did him homage. In recognition of their services, the Emperor gave the Roman army to Elen's brothers and they won many countries, cities and fortresses. They killed all the men and spared only the women. These wars of conquest lasted for many years: warriors who had joined the force as young man had white hair when the war ended. Then Avaon returned to Britain, but Kynan with his army stayed on the Continent. And to avoid their British tongue being contaminated by the women of the conquered countries, he had their tongues cut out. The land was called Brittany and its inhabitants *Bryttanyeidd.* This is the story of the dream of Maxen, ruler of Rome.[6]

Here the storyteller remembers the centuries of Roman rule, which in Britain lasted for five hundred years, but had ended seven hundred years before his time. It is not surprising, therefore, that he is a little hazy about the historic details and treats them with poetic licence.

Who were the historic protagonists of this dream story? Perhaps the storyteller had heard about old Welsh genealogies which mention a Roman prince named Maxen, and knew of the Roman general by the name of Maximus, the last Roman leader of legions on British soil. In AD 383 Maximus had been elected Emperor by his legionaries. Consequently he gathered the last of the Roman troops (and some British auxiliaries) and crossed over to Gaul, where he vanquished the Emperor Gratianus and slew him. A few years later he was himself overcome by the Emperor Theodosius, captured, imprisoned and executed for treason at Ravenna.

The historic prototype of Elen was the mother of Constantine the Great *(c.* AD 280–337), pre-dating Maximus by half a century. She became famous in history for allegedly having found the true cross of Christ at Jerusalem. Canonized by the Church, she was nominated patroness of all pilgrims to the Holy Land and was greatly venerated by the Crusaders.

The origins of Elen/Helena are disputed. According to some she was born in Asia Minor.[7] Others agree with Gibbon that she was a courtesan from Dacia.[8] Whatever her country of origin may have been, she was a strong woman and an important personality, both in Church history and in British legend. According to Constantine's biographer Eusebius, the Emperor was born in London in AD 274. Geoffrey of Monmouth, author of the pseudo-historic *History of British Kings* writes that Elen/Helena was the daughter of King Coel and succeeded him to the throne.[9] Admittedly, historians regard Geoffrey's work as pure fantasy, but in recent years certain archaeological discoveries have proved him correct at least in some details. If we read him in conjunction with Elen's contemporary Eusebius he seems believable in this case.

The Venerable Bede, an author of the eighth century, tells us that Constantius, the Roman governor of Gaul and Britain under the Emperor Diocletian, had a son, Constantine, by a woman called Helena, and that this son ascended to the dignity of Caesar and Emperor. Bede does not write who Helena was, perhaps because he thought her too well known and he did not go into details. However, the American medievalist R.S. Loomis is convinced that this Helena, the mother of Constantine, was also the model for Elen in *The Dream of Macsen*. It may be worthwhile, therefore, to study her more closely.

The British Helena

It seems that this British princess was born in the middle of the third century. "She was the queen," writes Geoffrey of Monmouth, "and she held this dignity by way of heredity from her father which nobody can deny." And he continues: "After her marriage with Constantius she had a son named Constantine."[10]

Historians have doubted both these statements, but a trustworthy witness for Helena's royalty is the chronicler Simon of Durham, who affirms that she was the mother of Constantine and that she built the first walls of London "in the year of our Lord 306."[11] And as we have seen, a network of roads are also said to have been built by her.

According to Constantine's biographer Eusebius, she was a strong Celtic queen in the vein of Boudicca. This is not to say that her character was above reproach and free of negative traits. On the contrary: in the great power games at the imperial court she appears not only as a woman of strength and circumspection, but also of the most ruthless ambition. This ambition was concentrated on her son Constantine I and her grandson Constantine II. She was the power behind the throne of these two British Emperors and it was because of her that Britain, up to then an unimportant colony, for one glorious moment came to occupy centre stage in Roman history.

Helena must have been a strong influence on Constantius, the father of her son, although it is not known whether he had actually married her. He was a career soldier coming up from the ranks, and was married to Theodora, daughter of the Emperor Maximian, who bore him several children. He may have seen political advantages in a liaison with the British princess, the legitimate heiress to the throne. Rome and Theodora were far away, and it appears that Helena was politically active for him, while having the wellbeing of Britain at heart. The fact that Constantine was elected Emperor at his father's death was certainly due to her influence, in detriment to the rights of Theodora's children, who were after all the grandchildren of Maximian, co-Emperor of Diocletian.

It is also of interest that she could educate her son in Britain and in the Christian faith, in spite of the persecution Christians suffered at that time. This indicates that she was no mere courtesan, as Romans used to separate bastards of high ranking men from their mothers and have them educated at Rome.[12] It must be said, however, that neither Helena nor her son was as pious as legend has it. Their canonization was largely due to their politics, which favoured Christianity: Constantine made Christianity the state religion and commissioned his mother to travel to Jerusalem with a Roman contingent in order to find the Holy Sepulchre and the "true Cross" of Christ. But in spite of her competence in politics and in pseudo-archaeology, Helena's reputation among historians is tarnished. When a plot against Constantine was hatched in Rome she saw to it that it was put down with the utmost cruelty. According to Eusebius she committed horrendous atrocities in order to save the throne for her son. One of her victims was her unfortunate daughter-in-law Fausta. Helena had engineered her marriage to Constantine in order to secure his succession to the imperial throne. Yet when Fausta was of no further use to her son, she had her accused of adultery and condemned to be boiled alive. It was the first time in history that an Emperor had signed a death warrant for his spouse and it set an unfortunate precedent.[13]

What do we know about the beginnings of Christianity in Britain? According to legend it had been King Coel's ancestor, king Arviragus who had given land to the Apostle Philip and to Joseph of Arimathea at Glastonbury for the founding of the Christian Church in Britain, and he had himself buried there. It is generally accepted that there was a Christian community in Britain long before the Gospel had spread to other parts of Europe. Therefore Helena too may have been Christian before Christianity was proclaimed the state religion by her son and she must have educated her son in the Christian faith, long before he had the famous vision of the cross at the Milvean Bridge in the night before the decisive battle against Maxentius in 312. In fact his father Constantius had been reprimanded by Emperor Diocletian for his laxity in the persecution of Christians in Britain, and we may speculate that this laxity was due to Helena's influence. Yet all we hear about the politics of mother and son has everything to do with power, and nothing with the Christian spirit of love and compassion.

In the wake of Celtic tradition the first Christian Emperor was very much under the influence of his mother, insisting on her title "Augusta," putting armies under her command and having coins struck with her image. He even founded a city, Helenopolis in her honour. On the other hand, by establishing a politically powerful Christian Church, both mother and son paved the way for the outrageous misogyny of the Church Fathers, causing centuries of persecution, vilification and enslavement of women, not to mention the spiritual stagnation later Church leaders inflicted on the West.

Welsh origins of the story

It goes without saying that the Welsh storyteller is unaware of these connections and of the historic irony of his tale: by making the princess Elen into a dream vision of Lady Sovereignty he deified the very monarch whose influence ended the freedom and integrity of women, the woman whose influence may have facilitated the closure of the great Mystery centres and of the Graeco-Roman universities of the time. Perhaps Helena was even behind the persecution of the Druids.

As mentioned before, the source material about Constantine

and Helena was taken up by Geoffrey of Monmouth and integrated into his *History of British Kings,* which was completed around 1136. Written in Latin this work was repeatedly translated into medieval Welsh. The earliest of these translations dates from the early thirteenth century and is known under the title *The Dingestow Brut.* Here is a summary:

> When King Coel of Britain died, (the Roman Governor) Constantius assumed the crown, married his daughter Helen Luydanc (Helen of the Hosts) and begat a son from her who was called Custennyn (Constantine). Custennyn followed his father on the throne, but he left Britain and conquered the Roman Empire from a tyrant by the name of Maxen. While he was absent from Britain, Eudaf, Count of Ergyr and Ewias (Herefordshire) took the sceptre of Britain. When he [Eudaf] was old, he sent an envoy to Maxen (Macsen Wledig), a cousin of Helen Luydanc, in Rome asking him to come and marry his daughter (also called Helen) and succeed him on the throne. Macsen Wledig came to Britain with a great fleet, met Eudaf in London, married his daughter and was crowned with the crown of Britain.
>
> Eudaf's nephew Kynan Meiriadauc had been hoping for the crown and rebelled against Macsen. He was beaten in several battles and made peace with Macsen. Five years later Macsen went to Brittany, conquered this country and invested Kynan with it. Then he vanquished the Emperor Gratianus.[14]

If this text sounds rather legendary, it nevertheless clearly distinguishes the tyrant Maxentius, whom Constantine vanquished, from Maximinianus, the Roman senator who came to Britain to marry the daughter of Eudaf (Octavianus). We note in passing that the marriage of the king's daughter becomes the *sine qua non* for the succession to the throne.

The *Dingestow Brut* was known to the author of the story in the *Mabinogion* and served as his template for the dream story. The two protagonists are first quoted in a manuscript by Nennius, which contains several genealogies of the tenth century. Two of these name the "true" Maxim Guletic with the addition: *Qui occidit Gratianum, regem Romanorum,* who killed Gratianus, the King of the Romans. So Maxim Guletic was the Emperor elected by his legions, who led them out of Segontium to Gaul, marched on Rome, but was beaten, imprisoned and executed. But the first of the family trees ends with Constantine the Great and Helen Luydanc, *qui de Britannia excivit ad crucem Christi querendam usque at Jerusalem,* who left Britain to search for the cross of Christ (and went) as far as Jerusalem.[15]

In these old family trees we sense the desire of the Welsh princes to deduce their origins from the powerful Roman generals who built the fortress Segontium (Aber Seint). And it is in these same manuscripts that we read for the first time the proud title "Helen Luydanc," Helen of the Hosts.

It seems that the old chroniclers were very much aware what the myth of Lady Sovereignty would mean in connection with the Roman Empire when they wrote:

> *Constantinus misit suam matrem, Helena, cum magno exercitu*
> *Ut exquirerat sanctum lignum crucis Domini.*
> Constantine sent his mother Helena with a great host
> to find the wood of the holy Cross of the Lord.[16]

When Maximus withdrew the last Roman garrison from Segontium in AD 383, the legions marched south between Carmarthen and Caerleon on the same road which even today is called *Sarn Elen,* Elen's Highway.[17]

The coins which Constantine had struck with the effigy of his mother, her title "Augusta," the troops he put under her orders, her legendary activities as builder of London's walls and roads in the west of Britain, all these vague memories coalesce to a fantasy which do not represent the dreams of a Roman Emperor, but rather those of a disenfranchized and powerless nation.

The scenes in the story which are set at Rome betray the childlike naïvety of an author who was obviously never there. They read like the description of a big city by a country boy who had never seen it. Similarly the author had no idea about the realities of battles fought in Roman times, nor did he want to know about them. R.S. Loomis describes the author's mind very clearly in these terms:

> Not greed or hunger for power motivates the Emperor to seek his British bride, only the dream of a beautiful woman fills him with burning passion. He finds her ... not in London, but beyond the mountains in Snowdonia, at a magnificent place at the shore of the River Seint. Thus evolved a new legend about the old Roman Fortress Segontium.[18]

The story of Macsen Wledig and the princess Elen is of disarming naïvety and this is the reason for its effectiveness even today. Seven hundred years after the end of Roman rule in Britain an author describes a British princess who is more powerful than the Emperor, who cannot live without her. For the love of her he is prepared to leave the Eternal City and to live with her in the wilderness of Snowdonia. Yet the ancient belief in the power of the maternal soil is especially mentioned: "And soil from Rome was brought there, so that it might be healthier for the Emperor to sleep and sit and move about."[19] Elen herself is unmistakably identified with British soil:

> Thereafter Elen thought to make high roads from one stronghold to the other across the Island of Britain. And the roads were made. And for that reason they are called the roads of Elen of the Hosts, because she was sprung from the Island of Britain, and the men of the Island of Britain would not have made those great hostings for any save for her.[20]

Clearly, the idea of Lady Sovereignty underlies this formulation. In Latin terms she is the "woman of destiny" who, though in the wilderness, has power to provide for the Emperor everything that made Rome great in the eyes of the contemporaries: city walls, military roads, and, last not least, a military force superior to the Roman legions. When Macsen loses his empire because of her, she accompanies him on his campaign like the best of Roman empresses, and with "her brothers" and "her Britons" she succeeds in reconquering the city for him.

The author describes a mythical dream world, romanticized beyond belief, but entirely Celtic in imagery and style. In contrast to *The Dream of Rhonabwy,* which describes an unbearably depressing environment, this dream describes a world of pure beauty, in which a divine woman takes centre stage. It is a "true dream" in the sense that the dreamer cannot escape its message and is driven to follow it, if his life is to be worthwhile. This also is a Celtic motif. We find it in the Irish saga of *The Dream of Oengus,* a story dating from the eighth century.[21] Just as Oengus, the Irish god of Love was the rejuvenated self of the Dagda so we can see in Macsen Wledig the personification of the ideal ruler according to the Celtic imagination: "He was the handsomest and the wisest of men, and the best fitted to be Emperor of all that had gone before him."[22]

A Celtic queen who is also Empress of Rome (and hence a goddess), whose name is Helena and whose brothers serve as her Dioscuri is an extraordinary phenomenon. As a woman of enormous energy and political astuteness, Elen brings to her husband a kingdom as her dowry. She establishes him again as ruler of Rome without ever hurting his male ego. Her two brothers reconquer Rome and the Empire for him, without ever fomenting rebellion. Elen with her brothers Kynan and Avaon thus form a mythical triad. Only towards the end of the story does the author permit us a glance behind the illusion: Kynan and Avaon reconquer Brittany for Macsen, and with truly biblical fervour all the men of the conquered country are slaughtered. "And they determined to cut out the tongues of the women, lest their language be corrupted."[23] This then is the reverse of the Celto-Roman glory, the dark side of the historic Helena. Or is it just one of those jokes about talkative women? The misogyny of the Christian Middle Ages has started — in spite (or because?) of the dream wife.

Perhaps Macsen represents the last vision of a matriarchal prince, ably assisted by a strong empress. Here the Goddess

Sovereignty seems to have merged with the memory of the world power that was Rome and of Helena Augusta, mother of the only Briton on the imperial throne. Constantine had told his chronicler Eusebius: "My beginning was in Britain!" At that time this was a proud confession. It said: "I come from a country which Rome calls barbaric. My father was Roman, but my mother was a British queen, and hence his equal."

This is how Geoffrey tells it:

> After King Coel's death Constantius seized the royal crown and married Coel's daughter. Her name was Helen and her beauty was greater than that of any other young woman in the kingdom.
>
> ...Her father had no other child to inherit the throne, and he had therefore done all in his power to give Helen the kind of training which would enable her to rule the country more efficiently after his death. After her marriage with Constantius she had by him a son called Constantine.[24]

With this statement Geoffrey reveals a royal rule which seems to have been forgotten by later monarchs: in British dynasties, princesses were educated to be rulers and not degraded to incubators for male heirs.

The author of *The Dream of Macsen Wledig* adheres to the same ideal. The British queen Helena Augusta, who led a Roman legion to Rome and on to Jerusalem was the woman who inspired him, and not Helena, the legendary saint. He did not care that she had discovered the "true Cross." She had built fortresses, roads and city walls; she had led Roman legions, and reconquered Rome and Empire for the Emperor! And that she had appeared to the ruler in a dream to call him to Aber Seint, this was the irrefutable proof that she was the Goddess, that she was Lady Sovereignty.

CHAPTER 10

Three Romances

The original meaning of the word *romance* signified a story told in the "romance language," the language of the troubadours in medieval France, Spain or Italy. They celebrate the valorous and amorous adventures of knights and ladies and the values of medieval *prouesse* and *courtoisie.* If we adhere to this definition, then P.K. Ford is right in omitting them from his *Mabinogion* translation. He writes:

> The three Arthurian romances, usually grouped with the *mabinogi* ... are excellent examples of medieval Welsh storytelling, but whatever their mythological underpinnings, they are undeniably romances.[1]

Yet as we shall see, it was the "mythological underpinnings" of the Welsh "romances" which gave them their depth and complexity.

What was it that inspired the best of French and German court poets to chose these stories for their own creative efforts? All three stories were translated and richly embroidered by that urbane author Chrétien de Troyes, court poet of the Countess Marie de Champagne and protégé of Duke Philippe of Flanders. In French the court epics taken from Welsh origins in Chrétien's work are entitled *Erec et Enide* (1170), *Yvain* (1177) and *Li Conte du Graal,* sometimes called *Perceval li Galois* (1182), the latter work remaining unfinished. These are precisely the stories we find in the *Mabinogion* under the collective title *Three Romances.*

They are: *Gereint Son of Erbin, The Lady of the Fountain,* and *Peredur Son of Efrawg.*

Chrétien's work was widely admired and court poets all over Europe translated it for their own patrons. In Germany, the Swabian Hartmann von Aue wrote his *Erek* and his *Ywein,* whilst the Bavarian Wolfram von Eschenbach recreated Chrétien's Grail story *Perceval,* as *Parzival,* the first German *Bildungsroman.* Compared with the work of Chrétien, Hartmann and Wolfram, the Welsh versions can seem naïve and archaic. Scholars long believed that they were translations from French and only after long dispute did they agree that the three stories are much older than the French versions, going back to a common source "X" which must be sought in Britain. "Source X" became a convenient cipher for story material contained in the so called "Matter of Britain" that must have once existed, but is now irretrievably lost.

To understand the basic structure of the *Three Romances* we must remember that they are not simple love stories. Originally they functioned as tales describing the duties of the chosen hero towards Lady Sovereignty and the consequences if those duties were neglected. In all three stories the relationship between the goddess and her earthly champion has been disturbed or forgotten.

In the eleventh and twelfth centuries when the stories were recreated, the Sovereignty of Wales was threatened from all sides by Gaels, Picts, Saxons and Normans. But the chosen hero had forgotten his duty or was never told about it, owing to the change from goddess religion to Christianity. Thus the hero had broken his promise to serve her and/or had neglected his cosmological task. The goddess and her hero had become redundant. Educated under patriarchy, the young champion is no longer initiated into his cosmic role and instructed in his duties. Unaware of their importance he ignores them. Instead of serving the Goddess of the Land in a sacred union, his relationship to her becomes a superficial love affair, an adventure, which may or may not end in the safety of a conventional marriage.

The importance of the relationship of the goddess and her champion in the old religion was first explored by the English scholar Jessie Weston in her book *From Ritual to Romance.*[2] Weston based her findings on folklore in formerly Celtic countries and her results were not accepted. In more recent years Glenys Goetinck has written a study on Peredur and reached the same conclusions as Weston, but with deeper insights.[3] Both authors agree that the *Three Romances* are centred around the goddess who manifests as a "lady in distress" or, in the case of Enid, as an ill-treated spouse. Yet it is possible to show that she is still Lady Sovereignty, identified with the land and its supreme mistress.

Like the *Four Branches* the telling of these three stories had originally been the prerogative of the bards, and they were used for the instruction of young princes and chieftains. When the great families of Wales had died out through never-ending warfare the bards lost their patrons. "Mere storytellers" appropriated their repertoire. This was hard for the bards, who had always looked down on the storytellers and had taunted them for their illiteracy and lack of education. Now both classes had to look for new patrons. They found them at the courts of the European continent.

The twelfth and thirteenth centuries were the golden age of the European court epic. This was the time when Europe awoke from the Dark Ages. The Angevin Empire under Henry II and Eleanor of Aquitaine reached from Scotland to the Mediterranean, that of the German Hohenstaufen emperors from the North Sea to Sicily. The contact with the Arab world during the Crusades, the poetry of the troubadours, the splendour of the great Courts and developing economic network, facilitated all branches of cultural endeavour. The courts of Central and Western Europe flourished. They all welcomed poets and had an insatiable appetite for adventure stories from strange lands. The so-called Matter of Britain, compiled by storytellers from Wales, Brittany and to some extent from Cornwall, was much in demand. Apart from the Arthurian cycles it contained the last remnants of the rich oral literature of the Insular Celts together with the pagan themes of the Lady Sovereignty and her hero. However, as the mythological content of the stories was no longer understood, they were combined with Christian themes (such as, in the legend of the Holy Grail, the dish used at the Last Supper) and adapted to the social problems of the time.

What interests us here is the relationship of the three Welsh Romances *The Lady of the Fountain, Peredur Son of Efrawg* and *Gereint Son of Erbin* with the same stories by Chrétien de Troyes and his German translators.

As it happened, Wales and later Brittany were annexed by their stronger neighbours. Welsh and Breton became despised languages, but their literature was appropriated by the conquerors. Because these tales are more naïve and archaic than their French counterparts, scholars long believed that they were debased versions of Chrétien's epics. In the Middle Ages, Wales was seen as a backward country, the Welsh language unintelligible to a society that conversed in French or Latin, and until very recently the *Three Romances* were regarded as poor imitations of Chrétien's work, and reminiscent of the *chansons de geste.* French scholars in particular approached these texts with unequalled snobbery. One modern critic went so far as to write that social conventions, such as washing the hands before meals had been introduced to Wales by the Normans.

Yet the French and German versions of *Yvain, Perceval* and *Erec* are all built upon Celtic mythological structures. Their Welsh origins should have been clear from the fact that the heroes of all three tales are either historic British characters or, as in the case of Gereint (Chrétien s *Erec)* are first mentioned in the Arthurian cycles. This does not mean that they were Arthur's contemporaries as the stories imply. Owain and Peredur hail from the most distant parts of Britain, from "the old North" where the goddess religion had lasted longest and the fight against the Saxon invaders had been fiercest. Both heroes may have been chosen in the hope that they may inspire the Welsh people to rally round the battle leaders and defend the land against the new invaders. Wales found itself in a precarious situation and the heroic service to Lady Sovereignty needed to be given new impetus.

By contrast the French versions of the three stories were probably commissioned by the Countess Marie de Champagne, daughter of Eleanor of Aquitaine, and served quite different political ends. After Eleanor's marriage to Louis VII of France was dissolved, she had married Geoffrey of Anjou, later King Henry II of England, and their united dominions reached from Scotland to the Mediterranean. This vast territory contained many different nationalities, yet most of her subjects were proud to be of Celtic or Celto-Roman origin, "and not Franks" as Eleanor was at pains to point out to Emperor Manuel of Byzantium, while accompanying her first husband, Louis VII, on his ill-fated crusade.

It seems that Chrétien's story of *Yvain* (in Welsh *The Lady of the Fountain)* had been commissioned to justify Eleanor's hurried remarriage after her divorce. On the journey from the court of Louis VII to her own capital Poitiers, her train was ambushed twice by ambitious young princes who wanted to marry her by force to gain possession of her domains. One of the aggressors was Geoffrey of Anjou, later to be her second husband and king of England.[4]

It is said that Eleanor presided at so called "love courts," where she acted as arbiter over the right behaviour of a knight towards his lady, and it appears that Chrétien's romances were part of her cultural policy, just like the book *About Love* by Chaplain Andreas (1170–1228).[5] Moreover, a woman of the calibre of Eleanor still realised the importance of ancient rituals for the masses of the people. Why else would she have included a symbolic marriage ceremony between her son Richard the Lionheart and St Valerie, patroness of the country, at his investiture as duke of Aquitaine?

The survival of the Goddess

We have seen that Church persecution had never been as severe in Britain as on the European continent. Consequently the pagan deities were never demonized into devils and witches as happened on the continent, especially under the Frankish Emperor Louis I (814–840).

Regardless of persecution, the old beliefs had not died out in early medieval times. Among the common people they had survived in the form of superstitions and the belief in elementals. In her valuable study of fairy belief, the French scholar Laurence Harf-Lancner writes:

> From the seventh to the twelfth century we find almost no mention [about fairies]. The most important source [of the fairy faith] is found around the year 1000 in the *Decretum* of Bishop Burchard of Worms. Book X, *De Incantatoribus et Auguris* and Book XIX *De Poenitentia* contain long lists of surviving pagan customs in the feudal age.[6]

The *Decretum* speaks of a belief in nocturnal witches' rides with Diana and Herodias, of tree and stone cults, of sacrifices to pagan deities, of magic and divination. All this seems to have been still very much alive at the beginning of the second millennium. Burchard was especially incensed about certain "supernatural women" whom he calls *parcae et sylvaticae,* that is "fairies and wild women of the woods." Harf-Lancner avoids calling these personages "former goddesses," but speaks about the formation of a "new mythological presence" which she analyses and separates into "positive and negative fairies." Positive fairies help a knight and reward him if he is obedient to them; negative fairies are those who punish him or keep him captive if he should oppose them or deny them his love.

Harf-Lancner's study is valuable and richly documented, but ignores the mythological structure of the goddess and her hero, from which fairies are derived. We have seen that J.J. Hatt rediscovered this structure through comparative archaeology, and Celtic scholars found it by comparing Irish and Welsh sagas.[7] The very idea of "negative fairies" points to the relentless persecution of pagan customs on the European continent, creating a fundamental difference between the preservation of pre-Christian relics there in comparison with the British Isles.

We notice the difference if we compare the story of the Scottish minstrel Thomas of Erceldoune (Thomas the Rhymer 1220?–1307) with that of the German *Minnesinger* Tannhäuser. While Thomas's sojourn with the Fairy Queen brought him eternal fame, Tannhäuser's love for Lady Venus in the Hoerselberg is punished by exile from court and eternal damnation. Assuming that the Fairy Queen and "Lady Venus" are the same otherworldly woman, we may ask why she is called "Lady Venus" in Germany, particularly when she dwells in a subterranean realm called "Hoerselberg" (Horse Mountain). The phonetically similar names of "Hoersel" or "Roessel" are both diminutives of the German word for "horse" and would point to the Celtic horse goddess Epona/Rhiannon, who had many sanctuaries along the Rhine and in the south west of Germany. By contrast the names Venus, Diana or Herodias were only known to the clergy, indicating that the fight against goddess worship was initiated by the Church authorities.

In Germany (which until 1648 included also Austria, Switzerland, Bohemia and the Netherlands) Pope and Emperor were agreed that the "old religion" could only be eradicated by mutual cooperation. Therefore German court poets feared to compose stories about mysterious women who owned magic fountains and controlled the weather. No matter how rich German folklore is in stories about fairies, elves, nymphs and other elementals, for sociopolitical reasons they never appear in court poetry.

Medieval England, Wales and Scotland lived in a cultural climate which facilitated a return to belief in the goddess. But she had changed. Now she appeared as "fairy," a word derived from French *fée,* Latin *fata.* In German-speaking countries the term was unknown, but the concept of otherworldly women was alive and well. In south and west Germany, the supernatural woman was called *Frau Saelde,* or *Frau Perchta.* Feared and revered by the common people, she came to their help or punished evildoers.

In keeping with the triple nature of the goddess, supernatural women often appeared in triplicate or even as three times three like the Muses. They were called *Salige Fraeulein, die Saligen,* meaning "Blessed Ladies." The Church was forced to tolerate the cult of the *Drei Bethen* or "Three holy Virgins" (Aubet, Cubet and Quere), and the equally legendary saints Catherine, Barbara and Margaret had their place in every church. None of these saintly women can be traced historically, but their cult was too popular for the Church to intervene. St Ursula, according to legend a British princess who was martyred by the Huns, was always suspect because her name connects her either with a bear goddess or with a horse goddess. Yet she was immensely popular and her cult inspired some of the most beautiful paintings in Gothic and Renaissance art.

Writing in 1866, the British clergyman Sabine Baring-Gould was particularly incensed by Ursula's survival as saint:

> Ursula is in fact none other than the Swabian goddess Ursel, Hoersel or Huersl to whom human sacrifices were occasionally made and who became the Venus of the Venusberg or Huerselberg, who entranced and debauched Tannhäuser.[8]

Generally speaking goddess worship in German countries suffered much greater repression than in Britain or France and this had its repercussions in medieval court epics. Other reasons for the changes in courtly literature were of an economic nature.

The economic problems of young aristocrats

To win in a joust or to be victorious on the battlefield is one thing; to be able to make a modest living is quite another. We read about the economic difficulties of young aristocrats in Stephen Knight's *Arthurian Literature and Society.*[9] In the patriarchal society of the Middle Ages, the dynamism of "Lady Sovereignty and her champion" suffers an inversion by the new law of primogeniture which had been introduced on the recommendation of the Church. While keeping landed property firmly together in the hands of noble families, the new law of inheritance left younger sons unprovided and in great economic difficulties. These young men had little chance of a future. All they had learned was to sit a horse and to fight. Their "knightly honour" forbade them to ply a trade or to start a business. The nobility lived off the produce of their fiefs, but these young men had no land and no chance to acquire any. As "knights errant" they could hire themselves out to a warlord or they could become clergymen, a career which most of them despised. The third possibility was to defend a noble widow or orphan maiden in distress, to risk life and limb on her behalf, then to acquire her land by marrying her. This was the dream of most landless young aristocrats, and therefore the favourite plot of romances. Unfortunately in real life there were not enough maidens in distress to save from dragons and ogres.

In reality, young women were often worse off, as Chrétien reveals with biting criticism. In his *Erec and Enide* we read how Enide's uncle thanks Erec profusely for deigning to marry his niece without a dowry.[10] In the episode of *Pesme Avanture* in Chrétien's *Yvain* story we hear about a count who keeps young women without dowry.

The Lady of the Fountain

First a short summary of the story in the *Mabinogion*:

The knight Owain leaves King Arthur's court in search of adventure. He has heard about a rain-making fountain which is guarded by a powerful knight.

He finds the place, activates the fountain by pouring water over it and so creates a terrible storm. The defender of the fountain arrives and challenges him, but Owain succeeds in wounding him seriously. The knight flees towards his castle with Owain in pursuit. They both make it over the drawbridge, but the portcullis falls down on Owain's horse, cutting it in two and Owain remains a prisoner, while the defender of the fountain dies of his wounds. The maiden Luned[11] arrives and recognizes him for a knight who once did her some kindness. She gives him a ring to make him invisible, which saves him from the men out to catch him. Through a window he sees the mourning countess, the Lady of the Fountain, and falls in love with her. Luned promises to recommend him to her lady, which she does. She explains to her that the fountain needs a new defender and nobody is better suited for the office than the man who overcame her husband. The lady reluctantly agrees and after some hesitation marries Owain.

After three years king Arthur arrives with all his knights and there is a great celebration. Gwalchmei/Gawain is able to convince Owain that he should come back to Arthur's court and find new adventures. The countess gives him three months' leave, but Owain remains with Arthur for three years. Then Luned arrives at Arthur's court and accuses him of unfaithfulness. Owain is overcome with guilt and seized with madness. He leaves Arthur's court and wanders through the forest, living like an animal.

A widowed countess finds him naked and unconscious. She heals him and invites him to stay with her. Owain rids her of her enemies, then leaves on a new journey of adventure. Wherever he goes he helps women in distress and rights wrongs. He also acquires a lion which comes to his aid in many a fight. At last his estranged wife accepts him again as her husband and he returns with her to Arthur's court.

In Britain the memory of the goddess seems to have been still alive in the eleventh and twelfth century, and mere allusions sufficed for audiences to understand the storyteller's meaning. In the Welsh version the name of the Lady of the Fountain is never mentioned. In his version, Chrétien de Troyes calls her Laudine, a name which has been connected with the fairy Undine or with King Loth of Lothian, the Orkney Islands. Gwyn Jones, the translator of the *Mabinogi,* and the Welsh scholar Glyn Ashton, knew that her name was Lleudine. *Lleu* connects with *lleuad,* "moonlight"; and *dine* with *dinas,* "castle": therefore her name would be "Moon Castle." We have already met with a similar name in connection with Arianrhod. In Lewis Spence's *Mysteries of Britain* we find the name *Caer Wen Glaer,* which translates as "Sanctuary of the Shining White Lady."[12] This was the place of bardic initiation in the wilderness of Eryri, Snowdonia, where Hywel, Prince of North Wales sought initiation in AD 1171. We may conclude that the rain-making fountain which the Lady Lleudine controlled was a sacred place, forbidden to the profane. Owain's seeking it out "just for adventure" was blasphemy and would have deserved punishment. Instead, in reading Chrétien's *Yvain* we are confronted with a series of monologues intended to explain and excuse Laudine's love for her husband's killer and much psychological introspection on

Yvain's side, betraying total ignorance of the story's mythological background.

We are spared all this in the Welsh version. Instead Luned, the countess's maid and confidante, convinces her mistress of the dire necessity for a new defender of the fountain. The countess understands that her marriage to Owain is not an *affaire de coeur,* but necessary for the protection of the fountain and therefore a duty. The only hint that the story takes place in the Christian Middle Ages is the fact that the countess "brought bishops and archbishops to solemnize the marriage,"[13] perhaps a humorous overstatement to conceal the pagan background and to poke fun at the Church's nuptial requirements.

Chrétien gave his story the subtitle *Le chevalier au lion* — the Knight of the Lion — unaware of the fact that Owain wears a golden lion as a badge on his coat long before he helps the lion in his combat against a serpent (a mythological motif with wide ramifications), and so acquires him as a companion. The lion badge identifies him from the start as a sun hero and hence a servant of the goddess. When he is seized by the *geilt,* the guilt madness so often experienced by Celtic heroes, he is healed by another countess, who remains nameless in the Welsh version. Chrétien introduces her as *la dame de Noroisons,* the Lady of the Black Birds, that is, the ravens. She is therefore Morgaine la Faye (Morgan le Fay), wife of the king of Lothian. An ambivalent figure, she was known as a sorceress and Arthur's half sister who seduced him and bore him Mordred. Through other stories, and through Geoffrey of Monmouth, we know that she was also Owain's mother, which makes him Arthur's nephew. Curiously, her divine status as the battle goddess Morrigan in Ireland was quite unknown in Wales.

As the Welsh narrator reveals at the end of his story, Owain owns a flock of ravens, which are his totem birds. Again, in *The Dream of Rhonabwy,* we read that Owain and King Arthur play a board game, while messengers arrive who tell of a battle raging between Arthur's men and Owain's ravens, in which the ravens carry the victory. This battle of the ravens indicates that Owain's relationship with Arthur was not always smooth and that he may on occasion have shared his mother's hostility against

Arthur. This is another sign that Arthur occupies a pivotal position in the fight against the goddess, a fact which is particularly obvious in Arthur's elimination of the Welsh Amazonian "witches."

As Morgaine's son, Owain has hero status by birth and his victory over the defender of the fountain seems preordained. His failure to return to Lleudine at the end of his furlough is therefore all the more inexcusable. Even more unpardonable is the use he makes of his new power position as Lleudine's husband and defender of the fountain. In the Welsh version we find the following paragraph:

> And Owain kept the fountain with spear and sword. This is how he kept it: whatever knight came there, Owain would overthrow them and hold them to ransom for their full worth; and that wealth Owain distributed amongst his barons and knights, so that his dominions had not love for a man in the whole world greater than their love for him. And three years he was thus.[14]

This form of ransom taking says much about the moral attitudes of the Middle Ages: the former hero of the goddess glories in his new status as robber baron. We may be prepared to excuse this behaviour with the poverty of Wales, but historians assure us that this was the accepted *modus vivendi* and so we resign ourselves to lose another illusion about noble knighthood.

The urbane Chrétien de Troyes knows nothing about such abuses. Instead he expresses his moral criticism with cool irony:

> So my lord Yvain is master now, and the dead man is quite forgot. He who killed him is now married to his wife, and they enjoy the marriage rights.[15]

The same marriage rights incidentally, of which Marie de Champagne wrote that they can never express the true love a knight and his lady feel for each other.[16] Again, according to Chrétien, Yvain blackmails Laudine to forgive him by shamefully misusing the weather working fountain:

> So he thought that he would go away from the court alone, and would cause such a storm of wind and rain that she would be compelled perforce to make peace with him; otherwise there would be no end to the disturbance of the spring, and to the rain and wind.[17]

In the Welsh story the author is satisfied to bring his hero and the countess back to King Arthur's court and from there to the land of his fathers and his Flight of Ravens: "And wherever Owain went, and they with him, he would be victorious."

Chrétien presents his Yvain as the exemplar of knighthood, a model for every aspiring knight. He is so successful that as well as figuring in Hartmann von Aue's German epic, Owain also appears in a Middle English ballad entitled *Owain Miles*.[18] Here the hero is subjected to a mystical initiation, complete with spiritual purification, fasting and a descent into the Underworld, whence like Dante, he reaches Paradise and after the three canonical days returns to Earth amidst the sounds of trumpets and cymbals, a perfected *miles Christi* or "warrior for Christ." Here the goddess has been made redundant because St Owain lives a life of monastic celibacy just like the Knights Templar.

Peredur of York

In no other court epic is the difference between Welsh, French and Middle High German versions more pronounced than in the story of *Peredur of Efrawg* (Peredur of York). Chrétien used the story to create his *Perceval li Galois* (begun in 1190) but died before he could finish it. His story ends in the middle of the Grail procession and we shall never know how he intended to resolve the Grail mystery. Wolfram von Eschenbach's *Parzival* (composed between 1195 and 1217) has been called "the first German *Bildungsroman*," a knight's development from youthful naïvety to mature manhood.

It seems that the Welsh author had similar intentions. Yet his hero's task is not so much about the achievement of perfect knighthood as about the duty of family vendetta and, more importantly, of redeeming his country from the Waste Land spell. Both tasks have fallen to him as the last surviving scion of the royal family of North Wales. If he can achieve them his country will be freed from foreign oppression, healed from all its woes and he will be able to celebrate the Sacred Marriage with Lady Sovereignty according to ancient Celtic myth. Yet a superficial reading of Peredur's adventures will not reveal these intentions. To understand the Welsh version of the story three things are necessary:

— a good grasp of the mythological symbolism of the episodes;
— an understanding of the political situation of Wales in the twelfth century;
— some knowledge of the initiatory tests a hero had to pass on his journey to the Otherworld, remembering that many of them are inner experiences and must be read as such.

Patience and tolerance for some chaotic writing will also help.

According to W.J. Gruffydd the name "Peredur" is a phonetic variation of "Pryderi," Rhiannon's son.[19] He also tells us that Pryderi's childhood name was "Gwri Goldenhair." But Gwri was the prototype of the Hero Gwalchmei/Gawain.[20] Peredur/Pryderi and Gwalchmei/Gawain are the two heroes of which Graves writes that they were inseparable friends, because they were succeeding each other to a sacrificial death at the end of the year. This at any rate would have been their destiny in pre-Christian times. It may also be the reason why the two heroes seem inseparable and leave the stage together at the end of the story.

The historical Peredur was the youngest of the seven sons of Eliffer, a tribal chieftain of North Britain. According to the *Annales Cambriae* he died *c.* AD 580. In the *Black Book of Carmarthen (c.* 1150) R.M. Williams found the following record: "The Grave of Mor, the magnificent and brave lord, son of Peredur Penweddig."[21] The title *Penweddig* means literally "Head Healer" or "Head of Healers" or possibly even "Healing Head." In Mary Williams' opinion this appellation of Peredur's refers to the healing of the Fisher King. But according to I.L. Foster it refers to his native district in North Cardigan, which is called "Penweddig."

If we consider how many riddles and innuendoes are contained in Celtic narratives it may be permitted to connect this name with the main motif of the story, namely "the severed head on the salver" which in this version is carried through the hall in place of the Grail. In any case "Head of Healers" and "Healing Head" have a common denominator in the verb "to heal," no matter whether the healing concerns actual wounds and ailments of the body or political and social ills. Perhaps Peredur's family was connected with a healing cult through a healing spring or rock, or perhaps as "the seventh son of a seventh son" he inherited a paranormal gift of healing.[22]

Peredur hailed from the mountain region of Snowdonia in the North of Wales and mountain dwellers are thought to be faithful to their traditions but "a bit slow on the uptake." This may be the reason why Perceval/Parzival (but not Peredur) is described as naïve, ignorant and foolish in the Continental versions. This is not the case in Britain: in his *Vita Merlini* Geoffrey of Monmouth gives Peredur his proper title: He is *dux Venedotorum,* Duke of Gwynedd, that is to say an important Welsh prince.

Loomis summarizes the history as follows:

> The semi-mythical Pryderi, Prince of South Wales was the original protagonist of the saga, including the dangerous mountain (Arberth) the Waste Land and the castle with the cup on the golden chain. The saga also contains motifs of the Irish cycles of Cuchulainn and Finn. Because of the phonetic similarity of the names, the saga of Pryderi became mixed with the (pseudo-) historic tradition of Peredur, Prince of North Britain. The new story which now only referred to Peredur, was taken to France by Breton *conteurs,* where it became known as the novel of Perceval. One version of the French saga was taken back to Wales, where a Welsh storyteller referred it back to the original historic hero and gave it the title *Peredur of Efrawg.*[23]

In the Welsh story we read that Peredur's father "had lost his possessions, his sons and finally his life through combats, tournaments and wars. And as often befalls him who follows the wars, he was slain, both he and his six sons." His wife, a sensible woman, thought to save her youngest son from the same destiny and fled with him into the wilderness.

> Never a one took she in her company save women and boys, and meek contented folk who were incapable of combat and wars and for whom such would be unseemly. Never a one would dare mention steeds or arms in a place where her son might overhear, lest he set his heart upon them.[24]

The name of this wise mother is not mentioned, but if we can trust Loomis, she is no other than Rhiannon, although the description of her character is much better suited to Parzival's mother, whom Wolfram has fittingly called Herzeloyde ("Heart's Sorrow"). She is but one of the many mothers who grieve for her sons and husbands.

As to the identity of Peredur's father, Hélaine Newstead has proved that his prototype is Bran, the British God of the Head.[25] One of the reasons for this theory is the fact that Peredur's father (whom Chrétien calls Bans or Brans de Gamoret), as well as Bran the Blessed are constantly mentioned in connection with the Waste Land motif. Admittedly, Peredur/Perceval is first of all the "son of the mother." But if anyone is a suitable candidate for his father it would be "the maimed king," the king who was wounded by a poisoned spear and is forever hovering between life and death. Such a figure is Bran, the God of the Head, whom we have met in the *Second Branch of the Mabinogi.* It is Bran's Head which presides at the feast of his warriors, and in the story of Peredur a severed head is carried through the banquet hall. Nobody explains its meaning to the young hero, and he does not dare to ask questions. But at the end of the story, when Peredur is already a famous warrior, a page appears, who kneels before him and gives him the following explanation:

> "Lord," said the youth, "I came in the guise of the black maiden to Arthur's court ... and I came with the head all bloody on the salver, and with the spear that had the stream of blood from its tip to the handgrip ... And the head was thy cousin's, and it was the witches of Caer Loyw (Gloucester) that had slain him. And 'twas they that lamed thy uncle. And thy cousin am I, and it is prophesied that thou wilt avenge that."[26]

Here we remember that at the end of the Branwen story, Bran's son Caradoc dies of a broken heart because he could not prevent his treacherous cousin Caswallawn from murdering the chieftains of Britain. If the page boy's explanation is correct, it would seem that the storyteller confused Peredur's cousin Caradoc with Caradoc's father King Bran. Pryderi / Peredur was not meant to avenge his cousin so much as rather his uncle Bran, the brother of his friend and stepfather Manawydan, who was also the brother of Branwen, the "matriarch" of Britain.

A closer study of the page boy's explanation reveals two important motifs: the bleeding head and the blood dripping spear. Both motifs recall the end of the *Second Branch:* Bran's head and the poisoned spear which caused his fatal wound. Yet Bran was not Peredur's cousin but his uncle, nor was he killed by the "Witches of Gloucester."

Glenys Goetinck, whose main study is the constellation of Lady Sovereignty and the King, believes the "Witches of Gloucester" may have been a code word for certain political enemies of Wales. Considering the difficult political situation of Wales during the Anglo-Norman invasion, her theory is justified. She writes:

> The hero and the whole nation are seeking the lost Sovereignty. *(Lady Sovereignty).* In his uncle's castle Peredur is shown his task symbolically ... At the end of the story we hear that the "witches of Gloucester" are the enemy: they have killed his cousin, whose bleeding head was shown to him and wounded his uncle.
>
> At the same time the *iarless vawr,* that is "the powerful

> countess" reveals that the witches besiege the castle ... Could it not be that these witches, instead of their traditional task to train heroes, are now representing the enemies of Wales beyond the border (that is in England) with their king and queen? In his uncle's castle a spear dripping blood is carried through the hall ... This could be a sign that open war has erupted. The bloody head recalls the head of King Llywelyn ap Gruffydd, a memory of his glorious combats and his tragic end, whereas the *gwr gwynllwyd* (the white haired old man) who converses with Peredur during the "Grail procession" could be the ageing Gruffydd ap Cynan (a hero of the Welsh resistance). The crying and lamenting shows the grieving of the people who have lost their leader.[27]

We have mentioned that the last king of Wales had fought valiantly against the English and Norman invaders and that his head was sent as a peace price to King Harold. But the people never forgot his deeds and when the English king Henry I died in 1135 the Welsh revived their resistance. This is the political background against which we have to regard not only the story of Peredur but the *Three Romances* as a whole. Wales found itself in a desperate situation and was yearning for a liberating hero who would free Lady Sovereignty from oppression, avenge all wrongs and dispel the curse of the Waste Land. In short, he would heal the land from all its ills — as *Penweddig* the Allhealer.

The journey to the Otherworld

Peredur spends his boyhood in the idyllic surroundings of Snowdonia, tending his mother's goats. When the young goatherd brings home two hinds which he thought to be hornless goats everybody marvels at his strength and fleetness. He meets some of Arthur's knights and thinks they are angels. They tell him who they are and that it is at king Arthur's court that one becomes a knight. This is the call of destiny for the young man. He sets forth on his journey towards a heroic life, unaware what is expected of him but trusting his inner guidance.

Unfortunately the narrator leaves this clear structure and instead accompanies the hero on a labyrinthine course which is difficult for us to follow. On this journey one adventure follows another and nearly all of them comprise archaic motifs. There is for example the episode of "the sons of the King of Sorrow." These men are killed every day by a monster, but always resuscitated in a reviving bath by their wives. Peredur is not allowed to follow them in their battle against the monster because he has "no loving woman to resurrect him," a parallel to the Cauldron of Life which originally belonged to Branwen's dowry.

Frontiers between elements, seasons or time (e.g. dawn and dusk) have always fascinated the Celts, and Peredur is the typical wanderer between frontiers, between this world of reality and the Otherworld of spirit and fantasy. After killing serpents and dragons, he tackles the monster Addanc, a gigantic beaver who ruins the land. The symbolism of the beaver consists in the fact that he can live both on land and in water — a wanderer between two elements. Then he reaches the border of the Otherworld:

> On the bank of the river he saw a tall tree.
> From roots to crown one half was aflame
> and the other green with leaves.[28]

Jeffrey Gantz comments:

> Of all the strange and supernatural images in the *Mabinogion,* none captures the essence of these medieval Welsh tales so concisely as does this vertically halved tree: the green leaves symbolizing the rich and concrete beauty of the mortal world, the flames symbolizing the flickering shadowy uncertainty of the Otherworld, and the whole emblematic of the tension and mystery which characterize all forms of Celtic art.[29]

At this point does the hero start a shamanic initiation journey? It may well be that in the Middle Ages there still lived people who understood the symbolism of such a path. And we notice that on this quest the hero is constantly led by supernatural women, whose advice, pleas and orders he follows blindly. The French Celticist Jean Markale notes:

> ... Given the traces of gynocratic system apparent in Celtic society, it is not unreasonable to suppose that [these women's] action recalls some former age when women as priestesses, lawgivers, even witches were able to impose their will by ritual, religious and magic means.[30]

Peredur's heroic character is also shown by the fact that, like Cuchulainn, he receives his highest training in martial arts by women, the aforementioned "witches of Gloucester." But times have changed: the witches are now branded as the "enemy" and he kills them, as they are killed in the story of *Culhwch.* According to Stephen Knight the murder of the so-called witches mark the final victory of patriarchy.

The Empress of Great Constantinople

Markale writes that all the women with whom Peredur has a love relationship were manifestations of the "Empress of Great Constantinople" and that in her person Lady Sovereignty and the Grail were united. This may be the reason why the story does not contain any mention of the sacred vessel: if reality appears, its symbol is no longer needed. In fact the motif of Lady Sovereignty appears very early in the story, but it is not easily recognized by the uninitiated. Here is a short description of the details:

Shortly after having left his mother, Peredur finds the pavilion which he mistakes for a church and where he meets a beautiful maiden. In the French and German versions this meeting is told as if he had taken by force the food and wine, kiss and ring. The Welsh version is quite different:

> And the doorway of the pavilion was open, and a chair of gold near the doorway and a handsome auburn-haired maiden sitting in the chair, and a frontlet of gold on her

> forehead, and sparkling stones on the frontlet, and a thick gold ring on her hand.
>
> And Peredur dismounted and came inside. The maiden made him welcome and greeted him, and at the end of the pavilion he could see a table and two flagons full of wine, two loaves of white bread, and chops of flesh of suckling pigs.
>
> "My mother," said Peredur, "bade me wherever I saw meat and drink, to take it."
>
> "Go then, chieftain," said she, "to the table. And God's welcome to thee." Peredur went to the table, and took one half of the meat and drink for himself, and the other half for the maiden. And when he had finished eating, he arose and came to where the maiden was.
>
> "My mother," said he, "bade me take a fair jewel wherever I might see it."
>
> "Take it then, friend," said she. "'Tis not I begrudge it thee."
>
> Peredur took the ring and he went down on his knee and gave the maiden a kiss, and took his steed and departed thence.[31]

The scene is of a childlike naïvety that is sadly lost in Chrétien's and Wolfram's versions. For the first time in his life Peredur meets a strange woman. Step by step he follows what his mother bade him, and he tells her that. The maiden is not in the least alarmed, but rather amused. In spite of his youth and his bizarre outfit she calls him "chieftain." One suspects she knows who he is and she has been awaiting him. The repeated formula "my mother bade me" has almost the ring of a password. It is meaningful that she permits him to eat and drink, willingly lets him have her ring and allows him to kiss her. Wine, ring and kiss were the sacral elements by which Lady Sovereignty initiated her chosen hero or the future king. Whilst the behaviour of Wolfram's Parzival is almost akin to attempted rape, Peredur kneels to the maiden as befits a sacramental rite. For the initiated of the time, Peredur is now the elect of the goddess.

Immediately after this episode we witness the insult to queen Gwenhwyfar by the Red Knight. The author's intention is to show that the relationship between knight and lady is out of balance. There were now men who no longer perceived themselves as protectors of women or champions of Sovereignty. On the contrary, they regarded women as their property, who had not even the right to speak to another man, as is shown by the episode of the Knight of the Pavilion. As to the queen, she has become a mere pawn through whom the king could be insulted and provoked to war. Not only was Lady Sovereignty dethroned; the relationship of the genders had been badly disturbed. It was time the goddess showed herself. And just as Rhiannon met Pwyll on the Gorsedd (the Throne Hill) of Arberth, so the mysterious "Empress of Great Constantinople" met Peredur on a sacred hilltop, and gave him a magic ring just as Luned gave Owain. Lady Sovereignty is here camouflaged as the Empress of Great Constantinople, a personage of a faraway country which is, however, not under the jurisdiction of Rome.[32]

After many adventures Peredur becomes the consort of the empress and rules at her side for fourteen years.[33] Incredibly, after twice seven years with the empress, the long enumeration of his adventures continues over another twelve pages. Only then is he entrusted with the central task of his life: to avenge his murdered kinsmen and thereby to free the land from the oppression of "the enemy," namely, from "the Witches of Gloucester."

He has acquired a *nom de guerre,* "Peredur Longspear" and we find him sitting with his comrades in Arthur's hall when the ugly black maiden arrives and curses him for not having asked about the meaning of the Severed Head and the Bleeding Lance.

> And hadst thou asked the king would have had health and his kingdom peace. But henceforth strife and battle, and the loss of knights, and women left widowed, and maidens without succour, and that all because of thee.[34]

Now at last does Peredur goes in search of the castle where he failed to ask the important question. In the Welsh story it seems that the Grail Castle and the "Castle of Wonders" are identical. It is the castle in which Gawain was submitted to such hard initiation tests, the abode of great women (among them Arthur's deceased mother Igraine) and the Amazonian witches. On his way Peredur kills the unicorn and throws the self-playing chess game (a symbol of his own destiny) out of the window "because his side lost." He kills the Black Oppressor and frees his prisoners. Finally he finds Gwalchmei/Gawain and the Castle of Wonders. It is here that the page boy explains to him the meaning of his adventures and tells him of the black deeds of the Witches of Gloucester. The story finishes with the killing of the witches by Peredur's hand — a deed which parallels the same episode in *Culhwch*.

The Witches of Gloucester

These so-called witches, whom we also find in the Irish sagas were probably priestesses of the old religion. They were proficient in astronomy, weather knowledge and geodesics, and they probably practised some forms of martial arts of the kind that are still found in East Asia as a spiritual exercise. It is a great pity that the intolerance of patriarchy eliminated their schools, as Western culture is the poorer for it. And here we find the central conflict in Peredur's story. Suddenly the great feat of vengeance and liberation for which he was prepared by all those helpful and mysterious women, is turned into a victory over the "witches." More, the victory over the witches is regarded as his ordained destiny.

What are we to make of this sudden turn about? Either Glenys Goetinck is right and "the witches" are but a code word for powerful enemies of Wales (who may well have been known to the audience); or the killing of the witches signals the final solution of a mighty order of priestesses and goddess religion in Celtic lands — or both.

Here again Arthur is called to help, but in the end Peredur achieves the deed himself. If we consider that the witches had been Peredur's teachers in arms and his benefactresses, his fight with them is an unexpected twist, particularly after he has warned them not to attack Arthur's men. It is also indicative that this last struggle takes place in the Castle of Wonders, the Grail Castle no less, a sanctuary presided over by priestesses whose task it was to train and initiate exceptional devotees.

Did the author intend to excuse Peredur's deed to the audience?

A close analysis of the Peredur story reveals the following: Arthur is the archetype of the patriarchal ruler, hated by his sister Morgaine who adhered to the old beliefs, herself a priestess of the old religion. The goddess as Lady Sovereignty and "the Land" is still the supreme deity in Wales. But her image has suffered an alienation: as Empress of Great Constantinople she has assumed features which reveal the naïve "dream of Rome," as it appeared in the story of the Emperor Macsen (see Chapter 9).

Her priestesses, the "witches," are standing in the way of the patriarchal system represented by Arthur and have to be eradicated. This is the reason why in the Peredur story they have been declared "the enemies" of the land.

Peredur, originally a matriarchal hero, stands at a turning point between two historic periods and is forced to make a painful decision. It seems that the salvation of the Land and Lady Sovereignty can only be achieved by Arthur the patriarchal ruler, yet his pragmatism denies the rights of the goddess. This is why Peredur's character seems so riddled with conflicts. Compared with the French and German versions, the Welsh Peredur is a tragic figure. For the sake of politics he must betray his belief in the goddess and her priestesses, and become Arthur's man. The Welsh author does not tell us that Peredur's mother "dies of grief," as Wolfram does. But his contorted style, his numerous hesitations, breaks and new beginnings betray his true feelings: he finds it hard to bring his hero to a finale which is obviously dictated by the *realpolitik* of his day and to which in his heart of hearts he cannot agree.

Gereint, son of Erbin

Of all the three romances, the story of *Gereint* — reworked in French as *Erec et Enide* by Chrétien and in German as *Erek* by Hartmann von Aue — is the most patriarchal in tone and attitude. Yet the hero Gereint is still led and protected by the goddess, as we shall see.

For scholars of medieval literature the slant of the story has always been clear: here knights are earnestly warned against excessive lovemaking. As in the First and Second Branches, a woman is punished for purely ontological reasons: she is a woman and she possesses erotic power.

Here is a short summary of the story:

> Gereint Son of Erbin and Prince of Cornwall, one of the best knights of King Arthur, leaves the court to avenge an insult of a strange knight against queen Gwenhwyfar, her maid and against himself. He overcomes the culprit in single combat and at the same time he wins the love of Enid, the beautiful but poor daughter of a local earl.
>
> He takes her to king Arthur's court and marries her. Then his uncle calls him back to Cornwall to defend the borders of his land. After having fulfilled this task he dedicates himself exclusively to his beautiful wife and thus neglects his duties as king and leader of his war band.
>
> Now his father, the old king, reproaches Enid for this failure and holds her responsible. Enid does not dare to pass his tactless remarks on to her husband and finds herself in a deep conflict. He misunderstands her shy attempts at an explanation and believes (of course) that she must have another lover.
>
> In order to punish her, he takes her on a journey of adventure, where she has to serve him as a squire and watch his prowess. She is not even allowed to speak to him or to warn him of impending dangers. The couple have many adventures and Enid has occasion to save him

> repeatedly from mortal danger. At last he is convinced of her love and loyalty and the story ends with a happy reconciliation.

Once again as in *Prince Pwyll* and in *Branwen* a woman is punished. In the earlier stories, the heroines suffer innocently because of calumniations. Now the motif has been changed: a woman is held responsible for the erotic excesses of her husband.

Enid is not described as a woman from the Otherworld like Rhiannon, nor as a "matriarch of Britain" like Branwen. She is poor, "without dowry and worldly possessions." It must have been difficult for the narrator to find a conflict for such an innocent girl. But he found it, and patriarchy has a new reason to condemn women: Enid is so beautiful that her husband loves her too much.

Being poor she did not contribute to the possessions of her husband and her beauty is her only asset. Therefore she is degraded to a sex object and held responsible for her erotic powers. While Rhiannon suffers through her motherhood and Branwen through the politics of her brothers, Enid is the victim of her sex appeal. The old king of Cornwall reproaches her for the amorous excesses of his son. This scene is missing in the French version, *Erec et Enide.* Neither does Chrétien mention Gereint's (Erec's) jealousy. His motivation is more materialistic. As we have seen in *Culhwch* a man has always the right to win a rich wife, but the same is not true for a woman. A woman who "catches a rich husband" is always condemned as a scheming opportunist. This is Enid's case.

The way Chrétien tells the story it is not clear why Erec takes his wife on such a dangerous journey. But the Welsh narrator leaves no doubt that Gereint's decision is caused by feelings of jealousy and revenge. He also makes it clear that Gereint is legally entitled to his action, although like Chrétien he is shocked by it. He does his best to describe Enid's gentleness, her patience, her loyalty and her forbearing love for her husband. It would be difficult to imagine Rhiannon or Arianrhod in a similar position.

The mythological background

The American scholar R.S. Loomis has mainly written about the story of *Erec et Enide* by Chrétien de Troyes, but he uses Welsh sources extensively. He comes to the conclusion that both protagonists come from British mythological background. In Gereint he sees a fusion of Pryderi and Gweir Son of Llwch, another Welsh hero. As to Enid such sources were more difficult to find, but not impossible. The name *Enid,* says Loomis, is an old Welsh word for "woodlark," a fitting name for a girl of Enid's character. But her further antecedents are surprising to say the least. According to Loomis, Enid is no other than Morgaine in Christian disguise. The disguise had become necessary because by now the Church was busy finding heresies everywhere, and what could be more heretical than the pagan icon of Lady Sovereignty and the King? Loomis defends his conclusion as follows:

> If an author wanted to use the tradition of Morgaine (that is the Goddess) for a long and realistic story he had to fulfil three conditions: Firstly he had to erase all traces of a fairylike and magical appearance, so that his heroine could not be suspected of connections with the devil. Secondly all mention of her lascivious and power hungry character must be avoided. Thirdly he must give her a name which did not evoke unseemly or repulsive associations.[35]

Here Loomis reveals what had happened to the image of the goddess everywhere. By Chrétien's time everything that pointed to her myth had been carefully erased and/or forgotten. A new female ideal was created: the paradigm of the ever loving, long-suffering, masochistic wife.

Enid loves Gereint to excess. She loves him in spite of his faults and his knightly deeds are of the greatest importance to her. She does not dare to express her opinions for fear of being misunderstood. Not only is her loyalty beyond doubt. She silently suffers her husband's injustices as his conjugal right.

In Celtic literature the story of Enid represents a radically new development and here we suspect the Church, the teachings of the Church Fathers and the harsh penitentiary books of Celtic monks. The doctrine of "the sin of Eve" imposed abasement and constant penitence to women and demanded of them attitudes which would have been regarded as dishonourable in pagan times.

Traditional Celtic bards and storytellers were not much concerned with Christian doctrine, least of all in the case of women and sexual love. This is shown clearly in a poem by Taliesin about Adam and Eve:

> ...
> Seven hours they
> Tended the Orchard
> Before Satan's strife,
> Most insistent suitor.
>
> Thence they were driven
> Through cold and chill
> To lead their lives
> In this world.
> ...
> Angels sent
> From God Almighty
> Brought the seed of growth
> To Eve.
> She hid
> A tenth of the gift
> So that not all did
> The whole garden enclose ...[36]

According to Taliesin, Satan wooed and seduced Eve, which cannot be reckoned as sin on her part. For him her real guilt lies in the fact that she hid the precious seedcorn God had sent her, betraying mistrust in God's goodness. It is clear that the traditional Celtic attitude towards women and women's sexuality is irreconcilable with that of Rome and the Bible.

GEREINT AND THE SPARROWHAWK

In the romance of Gereint and Enid the service of a knight to a lady is first mentioned, introduced by the episode of the sparrowhawk.

> Gereint pursues Sir Edern, his lady and his arrogant dwarf in order to avenge a deep insult Sir Edern committed against the queen, her maid and himself. As he carries no weapons he interrupts his pursuit to stay overnight in the house of Enid's father, an impoverished earl. He meets Enid and hears about the planned tournament for the price of the sparrowhawk. He borrows weapons from Enid's father and challenges Sir Edern.
>
> After having overcome him, he dedicates his price to Enid in recognition of her beauty and sends his opponent and his lad as prisoners to Arthur's Court.[37]

Having vanquished Sir Edern, Gereint wins a sparrowhawk and dedicates it to Enid, a gesture binding him to her as her knight. Yet according to the rules of knightly love this gift is unfitting for a future husband and foreshadows the conflict which becomes evident shortly after his marriage. It shows the fundamental change of the paradigm of the Goddess and her Hero. If Loomis is right and Enid is a Christianized version of Morgaine, Gereint's dedication of the sparrowhawk to Enid has the clear meaning that henceforth he will play the part of a tamed hunting bird. Yet this is the very role he must not play as her husband in a patriarchal society.

The relationship of the goddess to her Hero was mythic and symbolic. In ancient times it meant that the Hero was prepared to give his life for her. Only kings and noblemen were usually chosen for this role. In the Middle Ages this original was forgotten or ridiculed, the ancient sacred rites only tolerated as mummeries and children's plays. Yet the memories of the former glory which the part entailed was subliminally present in the dreams of young knights. Here for instance lies the reason for the dreams and antics of a Don Quixote.

But, as Joseph Campbell tells us, nothing is more dangerous than to take myths and symbols literally. The harsh reality of patriarchy sets different tasks for Man. His bravery, his strength, his whole carefully structured persona, *dignitas et gravitas* has the aim to win, to rule, to "stay on top" at all costs, also and especially in front of women.

Hence the conflict between Gereint and Enid erupts when Gereint objects to playing the role of the sparrowhawk. Enid has no part in this, but she is held responsible. In Chrétien's symbolic language we read: "She had no other riches and so she played with her sparrowhawk."[38]

His meaning is: every huntsman knows that one must never play with hunting dogs or hunting birds, as this will ruin them for work. Therefore if Enid plays with her sparrowhawk she renders it useless, just as Gereint has become "useless" in the eyes of his father and his war band. A change of roles seems appropriate and so Enid becomes Gereint's squire on a quest of adventure. She has to ride ahead of him in her oldest clothes and is not even allowed to speak to him when danger threatens. She has become as a hunting bird on a chain, humbly following his orders and submitting to his scolding. Besides it was known that female birds were more efficient in the hunt — provided they could be tamed. Such allusions were well understood, particularly by men: it was all a matter of taming the female falcon.

In the new order, then, the woman must never regard herself as the representative of the goddess, as Celtic and pre-Celtic woman may have done. She is conditioned for her serving role since earliest childhood. So we see Enid serving Gereint at their first meeting, taking off his boots, attending to his horse, shopping and cooking for him, and serving him at table. She was well trained for this role. After her marriage, she has to serve him in the role of a squire as a punishment for her alleged disloyalty. Her serving becomes calculated abasement by degrees — the begin of sexual slavery and masochism.

Only when Gereint learns to control his temper and to show compassion towards his wife does he become ready at last for his most dangerous feat, the famous "Joy of the Court."

The Joy of the Court

This adventure takes place at the court of Count Yvain/Owain and thus connects Gereint with the Lady of the Fountain. We have seen that Owain's fight for the weather controlling fountain was originally a fight for the right to champion the goddess. Here Owain appears as the initiator of a similar "otherworldly" combat. In Chrétien's version the founder of the combat is called King Evrain, in whom Hélaine Newstead sees another manifestation of Bran.[39] He rules an otherworldly realm on an island surrounded by a deep river.

Typically, the otherworldliness of the domain is indicated by an impenetrable wall of air (Chrétien) or a thick wall of fog *(Mabinogion)* and, as usual in such places, the heads of the previous ill-fated contenders are stuck on poles as tokens of warning. Both versions describe the place as a beautiful apple orchard, ruled over by a lady of great beauty. A further requisite of the place is a hunting horn. The knight who will carry the victory over the defender of the Court will blow the horn and end the game forever. The *Mabinogion* does not mention the name of this defender, but as usual, Chrétien is well informed. He tells us that his name is Mabonagrain, a name we have already translated: Mabon, *Mab ap Modron,* the Son of the Great Mother, plus *Grain,* the Sun. To judge by his name, the defender is the quintessential son/lover and sun Hero of the Great Mother, who has here been demonized, perhaps because of his pagan origin.

Gereint enters the pavilion in the middle of the garden and finds a maiden on a golden chair. He occupies another chair in front of her, and she warns him about sitting there. The defender of the garden arrives, scolds Gereint for daring to take his place and challenges him. The knights mount their steeds, lay in their lances and run against each other. Gereint unseats his opponent who asks for mercy. Gereint grants it under condition that "these games" will cease and the mist will disappear. He blows the hunting horn, the mist dissolves and all the magic is exorcised. Then the company gathers and peace is made among them all.

> ... Gereint went to his own domain. And he ruled it from that time prosperously, he and his prowess and valour continuing with fame and renown for him and for Enid from that time forth.[40]

The contrast with Chrétien's treatment could not be greater. There are long speeches and explanations, tears of Mabonagrain's lady who turns out to be Enide's cousin and is fulsomely comforted by her. But the irony of both endings consists in the contrapuntal opposition of the two couples: Gereint who keeps his wife a virtual prisoner is forced to see his error, and so is the Lady of the Orchard who kept her knight a "prisoner of love" and imposing the games on him with a view to keeping him forever. There is a moral in all this: the woman who keeps her lover a prisoner (even if only in a mythological sense) must release him, and the man who keeps his wife a prisoner must see his error and learn to trust her. This at least seems to be the hope of the author. We cannot but see in Mabonagrain and his lady a persiflage of Lady Sovereignty and her champion — a sure sign that matriarchal iconography is no longer understood and a new era has begun.

Enid

Finally a few thoughts about the person of Enid and her psychological achievement. Unbelievable as it may seem, her character was originally developed from the Celtic goddess Morgaine *(Mor Rigan)* the Great Queen. And indeed, she has kept some essential features of the goddess: her erotic potency, the Amazonian strength she displays as Gereint's squire, her healing and revitalizing power which helps Gereint's swift recovery after being mortally wounded. H. Goettner-Abendroth is right when she writes that in spite of her meekness Enid is "a dangerous woman," whose disloyalty could cost Gereint his life. Yet it is her greatness that she never usurps power over her husband, and nothing would be further from her thoughts than to keep him as a "prisoner of love" like her "cousin" in the Court of Joy. This may be the reason why Stephen Knight sees in the story an example of patriarchal sexual politics. In connection with Tennyson's treatment of the story in *The Idylls of the King*, Knight observes:

> Male narcissism, fear of effeminacy, a resulting control of women: the elements are central to the nervous sustenance of a patriarchal position and they dominate "Vivien" and "Enide," the idylls Tennyson first completed.[41]

Considering the stereotype of Celtic woman, and particularly the Celtic goddess as we meet her in Rhiannon, it is clear that this image has now been completely subordinated to the patriarchal ideal. The break is so complete that Tennyson, the poet of Victorian England, needed to add nothing and could only deepen it.[42] Yet hidden away in the description of the last act we notice another, perhaps unconscious change of symbolism: the former cornucopia from which the goddess distributed her rich gifts has now changed into the hollowness of the phallic hunting horn:

> And then Gereint came and sounded the horn, and the moment he blew one blast thereon the mist disappeared.[43]

And, we may add, so did the mist that had surrounded the Celtic goddess. Instead the smoke of the witches' burnings will soon be rising.

PART III

Arthurian Themes

CHAPTER 11

Ceridwen and Taliesin

From the point of view of cultural history the *Tale of Gwion Bach* and the *Tale of Taliesin* are most illuminating. Lady Guest published the story in her first English edition of 1849, although the manuscript from which it is taken dates from the early sixteenth century and is therefore at least two hundred years later than the rest of the collection. Although written down relatively late, it contains encoded descriptions of rites of considerable antiquity.

Patrick K. Ford dropped the *Three Romances* from his *Mabinogion* translation in favour of this unusual tale. His reason? He claims that the story of Ceridwen and Gwion Bach is one of the oldest relics of bardism and therefore much more important than the *Three Romances.* The author, Elis Gruffydd, a Welsh writer of the sixteenth century, was a historian who set out to write a world history. At the same time he collected examples of the almost forgotten medieval literature of Wales and included them in his *World Chronicle.*

The story is set in the sixth century, at the time of King Arthur and of the legendary King Maelgwn of Gwynedd. Elis Gruffydd claims to have known the tale in oral and written versions, but in his style as well as in his commentary the story carries his personal cachet, which adds to the special position it has always occupied in Welsh medieval literature. Other stories were reproduced many times by copyists, but here we have the personal work of a widely travelled author who adds his own interest, knowledge and social criticism. Gruffydd's main interest lies in the relationship of the Welsh bards to their goddess

Ceridwen and the initiation rites which every bard had to undergo.[1]

How was it possible that the naïve child Gwion, reborn from the bosom of the goddess, became Taliesin, the greatest poet of the Welsh medieval period? His poetic work makes him *the* Welsh national poet, at the same time legitimizing the whole bardic guild as saviours of the people from the abuses of the petty kings and their courtiers, and in particular of the "false bards," whose songs flattered the kings and demoralized the people.

In Elis Gruffydd's version the story has two parts: the first tells us about the boy Gwion Bach (Little Gwion), the second about Gwion's second birth as Taliesin ("Radiant Brow") and his youthful deeds.

The story of Little Gwion

In the days when King Arthur began to rule, there lived an earl called Tegid Foel. He had a fief in the region of Pen Llyn and the name of his manor was Llyn Tegid.[2] His wife was Ceridwen, and she had learnt the three arts of magic: incantation, shape shifting and prophecy.

Tegid and Ceridwen had a son, Morfran ("Great Raven") who was so ugly that they called him Afagddfu, the" Great Dark One" or "Utter Darkness." As he was so horrible to look at, his mother was sad and worried in her heart because she could foresee that with his looks he would never find friends among the nobles of the country. Therefore she thought to make him the wisest of all men. She knew the magic herbs that were required for the task and set to work.

She collected the necessary herbs at the right time and right hour, ready to boil them in a great cauldron. The elixir of wisdom had to brew for a whole year, and the fire must not go out by day or night. After a year and a day three drops of the brew would spill out of the cauldron, and whomsoever they hit, he would be the wisest man on earth and a great prophet. The residue of the concoction however would become a deadly poison, which would burst the cauldron and disperse over the countryside.

Ceridwen called a blind old man to guard the fire and a boy named Gwion Bach (Little Gwion) to help him. So they went to work: Gwion and the blind man tended the fire and stirred the cauldron, while Ceridwen went to pick the herbs which by and by she threw into it. After a year and a day Ceridwen went to get Morfran and made him stand beside the cauldron, so that he would receive the three drops of wisdom when the time had come. Then she sat down and fell asleep.

But when the three drops spilled from the cauldron they fell on Gwion Bach, who quickly had pushed Morfran aside. Then the cauldron burst with a loud bang and Ceridwen awoke. She saw Gwion and immediately knew that he had received the wisdom intended for her son. Gwion for his part had suddenly become wise and knew that Ceridwen wanted to kill him. He ran away as fast as he could and she after him. He changed into a hare, and she into a hound. He changed into a bird and she changed into a falcon. At last he changed into a grain of wheat on a threshing floor and Ceridwen changed into a black hen. She pecked up the grain and swallowed it. After nine months she gave birth to Gwion and the baby was so sweet that she did not find it in her heart to kill him. She put him into a basket covered with leather and pitch and threw the basket into a river or, as others say, into the sea.

The story of Taliesin

The scene changes. We hear that at that time the dreaded King Maelgwn Gwynedd held court in his castle Caer Deganwy in the North of Wales. In the vicinity there lived a nobleman called Gwyddno Garanhir (Gwyddno the Crane). On the shore at Conwy he owned a fish trap and each year in the night of Samhain (31st October to 1st November) such a great quantity of salmon was caught there that their sale brought ten pounds of silver.

Gwyddno had a son called Elphin (Elffin) who was a vassal of King Maelgwn and a great spendthrift. One day Gwyddno told his son that he could not give him any more money. But Elphin pleaded with him to let him empty the fish trap for his friends, as he had done in previous years and Gwyddno allowed it.

In the night of Samhain, Elphin came to the weir with all his friends. They had brought pack horses and were looking forward to a good catch. But they could not find a single fish. As they were about to turn home, Elphin saw a leather bundle in the water and pulled it out. Hoping for treasure he cut it open. But instead of gold and silver coins, he saw the face of a beautiful child. Surprised he cried out: "What a shining brow!" *(Tal iesin!).*

"Tal iesin, that is me!" said the child and smiled at him.

His friends taunted him that instead of a rich catch of fish he had caught a foundling. Elphin however had a kind heart and did not mind them.

The story tells that the child was Little Gwion, whom Ceridwen had carried for nine months and then brought into the world. From the beginning of Arthur's rule to the beginning of the rule of Maelgwn he had been carried by the waves, and that was nearly forty years. (Here Gruffydd interjects that this was rank nonsense and against all reason, but that these were the very words of the story.)

Elphin lifted the bundle with the child on his horse and rode home, all the while lamenting his sad lot. As the child Taliesin heard his words he began to sing a song to comfort him. In this song he praised his own gift of poetry, and promised that soon he would be very useful to his discoverer.

Elphin took the boy to his wife who welcomed him lovingly and cared for him. From this day onward Elphin prospered and soon he was one of the richest and most respected men at King Maelgwn's court.

After some time it happened that the king invited his vassals for the feast of Christmas and Elphin had to be there. All his guests praised the king, his generosity, his splendour, his bravery in war and the proficiency of his bards. The story goes on to explain the special accomplishments and duties of the court bards:

> At that time poets were received with great esteem among the eminent ones of the realm. And in those days, none of

> whom we now call "herald" were appointed to that office, unless they were learned men, and not only in the proper service of kings and princes, but steeped and skilled in pedigrees, arms, deeds of kings and princes of foreign kingdoms as well as the ancestors of this kingdom, especially in the history of the chief nobility. Furthermore, each of these bards had to have their responses readily prepared in various languages, such as Latin, French, Welsh and English, and in addition, be a great historian and good chronicler, be skilled in the composition of poetry and ready to compose metrical stanzas in each of these languages. On this feast, there were in the court of Maelgwn no less than twenty-four of these; chief among them was the one called Heinin Fardd the Poet.[3]

At this particular feast Elphin praised the virtue of his wife and the wisdom of his bard so highly that the king was offended by his vanity. He ordered Elphin imprisoned until the chastity of his wife and the wisdom of his bard could be confirmed. Then he sent his son Rhun, who was a great womanizer, to test the virtue of Elphin's wife. But Taliesin knew his plan and warned his mistress. She exchanged her garb with that of one of her scullery maids and even adorned the maid's finger with her husband's signet ring that he had sent to his wife as a token a short time before.

As Rhun arrived at Elphin's court, the maid disguised as the mistress sat in her lady's chamber. She rose from her seat, greeted Rhun pleasantly and invited him to sit down with her. He began to beguile the girl with seductive talk, while she preserved the mien of her mistress. The story says that the girl got so inebriated that she fell asleep, for Rhun had put a powder in her drink that made her sleep heavily and in this way he did his will with the maiden. If the tale can be believed, she didn't even feel him cutting off her little finger, around which was Elphin's signet ring. And afterwards he took the finger — with the ring on it — to the king as proof, telling him how he had violated her chastity and had cut off her finger as he left, without her awakening.[4]

Maelgwn was very pleased. He had Elphin brought from prison and in the presence of all his councillors he showed him the finger with Elphin's signet ring as proof of his wife's disloyalty. Elphin answered that he could not deny that the ring was his, but the finger could not be that of his wife for three reasons: firstly the ring would be too large even for his wife's thumb; secondly his wife was in the habit of paring her fingernails every Saturday, while this fingernail had not been cut for a month; thirdly it could be seen that the hand from which it was cut had kneaded rye dough within the past three days, which his wife had never done since her marriage.

The king was enraged at these words and ordered Elphin sent back to prison, asking him to prove that his bard was better than the bards at the king's court. In the meantime Taliesin comforted Elphin's wife and assured her that he would succeed in setting Elphin free. She asked him how he would do that and he answered her with a poem, which ended with a curse on King Maelgwn and prince Rhun:

> May there be neither blessing nor beauty
> On Maelgwn Gwynedd,
> But let the wrong be avenged-
> And the violence and the arrogance, finally,
> For the act of Rhun and his offspring
> Let his land be desolate,
> Let his life be short,
> Let the punishment last long
> On Maelgwn Gwynedd.[5]

Then he took leave from his lady and went to the king's court. Maelgwn sat in his banquet hall dining with his guests and courtiers as was the custom on high feast days. Taliesin mingled with the throng and sat down in a dark corner, close to the place where the bards had to pass when they came forward to pay their respects to the king and praise his largesse. When the time came for them to step forward he looked at each in turn, puckered his lips and made a sound like *blerum blerum* just like little children do. Nobody paid any attention to him, but when they all stood before the king, they puckered their lips, made faces at him and plaid *blerum blerum,* as they had seen Taliesin do. The king was astounded and thought they had had too much to drink. He ordered one of his noblemen to talk to them earnestly and to remind them of their duty. But they did not stop with their nonsense. Finally one of his squires took a food platter and hit the chief bard on his head. This had the desired effect and Heinin fell on his knees and asked the king's mercy. He declared that they were neither drunk nor mad. "But there is a little imp here in the hall. He looks like a little man and sits there in the corner."

So the king ordered Taliesin to be brought before him and asked him who he was and whence he came. Again Taliesin answered in verses and said:

Official chief poet
To Elphin am I,
And my native abode
Is the land of the Cherubim.
Johannes the prophet
called me Merlin,
But now all kings
Call me Taliesin.[6]

And as the king asked him further questions he recited his history, in an odd mixture of biblical, Christian and pagan themes:

I was with my lord
In the heavens
When Lucifer fell
Into the depth of hell;
I carried a banner
before Alexander;
I know the stars' names
from the North to the South
I was in the fort of Gwydion,
In the Tetragrammaton.

...
I brought seeds down
to the vale of Hebron;
I was in the court of Don (Dana)
before the birth of Gwydion;
...
I was a head keeper
on the work of Nimrod's tower;
...
I was three times
in the prison of Arianrhod;
...
I got poetic inspiration
from the cauldron of Ceridwen;

...
And I was nearly nine months
in the womb of Ceridwen; I was formerly
Gwion Bach,
but now I am Taliesin.[7]

This song impressed the king and his court deeply. Taliesin followed it up with another song, in which he explained to the king and his court why he had come and what he intended to do:

Provincial bards! I am contending!
To refrain I am unable.
I shall proclaim in prophetic song
To those who will listen,
And I seek that loss that I suffer:
Elphin, from the punishment
Of Caer Deganwy.
...
Elphin son of Gwyddno
Suffers torment now
'Neath thirteen locks
For praising his master-bard.

And I am Taliesin,
Chief-poet of the West,
And I shall release Elphin
From the gilded fetters.[8]

After this he chanted a prayer for divine succour, and immediately a great storm arose, so that the king and his court feared the castle would fall over them. The king ordered Elphin to be brought before him again, and as Taliesin sang another song, his chains fell off. (Here the narrator again registers his doubt.) Following this Taliesin sang the verses which later were called "The Interrogation of the Bards" and "The Satire of the Bards." In these verses he criticized the arrogance and hypocrisy of the so called false bards:

Minstrels of malfeasance make
Impious lyrics; in their praise
They sing vain and evanescent song,
Ever exercising lies.
They mock guileless men
They corrupt married women,
They despoil Mary's chaste maidens.
Their lives and times they waste in vain,
They scorn the frail and the guileless,
They drink by night, sleep by day,
Idly, lazily making their way.
They despise the Church
Lurch towards the taverns;
In harmony with thieves and lechers,
They seek out courts and feasts,
Extol every idiotic utterance,
Praise every deadly sin.
They lead every manner of base life,
Roam every village town and land.
The distresses of death concern them not,
Never do they give lodgings or alms.
Excessive food they consume.
They rehearse neither the psalms not prayer,

Pay neither tithes nor offerings to God,
Worship not on Holy Days nor the Lord's day,
Fast on neither Holy Days nor ember days.
Birds fly, fish swim,
Bees gather honey, vermin crawl;
Everything bustles to earn its keep
Except minstrels and thieves, the lazy and worthless.
I do not revile your minstrelsy,
For God gave that to ward off evil blasphemy;
But he who practises it in perfidy
Reviles Jesus and his worship.[9]

After Taliesin had proved the virtue of his mistress, showed his superiority as a bard and had liberated his master, he advised Elphin to bet against the king's horses. The king accepted the bet and a race was organized: the twenty-four best horses of the king against Elphin's mount. Taliesin himself chose the place of the race and before it started he told Elphin's jockey to throw his cap at the place at which he would overtake the king's horses. The boy did as he was told and after Elphin's horse had won Taliesin took his master to where the cap lay.

Then he hired people to dig at that place. After a while they found a cauldron full of gold coins. Taliesin handed it to Elphin saying: "Here is payment and reward for you for having brought me from the weir and raised me from that day to this."[10]

The king had Taliesin called into his presence and asked him about the beginning of the world and everything that would happen in the future. Everything that Taliesin told the king was written down in the books known today as *The Prophecies of Taliesin*.[11]

Thus so far the story of Little Gwion who became the bard Taliesin by the intervention of the goddess Ceridwen. P.K. Ford and others are particularly interested in the change from the naïve boy into the wise and judicious bard, who uses his art to combat the ills of the world. This change is attributed to Ceridwen, in this story at least no longer described as a goddess but as a sorceress. Yet the very fact that Ceridwen lives in or near a lake and owns a magic cauldron indicates that she is a supernatural woman. We also hear that she has a motherly heart: she is concerned about her son's handicap and she is incapable of killing the reborn Gwion, the boy who had once incurred her wrath.

The theme of abandonment of a child to the waves of a river or the ocean is a well-used motif, found in the life of many heroes from Moses to the founders of Rome. Some authors see in it the symbol of a purification rite and relate it to the baptism practised by St John. It seems that a similar "rebirth through water and the spirit" was in use as an initiation rite by the druidic order of bards. It may also have included a test of courage, as Davies explains: poets who aspired to the higher degrees of bardism were put to sea in a coracle and left to navigate through the dangerous surf. Old manuscripts reveal that this form of initiation was still practised in Wales as late as the fourteenth century.[12]

The Goddess of duality

Although it is Brigid who is usually worshipped as the goddess of poetry, it seems that in Wales this function was attributed to Ceridwen. She is the mother of an ugly son, but has also a beautiful daughter, Creirwy or Cordelia.[13] In the story of *Culhwch and Olwen* Creirwy has two semidivine suitors and on Arthur's behest they have to fight for her hand on every May-day eve until doomsday. Perhaps the contrast of Ceridwen's two children stands for duality in its many forms: light and dark, day and night, summer and winter, life and death. Indeed Ceridwen is not only the goddess of poetry but also a death goddess. We have seen that in the *Fourth Branch* she appears in her zoomorphic form as the lunar White Sow *Hen Wen* (the "Old White One") and leads Dana's son Gwydion to Nantlleu, the "Valley of the Moon." Here his murdered son Llew Llaw Gyffes awaits rebirth in the shape of his totemic eagle, while the White Sow feeds on his rotting flesh that falls to the ground. This repulsive image indicates the dual aspect of the Celtic goddess.

The pig has been a sacred animal from oldest times. Mocchus was the Celtic boar god in Gaul, and porcine symbols abound in Irish and Welsh sagas. Pigs are known for their fertility, but also for the fact that they devour their young. As the mother sow is known for eating her fallow, so the Great Mother brings forth her children and takes them back into herself at death. Celtic spirituality never shrank from the negative aspects of Life. On the contrary: death is accepted as a necessary part of life and a person of spiritual aspirations must never fear it.

Robert Graves derives the name "Ceridwen" from the Roman goddess Cardea: *Cerid wen* is the "white *(wen)* Cardea," "the goddess of the door hinges."[14] She is the deity who controls the opening and shutting of doors in a symbolic sense. She stands at the beginning and at the end of life and during each lifetime she grants or denies chances and opportunities. She also is the goddess who stands between the opposites, holding them in balance. And she is also seen as an early manifestation of Fortuna. Graves writes that Ceridwen was originally the pan-European barley goddess, and as such she shared features with Demeter as well as with Epona.[15]

In attempting to reconstruct the rites of the Druids from old manuscripts, Lewis Spence discovered that the druidic initiations had many parallels with the Eleusinian Mysteries, as far as they are known.[16] Quoting the antiquarian Davies, Spence writes that the first part of our story, the "chase" of Ceridwen after Gwion Bach is not a magician's contest as is often claimed, but symbolizes the sequence of the rites of the first or "lower" initiation. The postulant is "chased" by the goddess through the various degrees of perfection, until he can rest and grow as a seedcorn in her womb. These initiations took place at a temple, or perhaps a stone circle, in the mountain wilderness of Eryri in Snowdonia. As Grave attests, the transformations of Gwion Bach run in strict seasonal order: hare in the autumn coursing season, fish in the rains of winter, bird in spring when the migrant birds return, and finally corn in the summer harvest season.[17]

The higher degrees of initiation were taken at the sea shore of Conwy in north Wales, where the postulants, like the child

Taliesin, were abandoned to the surf in rudderless coracles. This ordeal was not entirely without dangers, but it seems that the men in charge chose their candidates carefully and those deemed worthy were probably put to sea at less dangerous places.[18] Only the sons of noble families were usually admitted. Hywel, Prince of North Wales, was initiated to the lower degrees in 1171, and prepared himself for the higher degrees administered under Gwyddno and his son. He composed a hymn of thanksgiving in which he praised the goddess as the Lady of the Moon, lofty and fair, slow and delicate in her descending course.[19]

Taliesin's ascent

It may well be that Little Gwion's lowly birth contributed to the special glamour of the story. A young servant boy who ascended to the highest perfection of bardism was certainly a rare occurrence. Mythologists like MacCullough deemed him a Celtic Apollo, which fits well with his name "Radiant Brow."[20] Perhaps Robert Graves comes closest to the truth when he writes that there were probably several Welsh bards who called themselves Taliesin. He writes:

> Gwion Bach Son of Gwreang Llanfair in Caereinion, a person of no importance, accidentally lighted on certain ancient mysteries and, becoming an adept, began to despise the professional bards in his time because they did not understand the rudiments of their traditional poetic lore, namely the service to the Goddess. Proclaiming himself a master poet, Gwion took the name of Taliesin, as an ambitious Hellenistic Greek poet might have taken the name of Homer.[21]

But that is not all. Graves continues:

> The pen-name "Gwion son of Gwreang" is itself probably a pseudonym and not the baptismal name of the author of the Romance. Gwion is the equivalent *(gw for f)* of Fionn

> or Finn, the Irish hero of a similar tale. Fionn son of Mairne ... was instructed by a Druid of the same name as himself to cook for him a salmon fished from a deep pool of the River Boyne, and forbidden to taste it; but as Fionn was turning the fish over in the pan he burned his thumb, which he put in his mouth and so received the gift of inspiration. For the salmon was a Salmon of knowledge that had fed on nuts fallen from the nine hazels of poetic art.
>
> The equivalent of Gwreang is Freann, an established variant of Fearn, the alder. Gwion is thus claiming oracular powers as a spiritual son of the Alder-god Bran. His adoption of a pseudonym was justified by tradition.[22]

Professor Ford is right when he ascribes great importance to the story of Ceridwen and Taliesin. The bard Taliesin has been studied and praised by many writers. One of the latest is John Matthews, who attempts to interpret content and background of some of his most difficult poems.[23]

As far as Ceridwen is concerned, she suffered the twofold destiny of Woman. On the one hand her cult survived among the bards of Wales until late in the Middle Ages: she was the goddess of bardic inspiration and the patroness of all those who were professionally concerned with the art of word and song. The Welsh princes were adepts at melding the worship of pagan gods and Christianity, and as we can see from Taliesin's poems, it was the bards who fostered this syncretistic trend. Taliesin himself saw his mission in advising the princes to return to the ancient ethic values, emphasising that the welfare of the country depended on a good and just reign. With advancing Christianity this duty fell progressively to the Church and as the great reigning houses died out so did bardism and the worship of the goddess Ceridwen.

The lower strata of the population had no knowledge or understanding for poetic inspiration. Life in medieval Wales was hard and there was little time for artistic pursuits. All that remained of the worship of Ceridwen was the image of the witch. It is true that in folkloric belief Ceridwen was also seen as a benefactress, the goddess who had brought barley seed, piglets and bee-swarms to Wales. But the irrational fear of the Death Goddess remained and people preferred to turn to "Christianized" goddesses such as St Brigid and St Madrun. The fear of the Death Goddess turned Ceridwen into an ugly shrieking hag, or into the "White Lady," the ghostly woman who announces an imminent death in the family.

With Ceridwen passes the last manifestation of the Celtic goddess from living memory. Worse, the feared and hated image of the Welsh witch with the conical hat — of the priestess — enters the folklore of English-speaking people throughout the world. Only in recent years do we witness a reverse trend. Witches are once more seen as wise women who live close to nature, dispensing counsel and healing power. And people everywhere are drawn to the solitude of nature in the hope to recapture some form of nature mysticism which was their Celtic heritage. The Swiss folklorist Kurt Derungs recommends the study of "landscape mythology" in the hope that it will help us recover the spirit of our ancestors and the strength of our roots. And so the circle turns on itself: the goddess Ceridwen, for centuries forgotten or feared as a malevolent witch, returns as the godhead of nature, recalled by men and women who invoke her transforming powers and her poetic inspiration.

CHAPTER 12

A Vindication of Gawain

Readers of the Arthurian cycles may judge Gawain the least deserving of all Grail seekers. In most medieval court epics he is described more as a womanizer than a fearless knight. Wolfram's version is typical: Gawain prefers to follow the capricious Orgeluse and to gain her favours in the dubious *Château Merveilles* instead of riding out with Parzival on the Quest for the Grail.

In his book *Gawain Knight of the Goddess* John Matthews attempts a vindication of this knight, and it is only fair that we discuss his results. The most important of Matthews' findings is probably the discovery that Gawain is the British incarnation of the Irish hero Cuchulainn, son of the Irish sun god Lugh and the princess Dechteire. Another of his claims is that according to an obscure Austrian court epic Gawain actually achieved the Grail and Perceval failed.

Most medievalists see in Gawain a stock figure, introduced as a dramatic contrast to his peerless comrade Perceval. Yet in the rich repertoire of Grail stories we also find other descriptions. One of the least known is in *Die Krone* (The Crown) by the thirteenth century Austrian Heinrich von dem Türlin. This rambling tale is no match for Wolfram's great epic, but Heinrich is one of the last true *Minnesingers* whose every word was intended as a praise of women. Introducing his story he writes that it was his intention "to gather jewels for a crown to womanhood" — hence the title.

This Austrian knows things about Gawain which cannot be found anywhere else in medieval literature. Working in faraway Carinthia could he have had access to sources unknown to Western court poets? His Grail episode was translated from Middle High German into English by Jessie Weston and J.D. Bruce[1] and is here abbreviated from John Matthews' book:

> Gawain had been searching for the Grail from a long time ... and now at last he reached a fair and beauteous land "so well tilled that naught was lacking of the fruits of the earth, corn and vines and fair trees, all whereby man might live grew freely on either hand ... it might well be held for an earthly paradise."
>
> Scarcely entered in this realm of wonders, Gawain saw a dwelling the walls of which were as clear as glass: but it was well guarded by a great fiery sword, and it seemed deserted, so he passed it by. Then after riding twelve days through woodland, he discovered his companions of the Quest, Lancelot and Calogreant, sleeping under a tree, and the three greeted each other joyously and told of their separate adventures.
>
> As night approached they were met on the road by a squire, who bade them accompany him to the lord's dwelling, where they would be made welcome and receive every comfort. The squire then rode ahead at full gallop, leaving the three knights to follow at an easy pace ... Within the castle was as fair a place as they had ever seen. In the great hall the floor was strewn with roses and the host, richly dressed in white and gold, reclined on a couch, while at his feet two noble youths played chess and made merry jests. The old lord made them welcome and seated Gawain beside him on a cushion of rose coloured silk. There was much pleasant conversation, and as night came a host of fair people began to gather; knights and ladies, minstrels and chamberlains to serve them.
>
> Their host kept his guests close to him, Gawain above and the others below him at the table, "and when all were seated, and were fain to eat, there came into the hall a

wondrous fair youth, of noble bearing. And in his hand he held a sword, fair and broad, and lay it down before the host."

While Gawain wondered at the meaning of this, cupbearers entered with wine for all. But the host neither ate nor drank, and when he saw that, neither did Gawain; but both Lancelot and Calogreant were so thirsty that they drank even though he bade them not to, and at once they fell into a deep slumber. Thereafter, though his host urged him to drink, he would accept nothing, but was on his guard, lest he too fell asleep — and it seemed at that moment that the hall became suddenly filled with a great host of people. Then there came into the hall a wondrous procession.

In the sight of all there paced into the hall two maidens fair and graceful, bearing two candlesticks; behind each maid there came a youth, and the twain held between them a sharp spear. After these came two other maidens fair in form and richly clad, who bare a salver of gold and precious stones upon a silken cloth; and behind them, treading soft and slow, paced the fairest being whom since the world began God had wrought in woman's wise, perfect was she in form and feature, and richly clad withal. Before her she held on a rich cloth of samite a jewel wrought of red gold, in form of a base, whereupon stood another, of gold and gems, fashioned even as a reliquary that standeth upon an altar. This maiden bare upon her head a crown of gold, and behind her came another, wondrous fair, who wept and made lament, but the others spake never a word, only drew nigh unto their host, and bowed them low before him.

Gawain looked with double astonishment upon this, for he found that he recognized the crowned maiden as one that he had seen before and who had spoken to him concerning the Grail and told him that if ever he saw her again in the company of five maidens, he should be sure not to fail to ask concerning what they did there.

As he mused thereon the four who bare spear and

salver, the youth with the maidens, drew nigh and laid the spear upon the table and the salver beneath it. Then before Gawain's eyes there befell a great marvel, for the spear shed three great drops of blood unto the salver that was beneath, and the old man, the host took them straightaway. Then came the maiden of whom I spake, and took the place of the other twain, and set the fair reliquary upon the table — that did Sir Gawain mark right well — he saw therein a bread whereof the old man brake the third part, and ate.

At that Gawain could contain himself no longer, but asked his host ... "What meaneth this great company and the marvels I behold?" At that every knight and lady in the hall sprang up with a great shout of joy, wakening Lancelot and Calogreant from their slumber. But when they saw the company around them, and the wondrous objects, they at once fell into an even more profound sleep ... Then the host bade the company be still and silent, and speaking to Gawain alone, told him the meaning of all he had seen:

"Sir Gawain, this marvel which is of God may not be known unto all, but shall be held secret, but since ye have asked thereof, sweet kinsman and dear guest, I may not withhold the truth. 'Tis the Grail which ye now behold. Herein have ye won the world's praise, for manhood and courage alike have ye right well shown, in that ye have achieved this toilsome quest. Of the Grail may I say no more save ye have seen it, and that great gladness that hath come of this your question. For now are many free from the sorrow they have long borne and small hope had they of their deliverance. Great confidence and trust had we all in Perceval, that he would learn the secret things of the Grail, yet hence did he depart even as a coward who ventures nought and asked nought. Thus did his quest miscarry, and he learned not that which of surety he should have learned. So had he freed many a mother's son from sore travail, who live and yet are dead. Through the strife of kinsmen did this strife befall, when one brother smote the other for his land: and for that treason was the wrath of God shown on him and on all his kin, that all were alike lost. That was a woeful chance, for the living they were driven out, but the dead must abide in the semblance of life, and suffer bitter woe withal. That must ye know — yet had they hope and comfort in God and His grace, that they should come even to the goal of their grief ... Should there be a man of their race who should end this their sorrow in that he should demand the truth of these marvels, that were the goal of their desire; so would their penance be fulfilled, and they should again enter into joy: alike they who lay dead and they who live, and now give thanks to God and to ye, for by ye are they now released. This spear and this food they nourish me and none other, for in that I was guiltless of the deed God condemned me not. Dead am I, though I bear not the semblance of death, and this my folk is dead with me ... And know of a truth that the adventures that ye have seen have come of the Grail, and now is the penance perfected, and forever done away, and your Quest hath found its ending."

Saying this he gave Gawain the sword which lay before him, telling him that it would serve him well always and never break. And he said that Gawain's quest was ended, and that as for the maidens: "'Twas through their unstained purity, and through no misdoing that God had thus laid upon them the service of the Grail; but now was their task ended, and they were sad at heart, for they knew well that never more should the Grail be so openly beheld of men, since that Sir Gawain had learned its secrets ..."

Therewith the day began to dawn and all the company faded from sight, save only for Gawain's two companions and the maiden who had borne the Grail ... And Sir Gawain was ... sorry that he saw his host no more, yet he was glad that the maidens spake, saying that his labour was now at an end, and that he had in sooth done all that pertained unto the Quest of the Grail, for never else in

> any land, save in that Burg alone, might the Grail have been beheld. Yet had the land been waste, but God had harkened to their prayer, and by his coming had folk and land alike been delivered, and for that they were joyful.[2]

Today Heinrich von dem Türlin is unknown even in German-speaking countries. Medievalists ignore him. We have to thank John Matthews for resurrecting a text which shows Grail and Grail achievers in a different light. Here the king's explanation mixes pagan, Christian and historic events. The king does not seem to be wounded or lamed and he holds himself innocent of the wasted land. God's punishment fell upon his people because of a fratricidal war — obviously an allusion to events in the German Empire at the time, and Gawain's quest had freed land and people from its consequences. Surprisingly it was the Grail's Queen herself who taught Gawain to ask the right question, yet Perceval is censored as a coward for not asking it, even without the benefit of her help.

Here the mythological framework as well as literary skill are missing. It seems that the poet has put together a jumble of Grail personages and, without knowing their original meaning, placed them into a limbo or purgatory from which Gawain set them free. Could this story be politically motivated? This is possible if we consider that the beginning of the thirteenth century was a time when House of Austria and the House of Anjou were separated by bitter enmity. It was the time when Henry II of England, husband of Eleanor of Aquitaine, had his chancellor, Thomas à Becket murdered.[3] During the second conquest of Jerusalem, Henry's son Richard the Lionheart revolted against the leader of the crusade, Duke Leopold of Austria and Carinthia. He was arrested, imprisoned and released only after payment of an exorbitant ransom. It is conceivable that the Duke of Austria or one of his vassals commissioned the work, which critics have condemned as "too long, too coarse and lacking in courtly manners."[4] Did Heinrich intend to compose an Anti-Parzival in opposition to Chrétien's and Wolfram's? This would explain his condemnation of Parzival as "a coward" who did not dare to ask the right question at the right moment. It is not intended here to compare the two German poets and given Wolfram's towering superiority this would be futile. Instead it is proposed to examine Gawain's relationship to the goddess in her various guises.

Gawain, Knight of the Goddess

At the beginning of the twelfth century Gawain was already famous in continental Europe. He is immortalized in a stone relief at a side portal of the cathedral of Modena dating from between 1090 and 1120. This Gothic sculpture celebrates Gawain (here called Galvagin) as the liberator of "Ginevra" (Gwenhwyfar),[5] a role usually attributed to Lancelot, who does not appear here. The relief shows that Gawain was known on the Continent before Lancelot, and that he was venerated as a saintly knight, worthy to be immortalized in a cathedral.

Is it possible to see in him also as a champion of Lady Sovereignty, a matriarchal hero? Matthews examines this question and answers it in the affirmative. Gawain is the son of Loth, king of Orkney, and of Morgaine (Morgan le Fay). This tells us that he hails from the Northern Islands, where paganism lingered longest and according to N.L. Goodrich he was a Pictish prince whose parentage pre-selected him for a heroic career.[6] Together with Cei he is also the oldest knight of King Arthur's entourage. We have met him as Owain's friend (or his brother) in *The Lady of the Fountain* and as Peredur's protector against Cei's rudeness. Like Culhwch he is Arthur's nephew, as Morgaine is Arthur's half-sister through Queen Ygraine. Therefore Gawain could have claimed Arthur's throne by matriarchal as well as by patriarchal right. Yet he never makes such a claim and is always represented as the king's most faithful knight.

In the *Mabinogion* Gawain is called *Gwalchmei,* a beautiful name phonetically as well as mythologically. It signifies "May Falcon," and shows him to be the chosen champion of the goddess, the Summer King. It follows that originally Gwalchmei was an important mythological figure, namely the son/lover of the goddess. Consequently Gawain is also the right man to champion her priestess Gwenhwyfar and her representative long before the appearance of Lancelot.

According to Norma Goodrich, queen Gwenhwyfar was also a Pictish princess and an ordained priestess either of the Goddess or of a Celtic form of Christianity which, like the Cathars, permitted ordained priestesses.[7] But everything about Arthur's queen points towards goddess worship, whilst also being compatible with Celtic Christianity. Her name signifies "White Phantom" and we may understand its meaning as "White Lady from the Otherworld." On the Continent the name *Gwenhwyfar* was not understood and underwent several adaptations: French *Guinièvre,* English *Guinevere/Jennifer,* Italian *Ginevra.* On the tympanum of Modena Cathedral, Guinevere is called *Winlogee* from Bretonic *Winlogen.* In the Latin story of *The Birth of Gawain* her name is *Gwendolin.* In all these forms we find the root *gwen, wen, win* or *gwin* "white," which is the Brythonic equivalent of Gaelic *finn.* The colour white was for the Celts synonymous with beauty, and consequently one of the many titles of the pan-European goddess is "the White Goddess." According to the Welsh Triads King Arthur was married three times, and each of his queens was named Gwenhwyfar, another triplicity pointing to the goddess.

Combing through the Arthurian cycles, both French and English, as well as Geoffrey's *Kings of Britain,* Norma Goodrich presents us with a wealth of new insights into the political constellation of the time. She points out that apart from the clergy, Gwenhwyfar was probably the only literate person at King Arthur's court, and that the keeping of the court archives was one of her duties stated in the marriage contract. She chose Lancelot as her appointed champion, because he was, like herself, of Pictish origin and hence well acquainted with Pictish laws, customs and, above all, Pictish goddess worship. According to Goodrich the name "Lancelot" is not French, signifying "Lot's Lance" or "Young Lance," as it is usually translated, but Pictish. He was a Pictish chieftain called "the Angus," Latinized into *Anguselus,* which in Old French became *L'Ancelot,* hence "Lancelot" — a surprising etymology, and a convincing one.[8] What French authors thought to be the quintessential French knight turns out to be a Pictish prince like Gawain.

For both men the queen was indeed Lady Sovereignty personified. Norma Goodrich maintains that the allegation of Guinevere's adultery originated through a mistranslation of the Gaelic word for "altar" as "bed" and claims that as high priestess Guinevere had vowed lifelong virginity. This explanation is disputable if we consider that pagan Celtic ritual demanded ritual union of the priestess queen and her champion as an integral part of the Spring festival. The Celtic concept of Lady Sovereignty was unknown in France and French court poets ignored the fact that Guinevere in her role as Lady Sovereignty had not only the right but the duty to celebrate a sacred marriage with the hero of her choice. From the matriarchal point of view such a union benefited the land and its people and inspired the chosen hero to a sacrificial death. Patriarchy saw in it sexual dalliance at best, damnable adultery at worst. The fact that it also weakened the position of the king was reason enough to condemn it. The question is, was Guinevere still a pagan queen, or did she represent a form of Christianity which accepted ordained priestesses?

As the *Prose Lancelot* shows, Guinevere, living at the cusp of paganism and Christianity, was caught between the opposing demands of both religions.[9] Had it not been for the unwavering loyalty of her champions Gawain and/or Lancelot, she would have ended on the stake for adultery and high treason. French authors make the most of Lancelot's seductive powers ignoring his Scottish/Pictish origin and the religious conflicts caused by his position at court. These conflicts are shared by Gawain, another Northerner of Scottish origin who asserts his dedication to the goddess by his shield: a white pentagram in a red field. The five-pointed star, emblem of the goddess since Egyptian times, was called the Seal of Morgaine (Solomon's Seal in alchemy) and has always been a symbol of divine protection.

The episode represented on Modena Cathedral shows Gawain attempting to save Guinevere from her abductor who is here called Mardoc. Chrétien describes a similar episode in the *Prose Lancelot* in which Gawain is accompanied by Lancelot.

Here the abductor's castle was only accessible by two bridges: a bridge of swords and a bridge "under water." Lancelot chooses the sword bridge, Gawain the water bridge and in this case it is he who rescues the queen. Commentators have related the sword bridge with the intellect, the water bridge with feeling and emotional values and concluded that Gawain was emotionally closer to Guinevere and also that inner liberations are better achieved through feeling values than through cold intellect.

More important than these psychological interpretations is a scene in Chrétien's *Perceval,* which is usually ignored by interpreters, but which gives us a better picture of Guinevere's real nature and Gawain's reverence for her:

> In Château Merveilles, Arthur's mother Ygraine asks Gawain about Queen Guinevere and he replies: "Ever since the first woman was created ... there has never been a lady of such renown which she deserves, for just as a wise master teaches young children, my lady the queen teaches every living being. From her flows all the good in the world, she is its source and origin. Nobody can take leave of her and go away disheartened, for she knows what each person wants and the way to please each to his desires. Nobody observes the way of rectitude or wins honour unless they have learnt to do so from my lady, or can suffer such distress that he leaves her still possessed of his grief."[10]

Markale interprets these words as meaning that Gawain sees in Guinevere not only a giver of all good gift, but also the initiatrix in a sexual sense. He writes:

> Since Chrétien's source material clearly contained many archaic elements this description of Guinevere furnishes further evidence that the cult of the Grail and, particularly, the ritual of the Quest holds traces of the cult of the ancient goddess represented in this case by the queen. As a woman she has control over life, over the

> food that makes life possible, over procreation, in fact total supremacy, which is administered by the king her husband or her lover-knights. In the light of this reflection, courtly love, its code and laws can hardly be just a form of amusement for the medieval nobility, but rather the poetic form adopted in the twelfth and thirteenth centuries by the cult of the *Magna Mater Omnipotens.*[11]

From this we may conclude that Gawain was indeed the champion of the goddess in the archaic sense.

Gawain in the Three Romances

In the story of *The Lady of the Fountain* as well as in *Peredur Son of Efrawg,* Gawain (here called Gwalchmei) constantly influences and advises the heroes Owain and Peredur. In Chrétien's *Yvain* his advice is sometimes negative: for instance when he warns Yvain not to spend too much time in lovemaking with his wife. Here his influence goes so far that some commentators infer a homosexual relationship between him and Owain or Peredur. By contrast Robert Graves believes that Gawain is the perpetual tanist, the companion and successor of the Year King destined for a sacrificial death and this was indeed the original role of the queen's champion. It is tragic that according to Malory his friendship with Lancelot ends in a blood feud, when Lancelot in saving Queen Guinevere from the stake inadvertently kills Gawain's two younger brothers who are innocent bystanders.[12]

Gawain's friendship with Peredur is more revealing. He is the only one of Arthur's knights who succeeds in waking Peredur from the love trance into which he had fallen at the sight of the goddess's colours black white and red, reminding him "of the woman he loved best."[13] Gawain understands the meaning of Peredur's trance and knows how to break it gently.

In this episode Peredur overcomes twenty-five of Arthur's best knights without ever waking from his trance. The last one to be unseated is Cei who breaks his arm and collarbone in the fall from his horse. Now it is Gawain's turn to go and wake Peredur and Cei taunts him with the words:

"Gwalchmei," said he, "well do I know thou wilt lead him by the reins ... Yet small renown and honour is it for thee to overcome the tired knight, fatigued with battle. And so long as thy tongue and fair words last thee, a tunic of thin bliant [fine linen] around thee will be armour enough for thee. And thou wilt not need to break spear and sword fighting with the knight thou mayest find in that condition."[14]

The contrast between Kei's and Gawain's mentality is significant and highlights the rude arrogance of the patriarchal warrior against the tactful understanding of the knight schooled in the goddess's service. Gawain succeeds in awakening Peredur, not as Wolfram has it by covering the divine colours with a cloth, but by "fair words," as Cei foresaw. The two men like each other immediately and become firm friends.

In the last part of the Peredur story we find both heroes in Arthur's hall, at the very moment when the Black Maiden appears on her mule to curse Peredur for not having spoken at the Grail Castle. At the same time she tells of a maiden in distress who urgently needs help. The Black Maiden is the same emissary we meet as Luned in *The Lady of the Fountain* and as Kundry in Wolfram's *Parzival.* Gawain is immediately prepared to come to the girl's aid, when another knight appears, accuses him of having murdered his lord and challenges him to a duel. Therefore the two friends depart in different directions: Peredur to seek the Grail Castle, Gawain to answer the challenge of the knight before coming to the aid of the maiden in distress. The scene is symbolic: Gawain has not one, but two worldly tasks awaiting him, whereas Peredur remains focused on the one and only, namely to find the Grail again and to redeem the land. Yet in the *Mabinogion* we never hear that he actually succeeds.

Similarly, Wolfram's *Parzival* "leaves us with the feeling that ... a decisive point has been omitted or suppressed ... What finally enables Parzival to achieve the Grail after his initial failure is never explained."[15] One could of course speculate that Wolfram saw the combat and reconciliation with Parzival's

Moorish half-brother Feirefiz (a figure of Wolfram's own invention) as the turning point.

Another solution is suggested by R.S. Loomis in his book *Wales and Arthurian Legend.*[16] Loomis draws attention to the fact that the moment we lose sight of Parzival, Gawain zooms into view with his adventures at the Castle of Wonders. And he asks: "Could the exploits of Gawain be a disguise for Parzival's initiatory experience?"[17] He claims that Parzival and Gawain are not only brethren in arms and Year King and tanist (as Graves suggests), but one and the same person under different names. We remember that Pryderi's (Peredur's) earlier name in the *First Branch* was Gwri Gwalt Adwyn, meaning Gwri Goldenhair. This name eventually becomes contracted into "Gawain." This leaves us with the mythological data that the hero variously called Pryderi/Peredur/Parzival as well as Gawain/Gwri Goldenhair is always the same Sun Hero, avenger of wrongdoings and redeemer of the Waste Land by his devotion and service to the goddess Lady Sovereignty.

Tragically his career is cut short and perverted by the ascendancy of patriarchy, or perhaps by the political necessities of the day. The priestesses of the goddess, now called "the Witches of Gloucester," have become the code name of the real enemies of land and people and therefore must be killed. In the Peredur story of the *Mabinogion* (which we may regard as the original *Parzival)* Gawain is again at Peredur's side and both men decide to ask for Arthur's help against the witches just as Culhwch had done. It seems that the former champions of the goddess are suddenly helpless without the great king's intervention, a sign that in spite of Morgaine's attacks against Arthur, patriarchy has carried the day. Peredur kills the witches, his former benefactresses, with the lame excuse "that it was prophesied." The story ends with the revelation that the last fight with the witches takes place at "the Fortress of Marvels."[18] Could it be that the final combat between Arthur and the pagan priestesses erupted at the same castle which Gawain delivered from the magic of the sorcerer Clingshor? Remarkably, here the story which originally contained initiation tales of a brotherhood of goddess champions abruptly turns into a tale about open warfare against her priestesses. It appears that the former champions have no choice but to change sides, declare themselves Arthur's men and take part in the 'final solution' of exterminating the priestesses which are suddenly called "witches."

Clingshor's kingdom

The English folklorist G.R. Phillips has attempted to locate the Castle of Wonders. According to him it is not situated at Gloucester, as the texts claim, but at Ingleton in northwest York, near what is now the Yorkshire Dales National Park. Close by is Ingleborough Hill, an outcrop once crowned by a pre-Celtic hill fort. In Roman times this fort was called *Rigdunum,* "King's Castle." According to Phillips the area exactly matches the topographical data described by Wolfram in Gawain's adventures.[19] The sorcerer Clingshor (Wolfram's Klingsor) never appears in the story, but his name is always mentioned with dread. The people call the area "Clingshor's kingdom," yet nobody knows who Clingshor was. Was he a pagan god or a druid who fought a lonely battle against the goddess or against advancing Christianity? It could well be that Clingshor was much older than the Druids, because here in the Yorkshire Dales we still find a certain matriarchal mentality, similar to that of other parts of Europe where matriarchy has lasted longer.

In any case it seems that Rigdunum was a pre-Celtic sanctuary dedicated to the goddess. This is the place where after many a hair-raising adventure, Gawain and Orgeluse are united. By passing the difficult tests of Château Merveilles he liberates her from the spell of the magician who, according to some, had used her as a decoy for unsuspecting knights. Gawain's ordeals in the Castle of Wonders — the magic bed, the self-shooting arrows, the fight with the lion — can all be interpreted as symbolic descriptions of initiation tests, similar to those imposed on the bards by Ceridwen. The Castle of Wonders must have been a place where different strata of beliefs and cult rituals merged.

Wolfram tells the story as a parallel to Parzival's love for Conduiramur, without however making any value judgements. Parzival too had been offered Orgeluse's favours, but he had declined, pleading his love for Conduiramour. Medievalists believe that Wolfram intended the name to show that a man who lusted after Orgeluse with all her wiles was never worthy of the Grail's vision. Reading Wolfram in a good translation it becomes clear that this is by no means the case.[20] To Wolfram, Parzival's love for his wife and Gawain's love for Orgeluse were of equal worth, even if the two women were very different. The name *Conduir amour* — "to lead by love" — is entirely Wolfram's invention. By contrast, *Orgeluse de Logroi* is a mythological name and one of the many sobriquets for the goddess. It signifies "the Proud One of Logres," and as we know, Logres is the Welsh name for Britain. In particular the name applies to old Brigantium, the tribal land of the pre-Celtic Pritenni and the later celticized Britanni. This tribe was especially devoted to the goddess Brigantia who, to judge from many European place names, was also worshipped on the Continent. Orgeluse de Logroi, "the Proud One of Brigantia," is none other than Sovereignty in her local manifestation. She had every reason to be proud and to demand the most heroic deeds from a knight who aspired to her service. Whether Wolfram knew what her name meant is a moot question, but it is indicative that the extermination of the Witches takes place in the Castle of Wonders as this fortress was her abode and the "Witches" her priestesses.[21]

Medieval authors such as Malory agree that after many adventures and tests Gawain finally wins the love of Orgeluse, that is, the local goddess of Brigantia. Yet in their telling she is the goddess no longer. She has been transformed into a lady of dubious character, a sorcerer's decoy and her favours do nothing to enhance Gawain's honour. The results prove the final victory of patriarchy. From a former champion of the goddess, Gawain's image in the Arthurian cycles was changed into that of a libertine, a layabout and a habitual seducer of women. The medieval court poets, makers of public opinion, had done their work well.

Gawain in Middle English folklore

Despite the medieval interpretations, John Matthews cites numerous further proofs for Gawain's status as "Knight of the Goddess." One of the most interesting is the affection in which he was held in popular narrative in medieval Britain, particularly in Yorkshire, the ancient centre of Brigantia, in contrast with the critical treatment afforded to Gawain in Malory's *Morte d'Arthur.* While Malory's Gawain is intended as a perfidious contrast to Lancelot the tragic lover, he survives in Middle English folklore as the most perfect of knights, surpassing both the Welsh Pryderi/Peredur/Perceval and the French/Pictish Lancelot du Lac.

And here we have to mention two stories which are unknown on the Continent: *Gawain and the Green Knight* and *Sir Gawain's Wedding.* It is significant that both stories are set in Central England, in the land of the Goddess Brigantia, where the localities mentioned in the stories are well known. The two tales must have circulated there for centuries until they surfaced in writing and became part of Medieval English literature, e.g. in Chaucer's *Canterbury Tales.*

Here is a summary of *Gawain and the Green Knight,* a Middle English poem which an unknown poet wrote around the year 1400.

The story begins at King Arthur's court in Camelot. During the preparations for Christmas there appeared suddenly a gigantic knight, all dressed in green, green of hair and skin and riding a green chaperoned horse. He carried an enormous battle axe and a branch of holly in token of peace. He declared that he had come to challenge the knights of Arthur to a test of courage. He offered his head to be cut off, if the knight who would strike the blow was prepared to offer his head to be cut off within a year and a day. None of the knights dared to accept the challenge, and when King Arthur declared himself ready for it, Sir Gawain arose and asked to strike the blow. He took the axe and cut off the giant's head. But to everyone's astonishment the giant picked up his head and put it back between his shoulders.

Laughingly he ordered Gawain to be at the "Chapel in the Green" within a year and a day to receive the counter blow.

The year passed much too quickly for Gawain. At last the time approached when he had to leave court and ride in search of the "Chapel in the Green." He wandered for weeks in the "Wilderness of Wirrell" and at last he came to the castle of Sir Bertilac, where he found a friendly welcome. He was told that the chapel he was looking for was only a few hours away, but in the meantime he was invited to rest and enjoy Sir Bertilac's hospitality. He met the beautiful chatelaine, Sir Bertilac's wife, and an ugly old lady who was however treated with great respect.

The next morning his host invited him to come hunting with him, but Gawain declined in order to rest from his long journey. Jokingly the two knights agreed to exchange everything they could win during the day. After Bertilac had left, his wife appeared in Gawain's chamber and tried to seduce him. Gawain permitted her a kiss, which in the evening he returned faithfully to his host. On the two following days the lady continued with her game, but Gawain steadfastly declined her favours. At last, beside her kisses, she gave him a green belt, promising that it would protect him from every danger. Gawain again returned the kisses to Sir Bertilac, but prudently kept the green belt[22] hoping that it would give him protection from the Green Knight.

The following morning he left in search of the Chapel in the Green. Sir Bertilac gave him one of his men as an escort and guide. On the way this man offered to take him to a safe place, but again Gawain resisted the temptation. At last they found the "Green Chapel," a moss covered grotto or former grave chamber. From afar they could hear an axe being sharpened and the Green Knight greeted them with taunting words. Gawain dismounted and knelt to receive the deadly blow. Twice the axe touched his neck, and the third time he received a slight cut. Then Gawain arose and declared that he had kept his word.

Now the Green Knight admitted that he was Sir Bertilac and the old lady in his castle had spellbound him in this guise. She was none other than Morgaine la Fay and she had invented the game to test Arthur's knights. Gawain had passed the test with honours, except that he should not have kept the green belt. He returned to Camelot a much wiser and more modest man. King Arthur and his knights honoured him greatly and they all decided to wear a green baldric in his honour.

The theme is ancient and comes from Irish literature where, in *The Feast of Bricriu,* the giant Curoi challenges the warriors in the same way, but only Cuchulainn accepts the challenge and keeps his word. He too is let off lightly by Curoi. Perhaps there is also a connection with the British God of the Head, well known to archaeologists and also as Bran Son of Llyr in the Second Branch of the *Mabinogi.* It may be that the saga has its origin in a very ancient ritual, perhaps even a human sacrifice, which was later changed into a test of courage.

Again Morgaine's enmity of Arthur and his court is clearly shown. Her appearance as an ugly old woman is repeated in the second story entitled *Sir Gawain and Lady Ragnall* or *Sir Gawain's Wedding.* The story is well known in England but not on the European continent.

Here is a summary of *Sir Gawain and Lady Ragnall:*

On a hunting expedition King Arthur found himself suddenly in the realm of the giant Gomer Somer Jour who threatened to kill him. Arthur could only save himself by promising to solve a riddle within a year and a day. And the riddle was: "What do women want most of all?"

On his return to court he met an ugly crone who promised to give him the answer of the riddle if Sir Gawain was prepared to marry her. To save the kings's life, Gawain agreed and the wedding of the odd couple was celebrated with great pomp and ceremony. In the wedding night, Gawain brought himself to kiss the ugly old woman, whereupon she turned into a beautiful maiden. She explained that her wicked brother Gomer Somer Jour had banned her into the ugly shape, until the noblest knight of Arthur's court was prepared to take her for his wife. Now it would be up to Gawain to choose if he wanted her to be beautiful by day for all the people, or by night just for him alone. After some argument Gawain told her that this question concerned her alone and that therefore it was up to her to decide.

The lady was overjoyed and said: "This is the answer to the riddle my brother gave the king to solve: the greatest wish of all women is *to have their own will."*

When Arthur returned with this answer to the giant, he was outraged and cursed his sister, Lady Ragnall, for having solved the riddle for him. Gawain and Lady Ragnall lived for many years in great happiness and a son, Guinglain, was born to them and he became an excellent knight at Arthur's court.[23]

According to Matthews both these stories belong to a ritual test which the chosen hero must pass. In *Lady Ragnall* the test consists in the acceptance of the goddess in her ugly aspect and in answering a riddle about women's integrity. It is not enough to be an invincible fighter. The goddess demands far more. In the story of the Green Knight the hero must show himself prepared to die for a given promise. Not only that: in the scenes of the bedchamber Gawain proves to be in complete control of his sexual impulses even while facing imminent death. At the same time he shows complete self control and perfect *courtoisie* towards Sir Bertilac's lady. These are new qualities for men who lived in an age of continuous warfare, and one may add, sexual deprivation.

The giant Gomer Somer Jour, the Green Knight and Sir Bertilac are different manifestations of the same mythological figure, otherwise known as the Green Man, the Lord of the Forest and the Animals, the primeval partner of the goddess, Cernunnos.

Matthews also points out the parallels which relate both stories to the *Four Branches of the Mabinogi:*

— Gawain/Pwyll/Arthur meet the Green Knight /Grey Hunter (Gomer Somer Jour/Arawn);
— The hero is given a difficult task to fulfil: single combat/sexual temptation, and a riddle to answer;
— Decapitation: Havgan, Green Knight, Bran Son of Llyr, Cuchulainn/Curoi;
— Wedding with an otherworldly woman: Rhiannon, Lady Ragnall;
— Birth of a son of the hero and the goddess/fairy: Pryderi/Guinglain as future tribal hero.

As we have seen, these elements return again and again in Celtic sagas and form the mythological framework in which the historic changes are played out. In fact Matthews cites nine stories with the same plot and structure and there are probably many more to be found in folktale collections.

According to John and Caitlín Matthews, Gawain and Arthur had to play the same role originally.[24] This is disputable considering their opposing ideology. But then John and Caitlín Matthews also deny the fact that Arthur and the Goddess of Sovereignty were fighting a battle royal for supremacy in Celtic realms.

It is interesting however that in the French story *Le bel inconnu* Gawain and the fairy Blanchemains have a son, "the Handsome Unknown," who is later told by his mother that his name is "Guinglain," a name suspiciously similar to "Cuchulainn," the Irish tribal hero. In an earlier version the fairy Blanchemains may well have been the goddess, whose love fulfils Gawain's heroic destiny.

The story of Lady Ragnall is a late version of the hero test we find originally in the Irish saga cycles: the test in which the future king must accept Lady Sovereignty in her ugly aspect before being accepted as her spouse and king. In the patriarchal world order such a test is no longer understood and has sunk to the level of farce. This is the reason why Chaucer had the story told by the merry widow of Bath. It is significant that the story of *Gawain and the Green Knight* is told frequently in the repertoire of Arthurian stories, whereas the story of Lady Ragnall had to await the second wave of American feminism to be resurrected for modern readers. Jean Markale, a scholar of Breton background, writes that the kiss Gawain gives to the ugly Lady Ragnall must be regarded as the first step of a heroic career. And he quotes the story of the Irish king Niall (see Chapter 1) who as the only one of his brothers was prepared to sleep with the old hag of the well and was rewarded with the kingship of Ireland. It has often been said that the two aspects, one ugly and the other beautiful, are symbolic of the appearance of the country (and by implication its Sovereignty) in summer and in winter. In temperate latitudes the ruler has to expect and accept this change. Markale however gives it another explanation: "The change of the old hag into a radiant beauty is in reality a change in Niall, and by implication in Gawain himself: these men now see Woman with new eyes."[25] Gawain is not a libertine and a philanderer. He is a true knight of the goddess who honours women's "own will" as Lady Ragnall taught him. Only men who have overcome the idea of male supremacy over women can claim to be truly in control of themselves and hence of their destiny.

CONCLUSION

The Once and Future Goddess

When the Indo-European Celts came to settle in Central and Western Europe they had to come to terms with the spirituality of the Neolithic farmers and pastoralists whose land they had conquered. Just as the invading Hellenes had to accommodate the goddess of the Pelasgians, the Celts had to find a way to merge the worship of their sky- and wood-gods with the belief in the power of the Triple Earth Mother. She was not only a great spiritual being, but also the Land personified and hence the lives of the conquerors depended on her and her fertility. Her names were many, and according to the season of the year she appeared as a beautiful maiden, the loving mother of a son and the wise old crone or death goddess.

By careful comparison of archaeological iconography and images on Celtic coins the French mythologist J.J. Hatt has shown one of the ways the two religions merged: the Earth Goddess was wooed and won by the sky god Taranis. She became his spouse and hence the Queen of Heaven, Rigani — a name of the same root as the Latin *regina* (queen).

But when spring and summer was over, the harvest done and winter began, the goddess wished to return to her abode under the earth and to her former partner Cernunnos, Lord of the Forest and the Animals. Taranis tried to take her back and war erupted among the gods. Some took the side of the goddess and some that of Taranis. As the years rolled on, so did the battle for the person of the goddess and of her son Maponos/Mabon. Farmers and graziers needed her blessing for the growing of their crops and the health of their herds. Therefore they never gave up her worship and that of her partner Cernunnos. As her presence on Earth was important during the growing season she was given a human partner and champion, her *heros* or Year King. She celebrated a Sacred Marriage with him, in which she was represented by her priestess, the queen, and he gave his life for her at the end of the year in order to accompany her to the Otherworld. In Greece this hero was known as Heracles/Hercules ("the Glory of Hera"), in Gaul he was Smertrius. In Britain and Ireland he had many names, one of which may have been Pwyll.

The name "Rigani," originally found only in Gaul, must have changed via "Rigantona," "Great Queen" to that of "Rhiannon" in Britain. Very early her image must have merged with that of the Celtic horse goddess Epona as well as with that of the pre-Celtic Earth Mother Modron/Matrona to form a complex deity who has many parallels and similarities with the pre-Hellenic barley goddess Demeter and the Roman Cardea or Ceres.

The First and the Third Branches of the *Mabinogi* show in a veiled form the story of Rhiannon's (Rigani's?) persecution by an importunate suitor. Could he originally have been a god of the invading Celts? His name "Gwawl" signifies "Light" and could stand for a sky god such as Taranis, "the Thunderer," possessor of the lightning bolt. Or was it "Lugh of the Long Arm," the sun god, whose name is also connected with "Light"? Rhiannon is shown as choosing an earthly spouse and teaching him royal wisdom. But neither she herself nor her son escapes the avenge of the snubbed sky gods. Finally it is the wisdom and moderation of Manawydan, a former Irish sea god, which succeeds in liberating Rhiannon together with her son, thereby ending the Waste Land or "Desolation of Dyfed." Manawydan represents a new heroic ideal which owes more to Classical wisdom and the Stoa than to the Celtic warrior image. It is aristocratic and élitist, comprising a wide spectrum of human experience.

We do not know when the ancient rite of sacrificial regicide or the sacrifice of his representative, the Year King, was abandoned. But the fact remains that in pagan times Celtic kings and chieftains considered themselves the true earthly spouses of the

Goddess of the Land, "Lady Sovereignty" and their ascension to the throne presupposed a symbolic marriage with her. The relationship of the king and Lady Sovereignty was the most important symbol in Celtic religion and had considerable political consequences. In this constellation the queen functioned as the representative of the goddess and as her priestess, a role greatly misunderstood in the Arthurian cycles.

Celtic kingship was not hereditary but by designation of the ruling monarch during his lifetime, or failing this, by election — a form of succession known as tanistry. Only morally and physically unblemished man could aspire to kingship, which was originally a priestly office, while the true power lay with the queen. If the king had been wounded in battle or was otherwise found to be unfit he had to abdicate. This relatively weak position of the king may have contributed to the readiness of Celtic kings to accept Christianity, where their power was greatly enhanced.

The story of Bran, himself a "wounded king," shows how he tried to secure succession for his son. It is indicative that Robert Graves identifies Bran with Cronos and that Bran himself, at the most dramatic moment of the story calls himself "Pierced Thigh," thus revealing the secret tragedy of the "Wounded King" who can no longer hold office. The necessity of a "royal footholder" for Math is another means by which an ageing king tried to remain in power.

In the *Fourth Branch* the dramatic impact results from the brother/sister conflict of Arianrhod and Gwydion. As the bard Taliesin reveals, the British goddess Arianrhod owned a "revolving" castle in the constellation of Corona Borealis, which was the abode or "prison" of dead kings, heroes and bards. Arianrhod as the keeper of heroic souls is the Death Goddess *par excellence.* Gwydion's attempt to make her the mother of his son against her will and knowledge is an insult to her powers over Life and Death and shows total ignorance of her original role.

Apart from her "revolving Castle" in the constellation Corona Borealis, Arianrhod was also connected with the constellation of Auriga "the Charioteer," representing the thirteenth sign of the Celtic zodiac. It was called the Spider and Arianrhod "Silver

Wheel" (Spider Web?) presided over it. The constellation is situated between Taurus and Gemini and its most luminous star is Cappella. The fact that in the British Isles fifteen stone circles were found to be aligned to this star indicates that the worship of Arianrhod goes back to the Stone Age and is therefore pre-Celtic. The legend that a web-spinning spider inspired King Robert the Bruce to continue his struggle against the English may allude to a special connection of Scottish kings with Arianrhod as Spider Goddess.

In the *Four Branches of the Mabinogi* and in the *Three Romances* we have perhaps of the most important remnants of Celtic mythology and goddess cult in Britain. The seven narratives are a treasure trove for cultural historians and it is here that we find the true origins of chivalry and Western gender relations. The other stories may be less important, but contain valuable information about the role and repertoire of bards and storytellers, whilst *The Dream of Macsen Wledig* is an interesting permutation of historic memories. Here the author is reminiscing on the time of Roman rule in Britain. It was a brief moment of glory when the British princess Helena became the mother of a Roman Emperor, and ruled the world through him.

One thing which is completely missing in the collection are the "Little People." Considering the many stories of dwarfs, elves and fairies in Celtic folklore this is surprising and hard to explain. It seems to prove that the *Mabinogion* stories were collected and edited with the sole intent of preserving the goddess faith in a veiled form. They survived perhaps because they were largely initiation tales and were originally intended exclusively for the nobility and especially for young aristocrats who could aspire to kingship, and heroic feats, a sacrificial death and a glorious afterlife. The tradition was continued in the veneration of Mary by the Knights Templar and other Christian militant Orders.

By contrast, the stories of the "Little People," whether referring to a pre-historic race, to so-called elementals, or even to the Latin *lares* were more of interest to the common people who had to accommodate them in their daily life and work. The fact that the tradition is remarkably similar throughout Europe lends them authenticity within the pan-European belief system, but they do not enter into the "inner circle" of goddess worship and ritual.[1] This in itself is an important sign of social stratification in pre-Christian as well as in feudal society. The elementals are still with us today, as they were never demonized to the same extent as the goddess, appearing in folk- and fairy tales as wicked witch and in the humorous guise of "the Devil's Grandmother."

Whilst Greek and Roman goddesses were allowed an ornamental role in classical education, the Bible abhors the goddess as "an abomination unto the Lord," and this anathema was also spoken over the Celtic goddess. It is little known moreover that the often quoted "god Mammon" of the Bible is none other than the Latin *Juno Moneta* whose temple in Rome also served as the Roman Mint: she was *Mammona iniquitatis,* the "Great Mother of Iniquity."

In spite of all this the cult of pagan deities continued under the new religion. The decapitated John the Baptist inherited the worship of Bran the God of the Head. Midsummer Day became St John's Day and the sun fires were lit in St John's honour. Another decapitated martyr is St James, whose legendary grave at Santiago de Compostela ("the Field of the Stars") to judge by its great antiquity, probably marks the sanctuary of an older pagan deity who may have been connected with the cult of the Head in another Celtic land, Galicia.

The continuation of goddess worship under Christianity would require a book by itself. While Cromwell's men successfully eradicated "mariolatry" in Britain, it is very much alive in Catholic countries where, according to C.G. Jung, it fulfils a psychological need. The Latin anthem *Salve Regina,* originally a hymn to Juno Queen of Heaven, admirably expresses the lament of the "exiled children of Eve" for her return. Even after two millennia of Christianity, the genius of Goethe was inspired to salute the Goddess at the end of his *Faust* drama:

> Virgin, Mother, holy Queen
> Goddess be Thou gracious!

EPILOGUE

A personal note

In the Australia of the Fifties I was classified as "hostile alien," ostracized and condemned to solitary confinement in Suburbia. Having grown up in the Tyrolean Alps I was pining with nostalgia for the mountains and reading was my only consolation. Once a kind neighbour lent me some paperbacks and told me that they were the legends of her native Wales. I was captivated. During my childhood I had suffered greatly from Fascist chauvinism, which forbade us children to speak German at school. I could sympathize with the Welsh in their struggle for their language and cultural identity. In those four paperbacks, the American author Evangeline Walton had retold the *Four Branches of the Mabinogi* in the form of historical novels (see *Further Reading).* Walton had understood that the many conflicts and riddles of the Four Branches were due to the culture clash between British matriarchal tribes and the "New Tribes' from the Continent which were organized according to the patriarchal system. Oddly, these ancient Welsh sagas had much in common with the legends of the Dolomites I had read in my childhood. In the Alpine wonder tales of the Raeto-Roman Ladinians and Grisons, the conflict of matriarchy and patriarchy also figured as the common denominator. Both saga cycles told of men and women of an archaic age: in both cases heroes wooed and won the love of a powerful otherworldly lady in possession of precious nature wisdom which she tried to save from the onslaughts of a new era. Whenever her sacred laws were broken there followed catastrophes of cataclysmic proportions.

In faraway Australia I had inadvertently stumbled onto the

sacred beliefs of my ancestors, before Christianity and before the advent of patriarchy. So God had not cursed us after all because Eve had eaten the apple! Suddenly my ontological limitations as a woman were gone and for the first time in life I felt a free human being.

Then, in the Seventies we were overwhelmed by a veritable avalanche of books centred on the topic of "matriarchy." Ethnology, archaeology, linguistics and other auxiliary sciences had discovered that the beginnings of Europe had been wrongly transmitted. Archaeological discoveries in Crete and Anatolia proved the existence of highly successful societies who were monotheistic, egalitarian and gynocentrally organized. The biblical wars of the patriarchal Israelites against the matriarchal Canaanites had been repeated in Asia Minor, in Greece and finally in far distant Central and Western Europe under the same premises. Only the names of the deities differed. The change from matriarchy to patriarchy was a long drawn out historic process which took place in different countries at different times, and in some parts it is still not quite completed. The first to draw attention to this important change was the Swiss J.J. Bachofen with his 1861 book *Das Mutterrecht* ("The Right of the Mother"). There followed Sir James Frazer with *The Golden Bough,* a study of ritual regicide, Robert Graves with his new interpretation of *The Greek Myths* and his 1974 work, *The White Goddess;* while the Breton Jean Markale, teaching at the Sorbonne in Paris, wrote of the high status of Celtic women. In 1980 there appeared in Germany a book by Heide Goettner-Abendroth under the title *Die Göttin und ihr Heros* ("The Goddess and her Hero"). Here the author attempted for the first time a structural analysis of this mythological process, but largely omitting Celtic mythology. When I drew her attention to the *Mabinogion* stories she suggested I undertake a closer study. Understandably perhaps, Australian universities were not interested in this research. But I found three Welsh scholars who became my guides and mentors in the task and to whom I am deeply grateful: Professor Gwyn Jones, co-translator of *The Mabinogion,* the Welsh author Glyn Ashton, and Professor Stephen Knight of Cardiff University. These men fired me with the necessary inspiration and through the untiring assistance of intervarsity librarians both in England and Australia I discovered many co-travellers who had come to the same conclusions.

There are few positive mythical stories or initiation tales for women in Western literature. As they were not deemed worthy of being written down, they were usually orally transmitted and told to devoted collectors who had them printed. Therefore they can only be found in the folk tales of the poorest regions of Europe, where matriarchy found its last refuge: near the subsistence farmers of the Alps and the Pyrenees, the fisher folk of the islands around Ireland and Scotland and perhaps in the Finnish *Kalevala,* an entire epic in rhymes, saved from oblivion in the nick of time by a Swedish collector. The Semitic religions with the story of Eve's sin have objectified women as the "weak vessel." Church Fathers and Reformers reinforced this idea to the detriment of society. Women were systematically cut off from their inner resources and kept in spiritual atrophy. In England women were legally at a par with children, idiots and criminals, in spite of the fact that the old British laws had once been collated by a woman, the British princess Marcia, and promulgated by Alfred the Great. Nevertheless the Feminine Principle remained strong within British mentality. Britain remained "the Motherland" and its best thinkers and poets are nourished from this source. Lately there have been signs that Anglo-American pragmatism shall not carry the day. Mythic figures like Rhiannon prove that feminine values do not preclude "empowerment" and inner strength. The study of the Celtic Goddess in all her facets can free us from an outlived mentality and bring unexpected new energies. Perhaps this book can inspire readers to embark on a similar quest.

The Goddess returns! Even in everyday life. The *Stuttgarter Nachrichten* of April 26, 2001, carries the news that an equestrian statue of Epona was recently unearthed near her ancient sanctuary in Stuttgart ("Mare's Garden") where incidentally the first motor car was built. The large effigy of the Goddess is to be re-erected at an important node of the Autobahn where it is hoped that she will protect motorists. All hail to the Great Queen!

References

Author's note: All quotations from German sources are in the author's own translation.

Introduction

1 *The Mabinogion,* Trans. G. Jones, p.x.
2 Jean Markale, *Women of the Celts,* London 1975, p.39.

Chapter 1

1 M.-L. Sjoestedt, *Celtic Gods and Heroes,* Berkeley 1982, p.51.
2 An example of this idea prevailing until recent times was the Doge's marriage to the Sea, celebrated annually at Venice.
3 Remnants of this ideology lingered long enough to allow Queen Victoria to ascend the throne of England, but debarred her as queen of her Hanoverian possessions in Germany, where the Frankish Salic Law prevailed.
4 Jan de Vries, *Keltische Religion,* Stuttgart 1961.
5 Eoin MacNeill, quoted in Patrick Power, *Sex and Marriage in Ancient Ireland,* Dublin 1976, pp.64ff.
6 Georges Dumézil, *L'Idéologie tripartite des Indo-Européens,* Brussels 1958.
7 Jean-Jacques Hatt, *Die keltische Götterwelt und ihre bildliche Darstellung in vor-römischer Zeit.* Exhibition catalogue "Die Kelten in Mitteleuropa," Salzburger Landesregierung, Kulturabteilung, Salzburg 1980, pp.52ff.
8 Hatt, J.J., *ibid.* p.54
9 Robert Graves, *The White Goddess,* New York, 1974, p.125
10 This is the traditional feast of All Saints and All Souls in the Catholic Church. The old Scottish Halloween signifies "Evening before the Feast of All Hallows" (= All Saints).
11 This purification refers to a ritual bath prescribed to Jewish women after having given birth.
12 In the Middle Ages this night became the evening and night before St Walpurgis Day. Walpurgis or Walburga was an Anglo-Saxon abbess and missionary in the land of the Frankish Kings, who died in 779 and was canonized soon after. Obviously she was neither a witch nor a Germanic goddess as is sometimes assumed, and it is quite by accident that her name became attached to this night of orgiastic pagan revelries.
13 On the European continent he was identified with Oberon, the king of the elves.

14 M.-L. Sjoestedt 1982, p.27 quoting Anwyl, *Transactions of the Gaelic Society,* Inverness No.26, p.44.
15 Quoted by Robert Graves 1974, p.284.
16 In Christian times all temples to Lugh / Mercury were rededicated to Saint Michael the Archangel and adversary of Lucifer. Hence all Lugh's former sanctuaries on mountain tops are now known as Michael Mount or Mont Saint Michel.
17 Proinsias Mac Cana, *Celtic Mythology,* Feltham 1983, pp.117f.
18 Robert Graves 1974, p.384.
19 It is a striking coincidence that the first motor car was built at the main centre of Epona's cult, in Stuttgart (Mare's Garden), South West Germany. The museum of this city has one of the richest collections of Epona altars and steles, found in or near the places where horses were once stabled. Like Isis, Epona was propitiated with offerings of roses.

Chapter 2

1 Anybody who has ever spent a summer in Austria or Bavaria is immediately reminded here of the summer festivals and processions organized by the farmers in honour of Our Lady.
2 Tacitus, *Historia* 5:22, quoted from *The Complete Works of Tacitus,* trans. A.J. Church and W.J. Brodrib, New York, 1942, pp.712, 717f, 728–31.
3 Jean Markale, *Women of the Celts,* London 1975.
4 Sir Ifor Williams, *Lectures on Early Welsh Poetry,* Dublin Institute of Advanced Studies, 1954, pp.45 and 48.
5 *ibid.* p.47.
6 Jean Markale 1975, Chap.2, pp.30ff.
7 Uwe Wesel, *Der Mythos vom Matriarchat,* Frankfurt 1980, p.145 (Author's translation).
8 *ibid.* p.129.
9 *ibid.* p.130.
10 Joseph Weisweiler, "Die Stellung der Frau bei den Kelten und das Problem des 'Keltischen Mutterechts'," *Zeitschrift für keltische Philologie,* Vol.21, 1940, pp.205–79.
11 Christopher McAll, "The Normal Paradigms of a Woman's Life in Irish and Welsh Law Tracts," in D. Jenkins and M.E. Owen (eds.), *The Welsh Law of Women,* Cardiff 1980 pp.7–23.
12 D. Jenkins, "Property Interests in the Classical Welsh Law of Women," in D. Jenkins and M.E. Owen 1980, pp.62–92.
13 M.E. Owen, "Shame and Reparation: Woman's Place in the Kin," in D. Jenkins and M.E. Owen 1980, p.45.
14 *ibid.* p.49, par.42.
15 R.R. Davies, "The Status of Women and the Practice of Marriage in Late-Medieval Wales," in D. Jenkins and M.E. Owen 1980, p.101.
16 *ibid.* p.103.
17 D. Jenkins, "Property Interests in the Classical Welsh Law of Women," in D. Jenkins and M.E. Owen 1980, p.85.
18 Owen M.E. *op.cit.* p.49.
19 *ibid.* p.49.

20 *The Laws of Hywel Da (The Book of Blegywryd)* trans./ed. M. Richards, Liverpool 1954, p.69.
21 *The Laws of Hywel Da, op.cit.* p.64.
22 *ibid.* p.66.
23 *ibid.* p.66.
24 D. Jenkins, *op.cit.* p.1, quoting law historian F.W. Maitland (n.d.).

Chapter 3

1 Lewis Spence 1979, pp.193–214.
2 Sir Ifor Williams 1954, pp.64f.
3 Sir Ifor Williams, *ibid.*
4 Robert Graves 1974.
5 Cited in Caitlín Matthews, *Arthur and the Sovereignty of Britain,* London 1989, pp.250–52.

Chapter 4

1 Sylvia and Paul Botheroyd, *Lexikon der keltischen Mythologie,* Munich 1992, quoting from the works of Jean-Jacques Hatt, University of Strasbourg, pp.277–80.
2 Ernest Bornemann, *Das Patriarchat,* Frankfurt, 1975, p.41.
3 Pigs were sacred animals for the Celts, and according to legend it was the barley goddess Ceridwen who first brought bees and piglets to Britain.
4 As Gwawl means "light, luminous" there may be a connection with the Gaulish Lugh, a name with the same meaning.
5 Relief of Epona found in Haus Furpach/Neukirchen/Saar now in the Museum für Vor-und Frühgeschichte, Saarbrücken, Germany. This relief shows the bag as a uterine shape, with an unmistakable vulva as its opening, a symbol of the goddess's life-giving powers. Reproduced in R. Fester, M.E.P. Koenig and D.F. and A.D. Jonas, *Weib und Macht,* Frankfurt 1980, Pl.24.
6 Christina Hole, *Dictionary of British Folk Customs,* London 1978.
7 *Pwyll Prince of Dyfed,* in G. & T. Jones 1949, p.9; in J. Gantz 1976, p.52.
8 There is another mountain called Arber in the Bavarian Forest. Its outlines on the horizon can be likened to the profile of an old woman and it is the locus of many legends about "the Old Woman of the Arber": she can be frightening or benevolent like a fairy or a goddess. The Bavarian Forest in South East Germany, now a National Park, is ancient Celtic territory.
9 "We have Giraldus Cambrensis's shocked account of an Irish kingship rite whereby the king symbolized his union with the land by a pretended coitus with a mare and bathing in the broth of her flesh. Giraldus wrote about twelfth-century Donegal!" (Caitlín Matthews, *Mabon and the Mysteries of Britain,* London 1987, p.33).
10 The *-u-* in Peredur is pronounced like the French *u.*
11 *Per-ce-val* is French for "through this vale."
12 It is important to remember that Wagner's opera *Parsifal* rests on quite different premises.

Chapter 5

1 To summarize, the classic life of a hero contains the following features:
a) At least one of his parents is a god or a goddess;
b) His conception follows some sexual or social irregularity;
c) He must achieve a heroic journey to the Otherworld (Underworld), or some unknown or hostile country and bring back a boon, a freed prisoner or some great treasure;
d) He becomes a prisoner and his liberation is achieved only with great difficulty;
e) He ends his days tragically, usually in combat.
As we see, all these conditions are fulfilled in Pryderi's life and recounted in the *Four Branches.*

2 Pen Arddun means "Shining Head," in a different translation "Head of the Shining Ones."

3 *Branwen Daughter of Llyr,* trans. J. Gantz 1976, p.67

4 "Matriarch" is Gwyn Jones' translation. Gantz translates the Welsh word *prifrieni* with "queen," "ancestor," although Branwen has no living descendants. It seems to be an ancient title which predestines her son to be king. The other two "matriarchs" were presumably Rhiannon of Dyfed (Pembrokeshire), mother of Pryderi, and Arianrhod of Gwynedd (Venedotia, Snowdonia), mother of Llew.

5 *Branwen Daughter of Llyr,* trans. G. Jones, p.26. Who does this "they" refer to: Ireland? Or both islands united? Under Irish or under British predominance? The reader is left to draw his or her own conclusions.

6 "Gwern" or "Fern" is the Irish form of "Bran." Graves uses *Gwearn* and *Fearn.*

7 Compare A. Aarne and S. Thompson, *The Types of the Folktale,* Helsinki 1981, p.242, No 707.

8 Proinsias Mac Cana, *The Mabinogi,* Cardiff 1977, p.59.

9 *Branwen Daughter of Llyr,* trans. J. Gantz 1976, p.77.

10 According to R. Graves 1974, p.66, the correct spelling of *Chronos* in this case is *Cronos,* "crow or raven." The name Bran means "Raven."

11 Graves 1974, p.233.

12 *op.cit.* p.171

13 Anne Ross, *Pagan Celtic Britain,* London 1974, pp.94ff.

14 It is interesting that in English churches decapitated saints, who carry their head in their hands are much more numerous than in continental Europe, where the severed head of John the Baptist filled the same function. It was venerated, particularly by women, until well into the time of the Reformation.

15 Anthropologists note that in some tribal societies twins were seen as omens of misfortune and were sacrificed.

16 *Peredur Son of Efrawg,* trans. J. Gantz 1976, p.242.

17 Robert Graves 1974, p.27ff.

18 S. and P. Botheroyd 1992, p.14.

19 *Branwen Daughter of Llyr,* trans. J. Gantz 1976, pp.78f.

20 S. and P. Botheroyd 1992, p.46.

Chapter 6

1. Gantz 1976, p.82.
2 *Manawydan, Son of Llyr,* trans. J. Gantz 1976. As for the "Three Ungrasping Chieftains," obviously taken from a Welsh triad, the meaning of the saying is unknown. It may be that Manawydan was excluded from inheriting property in consequence of a vow or for some other reason. Neither do we know the identity of the other two "ungrasping chieftains."
3 *Manawydan Son of Llyr,* trans. J. Gantz 1976, p.85.
4 *ibid.* p.85.
5 *ibid.* p.86.
6 Gantz observes in a footnote that the name Kigva was taken from the *Irish Book of Conquests,* where it appears as Ciocba, wife of a son of Partholon, leader of the first settlers in Ireland. See J. Gantz 1976, p.65.
7 *Pwyll Lord of Dyfed,* in J. Gantz 1976, p.65.
8 *ibid.* p.86.
9 *ibid.* p.86.
10 Wherever Gantz uses the word England, Gwyn Jones and Thomas Jones use the Welsh word *Lloegyr.*
11 *Manawydan Son of Llyr,* in G. and T. Jones 1949, p.46.
12 *ibid.* p.47.
13 Compare Chapter 1, J.J. Hatt's interpretation of the Gundestrup Cauldron and the myth of Rigani. See also Goettner-Abendroth, *The Goddess and her Hero.*
14 Quoted from John Matthews, *Taliesin,* London 1991, p.251.
15 *Culhwch and Olwen,* trans. J. Gantz 1976, p.165.
16 Proinsias Mac Cana 1977, p.60.

Chapter 7

1 Place names reveal that the cult of Dana was spread all over Europe: e.g. Danube, Denmark.
2 The syllable *-ven, -win,* Welsh *-gwyn* or *-gwen* means "white."
3 Robert Graves 1974, p.314, quoting Sir John Rhys.
4 According to the Irish descriptions of the Fomorians, this mysterious race seems to represent the forces of Chaos.
5 A shrine found at Risingham near Hadrian's wall is dedicated to a god Matunus, "the divine Bear," but nothing else is known about him (see S.& P. Botheroyd 1992, p.222).
6 According to R. Graves, a form of baptism was used in Britain even in pagan times. The translator Gwyn Jones observes that the name Dylan Eil Ton means "Sea Son of a Wave."
7 Lord of Pen Llyn, "Lord of the Great Lake." Ceridwen's husband has the same title. This may point to a connection of Ceridwen with Blodeuedd (cp. Chapter 11).
8 W.J. Gruffydd 1928.
9 Branwen's Tower, Weleda's tower, Ethne's tower; at that time the world seems to have been full of towers with nubile virgins. Perhaps these women were priestesses, who, like Merlin, lived in a tower all the better to study the stars.

10 Jean Markale 1975, p.130.
11 W.J. Gruffydd 1928, p.94.
12 Compare the novella of Heinrich von Kleist, *Das Fräulein von O.*, which treats the same problem.
13 See Graves 1974 and Joseph Campbell, *The Power of Myth and The Mythic Image.*
14 Graves 1974, p.448.
15 Taliesin, *The Battle of the Trees,* verse 6, line 119, quoted by Graves 1974, p.37.
16 *Math Son of Mathonwy,* trans. G. and T. Jones 1949, p.68.
17 Jean Markale 1975, pp.132ff; see also Markale 1993, p.163.
18 Graves 1974, p.371.
19 W.J. Gruffydd 1928, pp.267f.
20 Dante Alighieri, *La Divina Commedia, Paradiso,* Canto 33.
21 James Vogh, *The Thirteenth Zodiac,* London 1977.
22 Graves 1974, p.97.
23 Caitlín Matthews 1987, p.167.

Chapter 8

1 Knight 1983, p.15.
2 *ibid.* p.15.
3 *Culhwch and Olwen,* in G. and T. Jones 1949, p.95.
4 *ibid.* p.95.
5 *ibid.* p.96.
6 *ibid.* p.96.
7 "Shellhoofed," a form of grooming, consisting in filing the horse's hoofs in the shape of shells.
8 *Culhwch and Olwen,* p.97.
9 Knight, *op.cit.* p.24.
10 *Culhwch and Olwen,* p.98.
11 *ibid.* p.109.
12 Caitlín Matthews 1987, p.98.
13 *Culhwch and Olwen,* p.110.
14 *ibid.* p.110.
15 *ibid.* pp.110f. "Ol-wen" means "White Track," perhaps an allusion to the White Goddess.
16 In the land of the giants everything is reversed. Instead of saying "Where do you come from?" the giant asks "Where are you going?"
17 *Culhwch and Olwen,* p.112.
18 *ibid.* p.119.
19 *ibid.* p.136.
20 Caitlín Matthews 1987, Chapters 6, 8 and 9.
21 *Trioedd Ynys Prydein,* trans. R. Bromwich, University of Wales Press, Cardiff 1961.
22 W.J. Gruffydd, *Mabon and Modron,* in Y Cymmrodor XLII, 1930.
23 Caitlín Matthews 1987, p.152, quoting from *Trioedd Ynys Prydein.* For "cousin" read "nephew."
24 Gwri was the name given to Pryderi by his foster parents, before it was discovered that he was Rhiannon's son.

25 *Culhwch and Olwen,* pp.125f.
26 *ibid.* p.126.
27 J.J. Hatt, *Eine Interpretation der Bilder und Szenen auf dem Silberkessel von Gundestrup,* Exhibition Catalogue "Die Kelten in Mitteleuropa," Salzburg 1980, p.68ff. The mysterious migration of the salmons westward to an unknown destination may have contributed to this fantasy.
28 Glenys Goetinck, *Peredur, A Study of the Welsh Traditions of the Grail,* Cardiff 1975, pp.38f.

Chapter 9

1 The two translators spell the name differently. Gantz spells it the Latin way: Maxen (from Maxentius). Gwyn Jones chooses the Celtic spelling: Mac-sen.
2 *The Dream of Rhonabwy,* in G. and T. Jones 1949, p.138.
3 *ibid.* p.152.
4 *The Dream of Maxen,* in J. Gantz 1976, p.123.
5 Caer Lion = Caerleon on the Usk: Roman *Castra Legionum.* Caer Vyrddin = Carmarthen.
6 R.S. Loomis, *Wales and Arthurian Literature,* Cardiff 1956, p.4.
7 Edward Gibbon, *The Decline and Fall of the Roman Empire,* New York, p.433.
8 Modern historians agree that he was born at Naissus in Moesia (modern Ni in former Yugoslavia) which is possible if Helen accompanied Constantius on his campaigns.
9 Geoffrey of Monmouth, *History of the Kings of Britain,* London 1966, p.132.
10 *ibid.* p.138.
11 Stow, John, *The Survey of London,* revised edition London 1956.
12 *Catholic Encyclopedia,* Vol.IV, pp.295–301.
13 Pierre de Bourdeille, Abbé de Brantôme, *The Lives of Gallant Ladies,* London 1961, p.21.
14 Henry Lewis (ed.) *Dingestow Brut,* Cardiff 1942, pp..69–78.
15 Loomis, R.S. 1956, p.4.
16 *ibid.* p.5f.
17 *ibid.* p.4.
18 *ibid.* p.4.
19 *The Dream of Macsen Wledig,* in G. and T. Jones 1949, p.85.
20 *ibid.* p.85.
21 J. Rhys, *Lectures on the Origin and Growth of Religion as illustrated in Celtic Heathendom,* London 1892, pp.169–73, quoted in Lewis Spence 1979.

Oengus, the son of the Dagda and of the goddess Boann had a dream of a beautiful maiden, the most beautiful in Ireland. He had this dream every night, and Oengus grew steadily weaker for love of this maiden. All the physicians of Ireland were consulted and one of them guessed the reason of his illness. For a whole year they searched the island for the maiden, but could not find her until Bodh, the Elf king of Munster joined the search.

Bodh found her with one hundred and fifty other maidens as they were bathing in a lake. Her name was Caer and she was the daughter of Ethal, the elf king of Connacht. Oengus heard that every second year she changed into a swan, and he succeeded in finding her. He changed into a swan himself and brought her into his house which is the famous *sidhe* of Brugh Boyne, where she stayed with him for ever.

22 *The Dream of Macsen Wledig,* p.79.

23 *ibid.* p.87. In a footnote the translator Gwyn Jones explains that we have here an onomastic tale: the Welsh word for Brittany is Llydaw, implying the words *lled* "half" and *taw,* "silent, mute". It is to be fervently hoped his explanation of the gruesome detail is correct.

24 Geoffrey of Monmouth, *op.cit.* p.132.

Chapter 10

1. P.K. Ford 1977, p.*ix.*
2 Jessie L. Weston, *From Ritual to Romance,* Cambridge 1920, reprint 1980.
3 Glenys-Witchard Goetinck, *Peredur, A Study of the Welsh Tradition of the Grail Legend,* Cardiff 1975. For further background on this chapter, see Robert Graves, *The Greek Myths,* Vols.1 and 2, Harmondsworth 1960; and Introduction to *New Larousse Encyclopedia of Mythology,* 1968, pp.v–viii. See also Goettner-Abendroth, Heide, *The Goddess and her Hero,* Massachusetts 1995, pp.124–210.
4 Stephen Knight 1983, p.76.
5 Chaplain Andreas was Marie de Champagne's secretary at the same time as Chrétien de Troyes was her court poet.
6 Laurence Harf-Lancner, *Les Fées au Moyen Age,* Paris 1984; referring to Burchard of Worms, *Decretum, Patrologie Latine,* 1, CXL, col.831–54 and 950–1014.
7 See also Robert Graves, *The White Goddess,* and P. Mac Cana, "Aspects of the Theme of King and Goddess in Irish Literature," *Études Celtiques,* Vol.VII, 1953, pp.76–114, 356–413.
8 Sabine Baring-Gould, *Curious Myths of the Middle Ages,* London 1866. Reprint London 1977, pp.103–5.
9 Stephen Knight 1983, p.162.
10 Chrétien de Troyes, *Erec and Enide,* trans. W.W. Comfort 1975, pp.248f.
11 The name is spelt "Luned" in *The Lady of the Fountain,* "Lunete" in *Yvain.*
12 Lewis Spence 1979, p.197.
13 *The Lady of the Fountain,* in G. and T. Jones 1949, p.169.
14 *ibid.* pp.169f.
15 Chrétien de Troyes, *Yvain,* trans. W.W. Comfort 1975, p.208.
16 Kaplan Andreas, *Über die Liebe,* p.193. Marie de Champagne gave this answer to a letter which queried the strength of conjugal love.
17 Chrétien de Troyes, *Yvain, op.cit.* p.265.
18 Jessie L. Weston quotes the ballad "Owain Miles" from a manuscript published in 1837 by Turnbull & Laing, Edinburgh, without giving a date of compilation.
19 W.J. Gruffydd 1928, pp.324–27.

20 *Gwalchmei* is Welsh for "May Falcon," the traditional name for the Summer King.
21 Mary R. Williams, *Essai sur la composition du Roman Gallois de Peredur,* Paris 1909, quoted by Idris Llewellyn Forster, "Gereint, Owain and Peredur," in R.S. Loomis (ed.) 1959, pp.208–28.
"The grave of Mor, the magnificent and brave lord, son of Peredur *Pennwedig*"— The name *Mor,* meaning "big" or "tall," may have caused the misunderstanding which led Wolfram von Eschenbach to write that Parzival's father Gamureth had sired a black son with a Moorish queen, namely Parzival's half-brother. Feirefiz *(fair fils, meaning* "fair son") was the appellation given to Perceval by his mother in Chrétien's story, and this was the reason that he did not know his own name. In those times of family vendettas it was imperative that the names of children of famous fathers were kept secret, as we know from the Irish saga of Fion mac Cumhail.
22 As for instance told in the Welsh legend of the fairy of Llyn Fan Fach. This fairy married a shepherd who lived in the vicinity of the lake Fan Fach. She left him because he abused her, but to her sons she bequeathed her gift of healing as a family heritage. Quoted in Jones, Gwyn, *Welsh Legends and Folktales,* Harmondsworth 1979.
23 R.S. Loomis, *Arthurian Tradition and Chrétien de Troyes,* New York 1949, p.346.
24 *Peredur Son of Efrawg,* trans. G. and T. Jones 1949, p.183.
25 Hélaine Newstead, *Romanic Review* XXXVI 1945, p.214.
26 *Peredur Son of Efrawg,* p.226.
27 G.W. Goetinck 1975, pp.38f.
28 *Peredur Son of Efrawg,* trans. J. Gantz 1976, p.243.
29 J. Gantz, *Introduction to the Mabinogion,* p.9.
30 Jean Markale 1975, p.214.
31 *Peredur Son of Efrawg,* trans. G. and T. Jones 1949, pp.185–96.
32 The Orthodox Church of Byzantium left Rome because of a dogmatic argument in AD 1054.
33 *Peredur, Son of Efrawg,* p.217.
34 *ibid.* p.218.
35 R.S. Loomis, *Arthurian Tradition and Chrétien de Troyes,* New York 1949, p.118.
36 *The Tale of Taliesin,* ed. P.K. Ford, Berkeley 1977, pp.178f.
37 *Gereint Son of Erbin,* trans. G. and T. Jones, p.229.
38 Chrétien de Troyes, *op.cit.* p.19.
39 Hélaine Newstead 1939, p.106–30.
40 *Gereint Son of Erbin, op.cit.* p.273.
41 Stephen Knight *op.cit.,* 1983, p.162.
42 *ibid.* p.161.
43 *Gereint Son of Erbin, op.cit.* p.273.

Chapter 11

1 Lewis Spence 1979, pp.109–47, 193–213.
2 Llyn Tegid is the old name of Lake Bala in the North of Wales (Ford 1977, p.167).

3 P.K. Ford 1977, p.167.
4 P.K. Ford 1977, p.168f.
5 *ibid.* p.170; King Maelgwn of Gwynedd died of yellow fever in AD 547. Quoted in Chris Barber, *More Mysterious Wales,* London 1987, p.121.
6 P.K. Ford 1977, p.172.
7 *ibid.* p.172f.
8 *ibid.* p.174.
9 *ibid.* p.176f.
10 *ibid.* p.177.
11 *ibid.* p.178.
12 Lewis Spence 1979, p.202.
13 A stone statue of a Celtic mother goddess with twins at her breast is shown in the Museum Carolino-Augusteum at Salzburg (see Erich Neumann, *The Great Mother,* New York 1963, Pl.45).
14 Graves, Robert 1974, p.66.
15 *ibid.* p.75.
16 Lewis Spence 1979, p.202.
17 Graves 1974, p.400.
18 *ibid.* p.197.
19 *ibid.* p.196.
20 *ibid.* p 92.
21 *ibid.* p.75.
22 *ibid.* p.75.
23 Matthews, John *Taliesin. Shamanism and the Bardic Mysteries of Britain and Ireland,* London 1971.

Chapter 12

1 J. Weston and D. Nutt, *Sir Gawain and the Grail Castle,* 1903, quoted in John Matthews 1990, pp.148–51; J.D. Bruce, *Evolution of the Arthurian Romance,* 2 vols., Gloucester, Mass. 1958.
2 John Matthews 1990, pp.148–51. See also Matthews (ed.) *Sources of the Grail,* Floris Books, Edinburgh 1996, pp.239–46.
3 In 1173 bishop Thomas à Becket was canonized as a martyr by Pope Alexander III and enjoyed great popularity in Austria as "Sankt Thomas von Kandelberg" (Thomas of Canterbury).
4 Scherer, Wilhelm, *Geschichte der deutschen Literatur,* Berlin 1902, p.186.
5 Loomis, R.S., *Wales and the Arthurian Legend,* Cardiff 1956, quoted in John Matthews 1990, p.25.
6 Norma Lorre Goodrich, *Guinevere,* New York 1991.
7 *ibid.* pp.236f.
8 *ibid.* p.7.
9 *Prose Lancelot.* See *The Vulgate Version of the Arthurian Romances,* 7 vols., ed. H.O. Sommer, Washington, 1908–16.
10 Chrétien de Troyes, *Perceval li Gaulois,* trans. Foulet, Stock 1947 p.191, quoted by Jean Markale 1975, p.164.
11 *ibid.* p.164.
12 Sir Thomas Malory, *Morte d'Arthur,* abridged by A.W. Pollard, London 1917, p.461.

13 *Peredur Son of Efrawg,* trans. J. Gantz 1976, p.233.
14 *Peredur son of Efrawg,* trans. G. and T. Jones 1949, p.201.
15 Edward C. Whitmont, *The Return of the Goddess,* London 1983, p.166.
16 R.S. Loomis 1956, pp.35f, 154.
17 Quoted in Whitmont *op. cit,* p.167.
18 *Château Merveilles.* Gwyn Jones (1949, p.227 translates as: "the Castle of Wonders." Jeffrey Gantz (1976, p.257) translates as: "the Fortress of Marvels."
19 G.R. Phillips, *Brigantia, A Mysteriography,* London 1976.
20 A good translation, for instance, is that by A.T. Hatto, Penguin Classics, 1980.
21 As we have seen in Chapter 10, the designation "Witches of Gloucester" was localized to Wales and originated in the political situation of the time, when the English enemies of Wales concentrated their forces on the Welsh border at the fortress of Gloucester. In ancient times it had been the task of these priestesses (later called witches) to give young warriors the highest possible training in martial arts and from Irish sagas we know that they had their main centres in Scotland, then called Alba. But at the time when the Arthurian cycles took shape, their role had been forgotten. As patriarchy abhors priestesses as well as women proficient in magic and martial arts, their extermination was a foregone conclusion.
In Herder Lexikon, *Germanische und keltische Mythologie,* Freiburg 1982, a respected reference book, Cuchulainn's female teacher in martial arts, Scathach, is given as *"Waffenmeister"* (masc.), presumably because a woman proficient in martial arts is inconceivable.
22 The text speaks of "a baldric," a swordbelt.
23 Selina Hastings, *Sir Gawain and the Loathly Lady,* London 1985; Ethel J. Phelps, (ed.) *The Maid from the North, Feminine Folktales from around the World,* New York 1966.
24 John Matthews 1990, p.105; Caitlín Matthews, 1989, p.17.
25 Jean Markale 1993, p.151.

Conclusion
1 In AD 744 or 746 the Anglo-Saxon missionary to Germany, St Boniface (Wynfrith) in a letter to Pope Zachary, accused the Scottish Bishop Virgilius (Ferghil) of Salzburg of heresy, because Ferghil had written a book about the spheric shape of the Earth and the existence of elementals as "antipodes." Quoted in W.H. Marnwell, *Light from the West,* New York 1978.

Sources and Further Reading

Translations and editions of The Mabinogion:

The Mabinogion, trans. Gwyn Jones and Thomas Jones, London 1949, revised 1974, reprinted in Everyman Classics 1993. Introduction by Gwyn Jones and Thomas Jones.

The Mabinogi and other Medieval Welsh Tales, ed./trans. Patrick K. Ford, Berkeley 1977.

The Mabinogion, trans. Jeffrey Gantz, Penguin Classics 1976.

The Mabinogion, trans. Lady Charlotte E. Guest, Dover Thrift Editions 1997. An edition which doesn't include Lady Charlotte's endnotes on Welsh lore and mythology.

Evangeline Walton's retelling of the *Four Branches* was published under the following titles: *Prince of Annwn,* New York 1974; *The Children of Llyr,* New York 1971; *The Song of Rhiannon,* New York 1972; *The Island of the Mighty,* New York 1972.

Aarne, A. and S. Thompson, *The Types of the Folktale,* Helsinki 1981.

Barber, Chris *More Mysterious Wales,* London 1987.

Bornemann, Ernest *Das Patriarchat,* Frankfurt, 1975.

Botheroyd, Sylvia and Paul *Lexikon der keltischen Mythologie,* Munich 1992.

Comfort, W.W. (trans) *Arthurian Romances,* J.M. Dent, London 1975.

de Vries, Jan *Keltische Religion* Stuttgart 1961.

Dumézil, Georges *L'Idéologie tripartite des Indo-Européens,* Brussels 1958.

Goetinck, Glenys Witchard *Peredur, A Study of the Welsh Traditions of the Grail,* Cardiff 1975.

Goodrich, Norma Lorre *Guinevere,* New York 1991.

Graves, Robert *The White Goddess,* New York, 1974 .

—, *The Greek Myths,* Vols.1 and 2, Harmondsworth 1960.

Gruffydd, W.J. *Math vab Mathonwy,* Humphrey-Milford, Cardiff 1928.

Harf-Lancner, Laurence *Les Fées au Moyen Age,* Paris 1984.

Hatt, J.J. *Eine Interpretation der Bilder und Szenen auf dem Silberkessel von Gundestrup,* Exhibition Catalogue "Die Kelten in Mitteleuropa," Salzburg 1980.

Hatto, A.T. (trans.) Wolfram von Eschenbach's *Parzival,* Penguin Classics, 1980.

Hole, Christina *Dictionary of British Folk Customs,* London 1978.

Jenkins, D. and M.E. Owen (eds.), *The Welsh Law of Women,* Cardiff 1980.
Jones, Gwyn, *Welsh Legends and Folktales,* Harmondsworth 1979.
Knight, Stephen *Arthurian Literature and Society,* London 1983.
Loomis, R.S. *Arthurian Tradition and Chrétien de Troyes,* New York 1949.
—. *Wales and the Arthurian Legend,* Cardiff 1956.
—, (ed.), *Arthurian Literature in the Middle Ages,* Oxford 1959.
Mac Cana, Proinsias *The Mabinogi,* Cardiff 1977.
—, *Celtic Mythology,* Feltham 1983.
Markale, Jean *Women of the Celts,* London 1975.
—, *King of the Celts,* Rochester, Vermont 1993.
Matthews, Caitlín *Mabon and the Mysteries of Britain,* London 1987.
—, *Arthur and the Sovereignty of Britain,* London 1989.
Matthews, John *Taliesin. Shamanism and the Bardic Mysteries of Britain and Ireland,* London 1971.
—, *Gawain the Knight of the Goddess,* London 1990.
—, *Sources of the Grail,* Edinburgh 1996.
Monmouth, Geoffrey of *History of the Kings of Britain,* London 1966.
Neumann, Erich *The Great Mother,* New York 1963.
Newstead, Hélaine *Bran the Blessed in Arthurian Romance,* New York 1939.
Power, Patrick *Sex and Marriage in Ancient Ireland,* Dublin 1976.
Richards, M. (trans./ed.) *The Laws of Hywel Da (The Book of Blegywryd)* Liverpool 1954.
Ross, Anne *Pagan Celtic Britain,* London 1974.
Sjoestedt, Marie-Louise *Celtic Gods and Heroes,* Berkeley 1982.
Spence, Lewis *The Mysteries of Britain,* Wellingborough 1928, reprint 1979.
Vogh, James *The Thirteenth Zodiac,* London 1977.
Wesel, Uwe *Der Mythos vom Matriarchat,* Frankfurt 1980.
Weston, Jessie L. *From Ritual to Romance,* Cambridge 1920, reprint 1980.
Whitmont, Edward C. *The Return of the Goddess,* London 1983.
Williams, Sir Ifor *Lectures in Early Welsh Poetry,* Dublin Institute of Advanced Studies 1954.

Index

Carmina Gadelica

Hymns and Incantations from the Gaelic

Collected by Alexander Carmichael and presented by John MacInnes

The Carmina Gadelica *is by any standards a treasure house ... a marvellous and unrepeatable achievement. There will never be another* Carmina Gadelica.

Ronald Black, University of Edinburgh

The *Carmina Gadelica* is the most comprehensive collection of poems and prayers from the Gaelic tradition of oral poetry. Gathered by Alexander Carmichael (1832-1912) in the Highlands and Islands of Scotland, "from Arran to Caithness, from Perth to St Kilda." The poems had been handed down through the generations in a living oral tradition. This tradition and the way of life which sustained it have now disappeared but these poems and prayers live on to remind us of the faith of the unknown poets who composed them.

Previously available only as a bilingual text in six volumes, the Carmina in this one-volume edition of Carmichael's English rendering is an important contribution to the wider awareness of Celtic culture. John MacInnes' introduction puts the poems in the context of the life and folklore of the Gaelic community. This edition was published in 1992 and has already established itself as an essential book for all those interested in the culture of Gaelic Scotland.

Floris Books